What's in Your Hand?

What's in Your Hand?

Using God's gifts and talents to serve isolated people groups

By Elsie Bush
with John Bush

Bush
Publications

Copyright © 2023 Elsie Bush

All rights reserved. No part of this book shall be reproduced or transmitted in any form or by any means without prior written permission of the publisher. No patent liability is assumed with respect to the use of the information contained herein. Although every precaution has been taken in the preparation of this book, the publisher and author assume no responsibility for errors or omissions. Neither is any liability assumed for damages resulting from the use of the information contained herein.

Scripture quotations marked (NIV) are taken from the HOLY BIBLE, NEW INTERNATIONAL VERSION®, NIV® Copyright © 1973, 1978, 1984, 2011 by Biblica, Inc.® Used by permission. All rights reserved worldwide.

Scripture quotations marked (KJV) are taken from the KING JAMES VERSION (KJV). Public domain.

Hymn stanza quoted in Chapter 3 is from "May the mind of Christ, my Savior," by Kate B. Wilkinson. Public domain.

Photos included are the author's personal photos or from office work files. Cover photo: By the author - Helio Courier at grass airstrip in Peruvian jungle.

Information contained in this book was gleaned from the author's letters to family, prayer letters sent out over the years, from reports by colleagues, and from the author's memories.

Publisher's Cataloging-in-Publication Data:
Names: Bush, Elsie L., author. | Bush, John F., author.
Title: What's in your hand? Using God's gifts and talents to serve isolated people groups / by Elsie Bush with John Bush.
Description: Lancaster, PA: Bush Publications, 2023.

Library of Congress Control Number: 2023907055
ISBN: 979-8-9881538-0-1 (paperback) | 979-8-9881538-1-8 (ebook)

Subjects: LCSH Bush, Elsie L. | Bush, John F. | Missionaries--United States--Biography. | Missionaries--Bolivia--Biography. | Missionaries--Peru--Biography. | Missionaries--Kenya--Biography. | Missionaries--Congo (Democratic Republic)--Biography. | Jungle Aviation and Radio Service. | Aeronautics in missionary work. | Wycliffe Bible Translators. | BISAC BIOGRAPHY & AUTOBIOGRAPHY / Personal Memoirs | RELIGION / Christian Ministry / Missions

Classification: LCC BV3542 .B87 2023 | DDC 266/092--dc23

Editing by Hilda Bradney.
Editorial checking by Janet Morris.
Cover design by Nathaniel Dasco (coverdesignerpro) www.99designs.com.
Guidance, cover, and publishing arrangements by www.ebooklistingservices.com.
Contact the author at elsie_bush@wycliffe.org.

Dedicated to:

*Carol and Mike Barker,
my sister and her husband
who greatly enabled us to serve.*

And to

*Mission Support Staff
who are often the unsung heroes,
who enable missions to happen.*

Table of Contents

Introduction xi
Chapter 1 – Beginnings - Foundations for Life 1
    Tricky Flying 1
    Starting Out 2
    School Days 5
    Spreading my Wings 6
    College Days 8
    Great Expectations 10
    Harrisburg Christian School 13
    Red Sweater Girl 14
    John's Story 16
    Good Training 20
    Military Life 22
    Back to Civilian Life 26

Chapter 2 – Mr. and Mrs. - Preparing to Serve 27
Chapter 3 – Jungle Training Camp - Learning Survival Skills 34
Chapter 4 – Bolivia (1972-1976) - Life in the Jungle 48
    Going to Bolivia 48
    Spanish Study 49
    Jungle Life 53
    Our Work 59
    Bilingual Teacher Training 65
    Annual Conference 66
    Tools for Transportation 67
    New Experiences 69
    Guarani New Testament 74
    Machu Picchu 76
    Scaling Back 78

Chapter 5 – Peru, (1978-1979) - To Another Country 80
    Are You Willing? 80
    Off to Peru 81
    Back to Work 83
    House Hopping 92
    Translation Progress 93
    Bad News 95
    Never a Dull Moment 96
    Preparing for the Long Run 100

Chapter 6 – Peru (1980-1983) -- Frustrations and Blessings 102
    Our Own House 102
    Back to Work 103
    The Tour Guide 104
    Unusual Air Strip 106
    Frustrations and Blessings 109
    Captured 110
    Bent Wing 112
    Day by Day 113
    High Water 115
    Saturday Surprise 117
    Journal of an Unforgettable Trip 118
    Responding to Challenges 124
    Interrupted Meditations 129

Chapter 7 – Costa Rica and Peru (1984-1987)
- Contact and Completions 131
    Costa Rica 131
    A Series of Emergencies 133
    New Contact! 134
    Abandoned Child 141
    More Sickness 142
    Where is the Crew? 143
    Translation Milestones 148
    Nazca Lines 149
    Aviation Solutions 150
    Looking for the Moronahuas 151
    The Sunday Sink 152
    Special Guest Helper 153
    Progress and Challenges 154
    More Precious than Gold 159
    What if we Never Came? 160
    High River, Low River 162
    A Vital Service 163
    Finishing Before Furlough 164

Chapter 8 – Peru (1988-1992) - Progress Through Difficulties 165
    Ferry Flight 165
    Back Again to Peru 167
    Turtle Egg Time 168

Contents ix

    Words of Gold 170
    Problems and Progress 172
    Dangerous Times 175
    Cutting the Grass 177
    Pod Project Without Pod 179
    The Fleet 180
    Completions 182
    Conditions Deteriorate 184
    Cholera and Calamities 186
    Journal of a Tribal Trip 188
    Pressing Forward 199
    New Direction 200
    Finishing 200

Chapter 9 – Africa Transportation Service
- Those Barely Passable Roads 203
    Back Home 203
    New Program at JAARS 203
    In and Out of Africa 205
    The JAARS Team 207
    The ATS Program 208
    Delayed by Civil Unrest 211
    Moving into Production 212
    Meanwhile 217
    Many Involved 217
    Too Many Challenges? 219

Chapter 10 – Africa (1996-2000) - The Huge Continent 222
    Go Where? 222
    Do What? 227
    Flexibility 231
    Building Back Up 234
    Here We Go Again 237
    New Strategies 239
    Providential Banquet Tour 242
    Stuck in Entebbe 243
    Two Celebrations 244
    Mission Leaders Lost 249
    On the Road Again 250
    Pushing Forward 252

x   What's in Your Hand?

    Re-evaluating 253
    Side Benefits 254

Chapter 11 – Northeast Regional Office
- Mobilizing and Caring for Workers 258

Chapter 12 – Missions Fest Lancaster - Lets' Go Big 276

Chapter 13 – Mission Aviation Promotions
- Highlighting Technical Service 294

Epilogue 305

Abbreviations Used in the Book 307

Author biography 309

Introduction

Do what? Go where? Come along with us on our life journey--an adventure I never anticipated. Unaware to us at the beginning, God was preparing us for His service. Some of the training was hard, but profitable. While our journey led us through highs and lows, God kept us going, blessed by the fact that He could use us.

We served as part of a team, each of whom God had gifted in unique ways and prepared through experiences. He placed tools in our hands:

- pen and paper, typewriters, computers, printers, scanners
- hammers, wrenches, pliers, screw drivers, drills, saws, rulers, levels, compressors
- bicycles, vehicles, aircraft, engines, batteries, electricity, navigation aids
- radios, internet, software, communication tools
- stethoscopes, thermometers, blood pressure monitors . . .

Why? So that we could help bring God's Word to people groups with previously unwritten languages, the often forgotten and neglected ones. So that they too could know of God's love, His offer of salvation, and eternal life with God.

In the Scriptures, God asked a reluctant Moses, "What is that in your hand?" His ordinary shepherd's staff became a powerful tool to express God's glory to many cultures. Samson's donkey's jawbone became God's lethal weapon. Shepherd boy David used five stones and his sling to win Israel's giant enemy, Goliath, so that the world would know that there was a God in Israel. Jesus used a boy's lunch to feed a huge crowd. God wants to use the tools He has placed in our hands to accomplish His purposes and to bless others. That is the theme of this book.

God can use those with technical skills to help take God's Good News to every culture. God's mission needs more than preachers and teachers. He needs a myriad of giftings. John and I, along with multiskilled team members, have supported Bible translators to bring God's Word to people groups in their heart languages.

We sometimes found ourselves doing tasks we never dreamed of in places we hadn't anticipated. This book will take you behind the scenes to see ordinary tasks that enable missions to happen. I pray that as you catch a glimpse of the many ways our creative God used willing servants in the past, that you too can be encouraged to use your God-given gifts as He leads.

Chapter 1
Beginnings
Foundations for Life

―――――――――――――――✈

Tricky Flying

Flying an airplane has been described as hours of boredom, punctuated by periods of stark terror. Flight programs in remote jungle areas have a lot less boredom than most. JAARS pilots and mechanics are trained to deal with unique situations and challenging airstrips. In the 70s and 80s they also flew into uncharted territory without maps or GPS. We encountered many unexpected situations as we served Bible translation projects carried out in the most remote places.

Once on a busy day of flying in Peru, our pilots were taking bilingual teachers back to their villages after a Teacher Training Course at our Jungle Center. One of the pilots had a long flight way up north, very close to the Ecuadorian border, several hundred miles away. It was getting late in the day. After he had taxied up the river in the float plane and dropped the passengers off, he needed to get off the river and move to a lake for the night. He started taxiing back down the river. When he got close to the mouth, he accelerated to make what we call a step turn.

A step turn is a tricky maneuver where the pilot gets one float out of the water while the other one is still in the water, so he can make a turn around a bend in the river. This allows him to accelerate before and after the turn, gaining sufficient speed to take off. In this situation, as the pilot came around the corner, he realized that the wind was blowing in the wrong direction to make the takeoff. All he could do was chop the power. However, he wasn't down in the water enough, so the water rudders didn't have any effect, and he wasn't going fast enough for the regular rudder on the airplane to turn him. All he could do was go straight ahead—toward a big leaning tree which broke the wing halfway out!

Fortunately, the pilot was not hurt. He radioed in to explain his predicament. Word was passed to everybody at the Jungle Center to pray for the situation. The aviation team had to figure out what they could do. John needed to get help to him as soon as possible and get the plane to a place where they could work on it.

That was one of many challenges John faced during our time of serving with Wycliffe Bible Translators and SIL (Summer Institute of Linguistics). Serving alongside him, I also encountered my share of challenges. Come along with us and look behind the scenes to learn of the support services that make it possible to take God's Word to those who've never had it in their own language, and how John and I got involved.

Starting Out

An interesting and thought-provoking question was posed between bites of a delicious meal.

During my first year of teaching at Harrisburg Christian School in Pennsylvania, I was sharing an apartment with two other teachers. It was Sally's turn to prepare Sunday dinner, and we had invited a missionary couple from the church to join us, whose daughter attended our school. Sally had prepared Cornish hens, a rather elegant meal. We enjoyed chatting with our guests and hearing about their mission work. During our conversation, the question was put to us: "Which of you would be most likely to end up on the mission field?" Sally had a keen interest in missions. Nancy had a special gift for interacting with people on deep spiritual levels. But for myself, I really didn't think I'd ever serve God in another country. In my mind, I would have been the least likely.

True, back when I was a teenager, I had knelt by my bed and told the Lord that I would be willing to do whatever He desired me to do with my life—even if it was a difficult challenge like serving on the mission field in some strange place. But I was pretty sure that was a very remote possibility. Anyway, I thought I'd settled on my career and life decisions. I was serving the Lord by teaching at a Christian School.

So how was it that I ended up serving in missions? That turn of events will come out as I tell our story.

There's nothing like growing up in a small town in the 40s. In Bellwood, PA, we knew our neighbors, had a grocery store across the alley behind our house, and even a neighborhood store around the corner where we could buy a spool of thread, candy, or maybe an ice cream bar. The grade school to which my sister Carol and I walked was just half a block in one direction, and the high school about two blocks the other way. We came home at noon for lunch, while many students ate in the cafeteria. After our mother started working, we still came home and made our own lunch. We never locked the doors, so no keys were necessary.

Our father worked for a local plumbing business, then later installed heating and air conditioning systems. He was also a carpenter. He built our house when I was six years old. It was just the right size for our family, and we were so pleased to have our own home.

Mom loved to sew. When we were young, she made many of our clothes. She even taught me to sew when I was still in grade school. Later, Mom decided to get a job. She took a commercial sewing course, then worked in a sewing factory. After that, when Mom sewed at home, she whizzed those seams through the machine so fast we could hardly believe it.

Interestingly, Mom's brother, Ralph, had married Dad's sister, Martha. So, we were close to Uncle Ralph and Aunt Martha.

My father's parents lived just a block and a half from us. My granddad (Gampy) worked for a neon light business. He also had a part-time job as a janitor at the church we attended. One of his duties was to ring the church bell prior to the Sunday morning service. One time when I was with him, he let me help ring the bell. I pulled hard on the rope and then held on as it pulled me up high into the air. What fun! Only because my granddad was the janitor.

Grandma was a caring, stable part of our lives—always interested in us and what we were doing. She had significant spiritual influence on our family, concerned that we follow the Lord. There were things that we should and shouldn't do. Dancing and going to movies were bad. Grandma would be upset if a neighbor washed clothes on Sunday, hanging them to dry on the line for all to see. Although Grandma had her strict convictions, I loved her and wanted to please her.

There was a decorative plaque hanging on the wall in their living room that reminded us of eternal values:

> *Only one life,*
> *T'will soon be past.*
> *Only what's done*
> *for Christ will last.*

One cold winter (before we had our new house) we lived for a couple of months with my grandparents. I remember sitting on the carpet in their living room in the evenings listening to a program with Bible story dramatizations on the radio—a large wooden floor-model that sat in one corner. I liked to hear the stories and learned a lot of the Bible from them. Before falling asleep at night in their tiny upstairs bedroom, which I considered mine, I re-lived those stories in my mind. I had a very tender heart toward the Lord at an early age and sensed His love for me.

We attended the Olivet Baptist Church. Pastor Goehring's daughter Joyce took an interest in me. She gave me a lovely China tea party set, having outgrown it. On a couple occasions Joyce took me with her to the Sunday evening Young People's meeting held prior to the evening church service. At six years of age, I was really too young to go. One Sunday after a touching story by the teacher, an invitation was given to accept Christ as our Savior. Joyce took my hand and raised it to help me respond, but embarrassed, I pulled it down. What a zealous young evangelist she was! She made me think about my need to be saved.

On a hot summer day, neighborhood children ran through streams of water splashing out from a circular sprinkler in their yard. I joined them but didn't have fun, worried that if Jesus came and called people to heaven, I would be left behind. I went from the water play into our house and said to my mother, "I want Jesus in my heart." She knelt with me by the couch in our living room as I prayed to confess my sins and accept Jesus as my Savior. I was relieved to know I was ready should He come at any time. A year later, both my mother and I were baptized together by Pastor Herzog, who had followed Pastor Goehring at our church.

Church was a big part of our lives, except for Dad. We would coax and beg him to go, but he always had an excuse. We polished his shoes and tried various ways to make it easy for him, but only on a rare occasion would he go. We finally accepted his decision.

School Days

Mrs. Miller, my first-grade teacher at the Bellwood South Side Elementary School, had taught my father in first grade! Our second-grade school photos were taken immediately after a recess time, and my photo reflected that—with hair going in all directions.

From seventh grade on, my classes were in the Bellwood-Antis High School building. With my good friends, Joanne and Faye, we enjoyed many fun activities together. I chose the Commercial Course as I wanted to be a secretary. Our typing class became more interesting when the first two electric typewriters were brought in. Shorthand class also provided a skill I would later use. We all had to take Latin I in 9th grade. I opted to take elective Latin II in 10th grade, which was much more difficult but was good preparation for learning another language. Playing clarinet in the band and orchestra were wonderful experiences for me, helping to bring me out of my shyness.

Our new pastor and his wife made our church youth group a lot of fun, being personally interested in each of us. We enjoyed a variety of activities and became a closely-knit group. We grew spiritually, and it was a very formative time in my Christian life. Our group joined a monthly Christian Youth Fellowship with other church teens. Many from our youth group sang in the church choir. We also formed a youth orchestra which accompanied the singing in the Sunday evening services.

While I was a good student, I wish I had studied with more zeal. I did the work required—even those horrible long history book readings—but not enthusiastically. By my junior and senior years, I became motivated to get good grades. Our graduating class of 70 was just a nice size to know most of our classmates well.

Spreading my Wings

After high school graduation life was suddenly quiet. With no encouragement to go to college, I thought of being a legal secretary.

I went to the Unemployment Office in Altoona. I felt small and uncertain across from the agent's large desk. He found a few secretarial openings, but none appealed to me. I told him that I scored high enough on a high school Civil Service exam to be offered a good paying position at the U.S. Department of Agriculture in Washington, D.C. He then asked, "Elsie, are you taking that offer?"

"I guess so," I answered vaguely. It seemed better than local jobs. I hadn't given much thought of the logistics or living expenses in the capital city.

I accepted the Agricultural Department's offer. I would have to figure out the other parts later. When Uncle Ralph and Aunt Martha heard of my decision, they invited me to live with them. I can't imagine how my life might have been different, had they not extended that opportunity. They had just moved to a new home in McLean, Virginia, a D.C. commuting community. I would pay $50 monthly for room and board.

On the appointed day Dad loaded my new luggage into his car. I was numb, going through the motions, dimly aware of this life-changing decision. An hour on the way I had a stomach-churning realization. "Oh Dad, I don't have the papers from Agriculture telling me where to report." It was a hurried, unpleasant return as Dad drove us back home to find the necessary paperwork!

I shared a bedroom with my cousin Darleen. She and her brother David were in high school, while their little sister Debbie was a toddler. Uncle Ralph helped me get started, driving me miles out of his way to my work. He worked for the U.S. Weather Service. He suggested that I look

Beginnings   7

for a bulletin board with notices for carpooling. I found four older gentlemen who were patient with their new young partner-in-transportation. I paid my share of expenses, but soon they suggested I purchase a car, taking my turn to transport them.

Dad helped me purchase a beautiful 1956 Dodge. Then I asked one of the men to drive my car on my designated day. I had never seen so many vehicles on the roads at one time, so I was hesitant to navigate the rush-hour traffic. It took us a long hour even though the distance wasn't far. After a few months the men suggested I drive. I now felt comfortable, blending with every other car where two lanes merged into one as we inched forward. Once we crossed the Fourteenth Street Bridge, we only had to drive a couple blocks in the actual city traffic before heading into the Department of Agriculture parking area and to our assigned space.

I worked with another girl in the Oils and Peanuts Division of the Commodity Stabilization Service. Ellen was secretary to the Director of the Division. I was secretary to Mr. Davis, the Assistant Director. Beyond his office, a pool of accountant-type employees tapped with lightning speed on their adding machines creating constant clatter. They compiled statistics on oil and peanut production from across the country. We secretaries typed up their statistical charts—rows and rows of figures with several carbon copies. We also prepared "dockets" of information for policy decisions by higher authorities.

Our office window faced the street, with a nice view of city life. We could see the entrance to the U.S. Mint building across the intersection where the money was printed.

Sometimes Mr. Davis dictated

correspondence or reports, while I wrote in shorthand as fast as I could. One day I couldn't figure out a section of my shorthand. Ellen grinned and said, "Let me show you something." She took me to the waste can in Mr. Davis's office where he dumped his hand-written notes. I scanned them to find my troublesome section and so completed the job. After that, I remembered to check his waste can when I needed help.

Within a year my boss promoted me with an increased salary. Ironically, I wasn't to enjoy that for long.

When my home church pastor and wife, who knew Aunt Martha and Uncle Ralph, visited D.C., they overnighted with us. After catching up on my news, the pastor asked, "Elsie, when are you going to college?"

"I might just think about that," I told him. It was a life-changing question! I didn't want to continue my current routine into the future. I enjoyed attending my aunt and uncle's church, but hadn't connected well with the "young adults" there. I envied the college kids when they came home for Christmas vacation as they shared their Christian college experiences. A Bob Jones University student sparked my interest in attending there.

Since it was the beginning of summer, I had to act quickly if I wanted to enter college that fall. I wrote to Bob Jones University for an application. Before I knew it, I was accepted! When I told my boss of my plans, he was a bit upset, but did say that a college education was a good thing.

I needed to save money for tuition. Rather than buying nice clothes, I now saved every penny possible, carrying a packed lunch. I also applied for a college work/loan scholarship.

I had a short time at home before my next adventure. My pastor was delighted to hear that I was headed for college. I mentioned my interest in studying art. "Oh, you don't want to do that," he said, "That's what the way-out-kids take. You might get in with a strange crowd."

In September Dad, along with family, drove me to Greenville, South Carolina. They settled me in my dorm room, then headed back to PA.

College Days

I shared a room with three girls. Gloria, our room leader, gave me helpful advice for finding an on-campus job with their work/scholarship program. Secretarial jobs were only year-round, so I first worked at the

Snack Shop, and later in the library. I loved being around the books, and often wished I had time to just sit and read.

My original intention was to attend one year, taking interesting classes like Interior Decorating, Piano, Art. However, my class advisor explained, "This is the program that freshmen take. If you're not sure of a major, you can decide that next year." She suggested a Humanities major. Later, when I planned to continue for more years, I changed to Elementary Education.

I did enjoy college life and was grateful for the opportunity. Classes were interesting, but I had to work hard for good grades, endeavoring to make the very best use of my time.

Each year I ran out of funds. When I reluctantly wrote home, Mom kindly sent what I needed. To save money, I washed my laundry by hand in the dorm laundry room and hung it on racks to dry. I skipped extra snacks, only buying necessities like toothpaste and textbooks. Fortunately, our meals were included with tuition.

I needed a good summer job to earn funds for each year. The first summer I worked part-time at Fishers Department store near home. But the pay wouldn't cover my tuition. I contacted Miss Spates at the Agricultural Personnel Office. She told me to come immediately to help in her office. So, I went back to the good-paying government work for the rest of the summer, and I was welcomed back to join Uncle Ralph's and Aunt Martha's family.

After my sophomore year, I went directly to work in the Personnel Office at Agriculture and was able to participate in a summer government college program. Once every two weeks we were invited to attend a special presentation at one of the government agencies. These programs espoused the virtues and values of their specific agency and told of opportunities for college grads to make a career with them.

By this time, I was committed to graduate with a B.S. in Elementary Education. Since I worked many hours, I had little time for extra-curricular activities or social life.

For the summer after my junior year, I was determined to find a job in the Bellwood area and stay with my family. I realized that after graduation I didn't know where I would teach. I applied at a new factory near Bellwood, which only offered production work. What a new education for me! James Industries was the maker of the famous Slinky toy. I first packaged Slinkies—

as fast as possible! Soon I moved on to connecting plastic frog pull toys. My coworkers' rough language made me blush, but I admired their hard work. Heat from the production furnaces made us perspire profusely. I learned to appreciate the hard labor needed to keep industry humming.

Recruiters came to our campus representing their Christian schools to graduating education majors. The friendly group from the Virginia Beach area needed a fourth-grade teacher. After checking other options, I chose to teach in Virginia along with Dottie Bullock who would teach 7th grade. The salary would be minimal, only $200 a month before taxes, but housing was provided. I had no idea how that decision would affect my life.

Great Expectations

My sister Carol was to graduate from high school the same year I finished college. *Wouldn't it be fun to live together in Virginia Beach! She could get a job there, probably secretarial, and I would teach school.* Our plan seemed like a great idea. Since housing was part of my benefits, I asked if we could share housing and expenses.

A week before school was to start, we packed my car and Dad's car with our gathered household items. In a two-car caravan we drove to our new adventure. As we found our way to the new address, the area looked run down. The principal was working on a school bus engine in the church yard. The school used a country church's facilities, not a nice school building as I expected. My classroom would be a small Sunday School room.

"I've been busy getting things in shape for school," said the principal. "Sorry we haven't had time to get your place cleaned up." He showed us to one side of a duplex house that was just across the road from the church. "It's convenient that the property belongs to the pastor," he said. "Two other teachers live in the second-floor apartment of the pastor's house, just over there."

Our new home was, at that time, hardly livable—such a disappointment. My expectations were shattered.

The principal, along with Mom and Dad helped us unload our belongings, with subdued conversation. Then they needed to be on their way. I had never seen Dad with tears in his eyes before. In a shaky, hoarse voice through the car window, he told the principal, "Take care of my girls."

I could imagine his thoughts: *My daughter spent four years in college for this?*

For the next days we tore up several layers of deteriorated floor covering in the kitchen, tried to clean off built-up wax, and cleaned all over. We wanted to make it at least livable before school started.

Dottie arrived to share the apartment above the pastor's house with Etta who had already taught for a couple of years. They helped us clean. The bathroom needed new paint. The principal gave us some school-bus yellow paint and some white to lighten it, a couple of brushes and a can of gasoline to clean them. We found it took a lot of white and a little yellow. While painting in the small unventilated bathroom, we were overcome with gasoline fumes. Coughing and gagging, we had to leave. *(To this day the smell of gasoline turns my stomach.)* There was no closet, so we hung our clothing on clothes racks on the back enclosed porch.

It was expected that we would attend this church. The first Sunday as we entered, the pastor asked Dottie if she would sing a solo. Dottie was surprised since she didn't sing solos. "Oh, the teacher before you used to sing, and I thought maybe you would too."

Oh, dear God, I prayed. *What have I gotten myself into?!?* The school year was starting, and I felt so unprepared. All my prep time was used to make our house livable.

I had squeezed a teacher's desk and nine student desks into my 9-by-9-foot classroom, literally wall to wall. The Virginia heat was exhausting. Perspiring, I dressed for school. When I sprayed my hair into place with White Rain, breakfast was churning in my stomach. *(Years later, the aroma of White Rain hairspray still gave me a nauseating rush of adrenaline.)* Facing the day, I had to go forward. I was not coping well with my first teaching job.

Dotttie also had challenges. With no advanced notice, she was told that she'd have a new student that day in her 7th grade class. He had been expelled from public school, and hopefully she could help straighten him out. Unfortunately, this boy turned Dottie's class upside-down. His bad influence was more harmful than our ministry to him was helpful. Finally, when Dottie could take it no longer, they found another place for the boy.

12 What's in Your Hand?

There was another larger Christian School in the area—Norfolk Christian School. It was well run and very well thought of. I wished I was teaching there.

As Thanksgiving time came near, Carol and I planned to visit Mom and Dad. "I hate to tell you this," Carol said, "but when we go, I'm not coming back." I was disappointed, but I could hardly wish her to stay. Our big plans had not turned out as we had hoped. I felt like I had gotten her into a bad situation. *(Recently she told me that she didn't see it as a wasted experience. She had enjoyed fixing up the house and had learned how to do a lot of new things—which she later used to fix rental properties.)*

Dottie and Etta were asked to move in with me since my place was larger than theirs. There wasn't room for three single beds in the bedroom, so we added a cot which we folded up during the day for walking space. We rotated monthly turns on the cot, meal preparation, and chores.

Throughout that school year we shared many new experiences. When the weather cooled, we learned the tricky procedure to light the kerosene stove in the living room. When we saw mice droppings, I set traps. We'd hear a snap and scuffle in the night, and Etta emptied the traps in the morning. During the flying ant season, they filled our back porch, falling like snow over our hanging clothes. To relieve stress, Dottie and I walked in the mall. Life there seemed normal and carefree.

One day I received a letter from the Harrisburg Christian School. (I'm not sure how they got my address.) They asked why I hadn't applied the previous year. I wrote back explaining that they hadn't included an application with their correspondence. A subsequent letter included an apology and an application. "We are better organized now," they said. We set a time for an interview during my next trip home.

Mom and Dad drove me to a house in Harrisburg for the teaching interview, which was a delight. Harrisburg Christian School (HCS) would be moving into a newly completed building for the next school year. It was a parent-run school, with an elected board. I was offered the opportunity to teach second grade and happily signed the contract.

I felt like I had hope for the future. I completed the year and prepared to move my belongings back to Pennsylvania. Looking back, it was the hardest year of my life. Could I have done more to help the school be better? Or was it all I could do to carry on? In fact, that year was good training for living on the mission field. Back then, I didn't expect to be doing that.

After that stressful first year of teaching, I headed back to Pennsylvania. That summer I worked at a Christian camp, Mt. Lou San, located adjacent to the Christian school. That gave me some summer income and helped me get acquainted with local people. My job was Registrar, which basically involved helping the Director's wife with various record-keeping duties as well as working shifts in the gift shop.

At the end of the summer two other teachers and I found a second-floor apartment to rent on Balthaser Street in Linglestown. Sally was also new to the school, having just graduated from Bob Jones. I knew Nancy from Camp Lou San; she had taught at the school one or two years already. We had fun setting up our new home with our gathered furniture and belongings. We planned a rotating chore schedule. We were ready to start the school year.

Harrisburg Christian School

My classroom was large and bright. It was well equipped with built-in cupboards, shelves, coat racks, large chalk boards, bulletin boards, and even a piano. I organized supplies and made lesson plans. I had already met some of the parents and students who attended the Brookfield Bible Church.

Second grade offered opportunities to do a lot of fun things—especially as we learned about "Community Helpers." We made our own Post Office in the back corner of the room. We had a "Twoville Grocery Store" and created a little town on the floor. We had reading groups and activity corners, learned new math, did fun art projects, play-acted Bible stories, and had a rhythm band in music class. After the lunch recess the children rested while I played a story or song on our record player.

"We should have a school yearbook," enthused a teacher. We teachers formed the staff, and students helped. A parent/printer guided us. I enjoyed working on the layout (skills which I later used). The book became an annual school tradition.

When our new apartment parking restrictions necessitated finding another living place, a parent helped us locate a cute ranch-style house. It had personality, a fireplace with a white stone hearth, living-dining-kitchen area, garage, and three bedrooms. Sometimes we prepared ethnic meals, inviting guests. Although a push-mower was provided, the grass often got rather high between cuttings. But a solution was on the horizon to deal with that.

Red Sweater Girl

A church family invited us to their home for an after-church dinner. Surprisingly, they had a telephone call that was for me. It was Harry Jones from our church. "Someone would like to talk with you," he said. It was John Bush who also attended our church.

"It's such a nice day. . . . Would you like to go for a ride?"

I knew who he was but had never talked to him. I did remember that Pastor Burtner had interviewed this young serviceman in a Sunday evening service. John had shared that he planned to be a missionary, involved with aviation.

John came by and we drove around the countryside. He seemed a responsible and serious person and used big words. We got acquainted.

John was stationed at the nearby New Cumberland Army Depot finishing up the last months of his Army time. This was the first of many dates.

I later learned that Harry had asked John if there were any girls at church he'd like to meet, and John had said, "Yes, the one in the red sweater."

When John visited me at what he called our "hen house," the grass was very high—out of control. I was very impressed when he offered to mow the grass.

The following school year, my former camp roommate, Carol, joined Sally and me. Carol taught Physical Education and was a sports coach in a public school. She played the guitar, and we enjoyed jam sessions when we harmonized singing. Our social life picked up as Sally and Carol also dated young men from our church.

One day John, in hunting clothes, knocked on my classroom door. "Would your students like to see the deer I shot?" he asked. Sure enough, a deer sprawled across his car hood. "Oooooo, he's bleeding," said one of the girls. The boys enjoyed seeing John's trophy.

As we continued our friendship, I knew John's goal was missions. I wasn't sure if I could live in a thatched-roof mud hut in the jungle, eating strange foods. I wanted to be comfortable in a nice house, speaking English. These thoughts weighed heavily. *I'm not being fair to John,* I realized. Finally, I said to him, "You're going. I'm not going, and I don't want to keep you from going." So, we broke our relationship.

Months later, John again asked me for a date. "You're living dangerously," I responded. But he said he wasn't worried. I felt I'd honestly communicated to him my feelings, but if he was OK with my hesitation, then together we would trust the Lord to guide us. (I didn't realize it then, but God had been placing many tools in my hands that could be used in a needy area of God's world.)

We became close and John asked me to marry him. "But missions is my life, so that's part of my package," he clarified. I told him I'd have to work through some issues.

We went to Pastor Burtner for advice. "I feel that in a marriage, God leads through the man," he advised. "Elsie, what do you consider is God's call? A bright light like Paul experienced on the Damascus Road? If God has brought you both together, would you consider that God is calling you through John?"

I thought of my desire to live in a nice house. Would I ever have that? I remembered when I was hosted in a beautiful home for two evenings. I admired the magazine-perfect décor. Our hosts were lovely Christians. *That's what I want to be like*, I told myself—and the Lord. *I could send money to the missionaries.* But, when the couple shared some of their heartaches, I realized their lives were far from perfect.

Nice homes, nice people, are not the most important things in life! Could I serve God with John and trust Him for my desires as well as for my needs?

So . . . it was over a root beer float at Howard Johnson's restaurant that I told John that, with the Lord's help, I could do missions with him. When we went out to the car, John opened the glove box and pulled out a little box. There, inside, was a diamond engagement ring. He placed it on my finger—a perfect fit.

John's Story

John was born in Elmira, NY. His father, Fred, worked as a truck driver for Cotton Hanlon in Odessa. Then they sent him to the Adirondacks to manage a lumber mill at Forth Lake, near Lake George. He built a house there for his family.

When John's mother, Claire, was expecting her third child, she didn't feel well and was being treated for heart issues. She and John's dad weren't getting along. She decided to take the children (John and his older sister Karen) and go to her parents in Corning, NY. She stayed at the home of her mother and stepfather, Bessie Champney Witter and Dr. Charles Witter, a chiropractor. After Joette was born, they stayed on a while, then moved to Savona, NY, living in rented houses, one with a leaky roof. She received some child support from Fred but had no other income.

One Sunday morning, John's mother was determined to attend church after a rainstorm. She loaded the three children into a baby carriage and pushed them through flood waters. After church, someone kindly took them home in a vehicle.

Later, Claire moved with the children to Thurston, NY, and attended a small church across the street. A wood-burning kitchen range provided heat for their house. John remembers having the important chore to chop firewood with a hatchet and axe at four or five years old. Claire planted a garden to help provide food. Their bathroom was a little outhouse.

The children enjoyed jumping off large maple tree branches into piles of fall leaves. John and Karen liked to climb an apple tree, but Joette was too small to reach the first limb. Once they tried to help her by dropping a rope around her neck to pull her up! Fortunately, Claire rescued her in time!

John started first grade and enjoyed riding the bus to school in Campbell, along with Karen. Then Claire moved again, this time to Thurston Hill. After having a heart attack, Claire continued with heart problems. When she needed surgery, she arranged for Joette to stay with her parents, Karen with a friend, and John with a nearby elderly couple. Shockingly, Claire died during the operation! It was a difficult time for everyone.

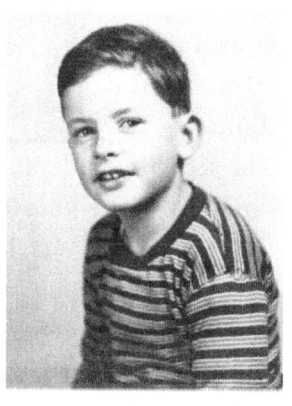

After the sad funeral the children stayed with Grandma and Grandpa Witter. John climbed onto his grandmother's lap and said, "You're our mother now."

Permanent living was discussed, but their father wanted the children to come to the Adirondacks with him. A bitter contest in court ensued. Fred's brother and sister testified that the children would be better off raised by their grandparents. Fred was an alcoholic and hadn't even seen the children for years. The court judge felt that the children should live together. The best option was with the Witters in

a nice home situation rather than a rustic lumber camp. So they settled in to form a new family.

Their Bridge Street home was large and nice, where Grampa had his chiropractic office. The children enjoyed the large porch, living room, and kitchen with an adjacent pantry well filled with canned goods and other foods. They ate meals around a large table in the dining room.

The second floor housed bedrooms for everyone with large closets, and a sun porch where John liked to sleep on warm evenings.

For several years, John and his sisters spent part of their summer with their father at the lumber mill. Later he managed a beer joint and lived in quarters adjacent to it, which wasn't an ideal place for the children.

John's grandparents gave them a stable home. The children had a good upbringing and attended a good school system. John has fond remembrances of holidays with visits from cousins David and Curt. Their older cousins (Frank, Marie, and Ann) would sometimes come too—especially for family reunions.

John enjoyed visiting his cousin Jack in Quarryville, especially riding his pony, Patches. He fed the goats which often butted him from behind. Uncle Lyman, a veterinarian, sometimes took John along on barn calls. John thought that he'd like to be a vet.

John sometimes helped his grandmother with cooking. He learned to make bread. He would place the dough on a bread board on a narrow table. As he kneaded the dough, John would let it hang down over the edge and then retrieve it just before it hit the floor, while his grandmother watched anxiously from her chair in the dining room. John liked to help prepare their Thanksgiving turkey. One year he placed it in the oven before going to bed. Later, he smelled smoke. He ran into the kitchen and discovered he had forgotten the giblets he was boiling. Only ash was left, and the whole house reeked of smoke. He opened windows to get rid of the smoke, despite the very cold day.

John joined a Cub Scout troop which met at Grace Methodist Church. He worked hard to earn badges and worked all the way to Explorer Scout.

For six years John faithfully delivered the Corning Leader newspaper, first one country route, then two. His customers increased from 60 to 100. Later he switched to a city route. Collecting weekly payments, any excess was his—not a big amount, but it taught him responsibility.

When John begged his grandparents to let him play football, they protested, afraid he would get hurt. But he persisted, and they let him do it. He earned a letter his senior year. He enjoyed playing and has liked watching football ever since.

Often the family took a Sunday afternoon drive. Grandma relished revisiting places where she had taught school. One time, when in Trout Run, near Steam Valley Mountain, Grandpa wasn't feeling well, and a gas attendant offered to drive them home. After that their driving trips were closer to home. Later, Grandpa took John to Bath, NY, for his driver's license. Returning, he allowed John to drive for the first time his prized Hudson Hollywood Hornet with a continental kit on the back. Grandma never learned to drive but wore a hole in the floor mat on the passenger side where she braked.

When Grandpa's health continued to deteriorate, he travelled to Canada to be treated for pancreatic cancer. However, he died during John's senior year.

John worked for a time at a Christian bookstore located across town owned by Harold Royce. It was a long walk to work every day. One rainy day, John asked his grandmother if he could drive the car to work. "You're not taking that car out and get it all wet," was the answer, so he walked in the rain.

After Karen graduated, she worked for the United Gas Company in Lancaster, PA. Grandma's health had begun to deteriorate. She sat mostly in the dining room where she could guide John and Joette in their kitchen chores. She read a lot and enjoyed Reader's Digest books.

The children had been attending church with their grandparents. They also participated in release time Bible classes at their school held by the Bible Club Movement in the Corning area. There John really learned about Jesus dying on the cross for peoples' sins. Later, John's friend Keith Thompson invited him to go with his family to a Billy Graham Crusade in Elmira. John gave his life to Jesus, as Savior and Lord. He didn't then know what that commitment would mean for him.

John realized, with a change of pastor, that his church didn't focus on Scripture, and that many sermons seemed to be like Reader's Digest stories. John heard a church matriarch congratulate the pastor saying, "I'm so glad you don't teach the slaughterhouse religion." That was an eye-opener for John, and he felt he didn't belong there. He started to attend North Baptist Church, closer to home, as did Joette.

Pastor Edwards clearly taught the Scriptures and was a gifted musician who often played his trombone or violin in the evening service, or even a saw! John's faith grew, along with his desire to serve the Lord in some way.

John read books about the five missionaries who were killed while contacting the Auca Indians in Ecuador in 1956. He could not get rid of the feeling, *who's going to take up the torch and carry on?* He said, "God is pointing His finger at me. I ought to get involved."

One of the high school teachers, Ernestine Booram, heard of John's interest in aviation and in serving the Lord. One day, by accident (but truly God's providence) the mailman placed a LeTourneau promotional flyer in the Boorman mailbox. It was about a technical institute in Texas, about to become a college. Mrs. Booram asked neighbors, to whom the flyer was addressed, if they could share the flyer with John. "If you're interested in aviation as a career, write to them," she counseled John. He followed her advice, which led to his enrollment in their Aviation Technology Course.

Good Training

To save funds for school tuition, John worked hard at the bookstore. Mr. Royce also gave him work at his home cleaning up an area that had been used for the disposal of cans, jars, and junk from the previous owners. John even shingled their roof.

That fall, it was difficult for his grandmother to say goodbye. John had been doing a lot of chores to help in the absence of Grandpa. Only Joette was left to help Grandma, which was more of a challenge than anyone knew as Grandma suffered with increasing dementia.

John received a partial scholarship from LeTourneau, but it was to be spread out over his time there. He needed to find work. He and his roommate, Ron Durie, applied at the Golden Point restaurant (similar to McDonalds). The owner, Dan Morton, was a fine gentleman who gave John extra work cleaning around his house. At first John used a borrowed bicycle from another student to get to work. Later Dan got a used car that he let John use for transportation. (When John graduated, Dan even helped John find a car to buy.)

John became quite the efficient short-order cook. He tells of cooking 144 Hamburgers at one time on the large grill (a possible exaggeration)! During rush times they really had to move! Even today, when John helps in our kitchen, he zips around making every movement count. I just get out of his way and enjoy the results.

Several professors greatly impacted John: Dale Crane and Glenn Ellis who taught maintenance, and Dr. McKinley who taught Bible courses. Because of long work hours, John sometimes fell asleep in his first-hour class, and when called upon with a question, he tried to come up with a reasonable answer. The student body at that time was comprised mainly of males, with just a few females. So, John had little distraction from his studies in that area.

After graduation, John wasn't sure where to look for work. His grandmother now lived with Uncle Ferris and Aunt Dot in Clarion, PA. Since John's sisters, Karen and Joette, both lived near Lancaster, he headed to that area. Joette was attending nurses training at Lancaster General Hospital (where their mother had graduated). Karen was living with her cousin Ann. John slept on a couch at Ann's house for a while as he looked for a job and a place to live. Enroute to check on a job, he noticed there was a little airport at New Holland. On a whim, he stopped there and met operator Al Stover who hired him part-time. He also found Christmas seasonal work at Watt & Shand Department Store, selling men's clothing. He enjoyed competing with their top salesman. They wanted to hire John full time, but his heart was with aviation.

On the newly paved airport runway, John helped plow snow and de-ice planes. For housing, he found an over-the-garage apartment to rent in nearby Leola. He settled in and was doing well. But that wasn't to last for long.

When Karen's fiancé, Richard Hackman, received military draft papers, John realized that Uncle Sam would soon look for him. John checked with the Recruitment Office, took required exams, and signed up for the training he wanted. As it turned out, his draft papers arrived the very morning he had gone to enlist. The next three years of his life would be in the Army.

Military Life

February 28, 1964, found John on a train to Harrisburg with area recruits, then on to New Cumberland Army Depot for physicals. Since John was the oldest in the group, he was put in charge to see that they all got to South Carolina via train. With no previous experience in Army discipline, this was a challenge. From the train windows they saw heavy snow blanketing the countryside. In Virginia their train was put off on a siding where they waited for eight hours. Finally arriving around midnight, the sleepy Columbia, SC, staff unhappily processed the recruits.

Early the next day John's group, dressed in civilian clothing, waited outside in the cold. A burley sergeant in a 2½ ton truck squealed to a stop and yanked down the tail gate. "Fill it up," he shouted. After six climbed up into the truck bed, the sergeant looked despairingly at the uninitiated men. "I said fill it up!"

"It's full," the men called back. Whereupon the sergeant jumped back into the cab, gunned the engine, and popped the clutch, shifting the six to the back. Then he stomped on the brakes, throwing them sprawling forward.

He yelled to the remaining recruits, "Get in there!" And they knew he meant all of them. Somehow, they piled in, following his orders.

John did basic training at Fort Jackson. But all along he was keeping his goals in mind to serve in mission aviation. On a three-day pass he found a bus to North Carolina to visit the JAARS Center, the technical service department of Wycliffe Bible Translators, known at that time as Jungle Aviation and Radio Service.

John had used about all his money for bus tickets, so at Monroe, NC, he called the JAARS Center and asked for a ride. They kindly took him to the Walkup House, a former mansion then used as a guest house. The staff welcomed John with a tour, including the aviation program and hangar facility. *Maybe someday I'll join the JAARS team*, he thought as he got on the bus and headed back.

Graduating from basic training, John visited Karen and Joette. Then he went to Fort Eustis, VA, to train in instrument overhaul, repair, and calibration, which became his military occupation specialty (MOS). As he came out top of his class and already had his civilian A&P (Aircraft and Power Plant license), they kept him to teach engine overhaul and repair to new recruits.

During his time there, one of the lieutenants encouraged him to put in an application to OCS (Officers Candidate School). As it took a long time to process this, John asked to go to Non-Commissioned Officers School in Fort Knox, KY, as a prep school for OCS. The top three graduates would receive promotions. Despite coming out as number four, his commander promised him the next stripe available.

Army orders arrived for John to serve in Korea. Right before his departure the promotion rank came down. His Aunt Dot helped sew the patch on his uniform.

Arriving in Korea he was told, "We don't have an aircraft instrument shop, never had one and never will." Since John had civilian ratings they asked, "Well, where would you like to work?" John felt his experience on props and rotors was limited, so he asked to work in the propeller overhaul shop.

A month later the sergeant said, "Hey, we've just received a mobile instrument overhaul shop that needs to be inventoried."

John found $12,000 worth of equipment with no directions on how to set it up. He was permitted to hand pick a crew to help. He had fun getting all the equipment organized and functional. He found barometers and monometers, but no mercury needed to operate them. He requisitioned 20 pounds of mercury. Surprise, a couple months later 200 pounds arrived!

John found a way to trade mercury with Air Force staff at Osan Air Base in exchange for the supplies he needed to complete the shop set up, then functional with equipment worth about $100,000.

John had pre-determined that he was going to continue to have daily devotions wherever he was in the military—that he would not put his faith "on the shelf" for the three years. When he sat at his bunk with Scriptures opened, some of the guys made fun of him. But a few asked about joining in Bible study. They were able to meet in the Day Room, and the class grew as some from other companies heard about it. Officer Randy Acton invited the group to use the Officers' Room on Sunday mornings. Later the Navigators organization came to Korea, so John moved their study into the Navigators' program.

(Randy later taught Navigator courses and has continued to be a friend to this day. Navigators serve on military bases, college campuses and inner cities with the theme, "To know Christ, make Him known, and help others do the same.")

There was a Korean orphanage near the base which housed lots of children with not much money for food or to heat their run-down facility. With permission, John solicited fellow soldiers for donations on payday. He worked with a couple men from other companies and took food and heating supplies to the orphanage to keep them going.

John's unit lived in a Quonset hut (which looked like a giant tin can, sliced in half lengthwise). With no insulation, it was heated with a 50-gallon drum into which kerosene was fed from a five-gallon jerry can. This provided heat until about 3:00 a.m. when they felt the cold, sometimes with snow blowing through cracks around the windows.

One day word came down that they were to have a big I-G Inspection the next day, when the Inspector General would come in with white gloves to check everything and look for any dust. The men meticulously cleaned up their Quonset. Some hung up their uniforms to avoid wrinkles. During that night John awoke and smelled smoke. To his horror, he saw flames leaping out of the top of the barrel stove. The Quonset was filled with smoke down to three feet from the floor. John quickly got the fire extinguisher, yelling "Fire, fire!" Everybody ran out as he sprayed foam on the barrel. Hitting the super-hot surface, foam splattered all over, even on some uniforms. Everything was now a big mess. How would they ever pass inspection? They explained what had happened and were relieved when the inspectors never entered their Quonset.

During this time, tensions rose in Vietnam. Then most of John's battalion were sent directly there—including all the E-5s and above. Then when the next E-5 stripe came down, the company commander got it for John. John had actually been working in an E-6 slot but wouldn't receive that rank since he wasn't planning to make a career in the Army.

Then John was reassigned back to the New Cumberland Army Depot near Harrisburg, PA, for his final eight months. Before checking in, John looked for a good church in Harrisburg. He asked advice from Pastor Crichton of the Calvary Independent Church in Lancaster, who recommended Brookfield Bible Church, where J. Howard Burtner was pastor. Before reporting for duty John checked out the church location. This proved to be providential, since that was the church I was attending.

At the Depot, John overhauled instruments, working with civilians. Then they asked him to head up repairs on a Beechcraft C-45 airplane (like a Beach 18 civilian model) which had been in Germany. John was permitted to hand-pick a crew to rebuild the plane. He chose guys whom he felt would be willing to learn and work responsibly. Most enjoyed the aviation work, and three of the men considered making it a career. One weekend John drove Bill O'Brian and two others to check out Pittsburg Institute of

Aeronautics. All three men decided to go there. Bill later earned his A&P, pilot, and commercial licenses. He eventually worked as an inspector for the FAA (Federal Aviation Administration) and remained a good friend.

During John's final months of duty, his work slowed down. With time on their hands, several men found part-time local work to augment their limited income. John worked odd hours refueling planes for L. B. Smith Aircraft, a Cessna dealer and fixed-base operator in Harrisburg.

John had enjoyed his time in the Army, gaining multiple experiences at the expense of Uncle Sam. Although there had been hard times and challenges, he was glad he had enlisted and thankful for all he had learned while serving.

Back to Civilian Life

With the goal of paying off college debts, John worked for AMP Inc., a manufacturer and producer of electrical/electronic connection devices, which conducted experimental testing and product development of printed circuit boards. John helped maintain their fleet of eight executive twin-engine Beechcraft Barons. He lived in a mobile home adjacent to the airport, where planes flying overhead were like music to his ears.

He used GI Bill funds to take flight lessons and dated me in his spare time. Earning his Private Pilot's license, he took me for a flight, flying low over my house and school. I was happy when he returned towards the airport since I felt queasy. But when he headed in another direction, I had to ask, "Do you have any of those little air-sick bags?" He looked disappointed as I used one, and I was sorry to dampen his enthusiasm.

John flew whenever possible. That Thanksgiving, he took Karen, Rich, and me to visit Uncle Ferris and Aunt Dot. Another time, he and a friend suddenly entered icy conditions and the windshield clouded, so they opened windows for visibility. The buffeting wind made his friend lose his lunch into their map, which then flew out the window. A comical, yet dangerous experience. Finally, they landed safely. A few close calls made John evaluate whether he wanted to pursue being a mission pilot or an aircraft mechanic. I was thankful he decided to be a mechanic, and I prayed that God would enable him to keep mission planes safely prepared to fly in whatever remote area of the world we would serve.

Chapter 2
Mr. and Mrs.
Preparing to Serve

———————————✈

After we were engaged to be married, Pastor Burtner asked us if we would lead the youth group at the church. Since we each were members in our home churches, we became "associate members" at Brookfield so we could take on this responsibility. Most of the 20 teens were well established in their faith. One of the teens, Karen, had found a youth curriculum published by Word of Life which we reviewed and liked. The Church purchased these materials for our Sunday evening meetings.

At one event we showed them a filmstrip about the rugged jungle camp training we needed to take if we joined Wycliffe Bible Translators. I think most of them decided it would be a rough experience. Maybe they noticed that I was a little fearful of what might be ahead. I hoped they sensed my determination to face challenges for mission service in remote areas. Several of those young people later went on to serve in missions.

We set April 13th as our wedding date—the day before Easter, 1968. We hoped for a nice spring day, but surprisingly it was a scorching hot day and very hot inside the church. We appreciated all those who came and those who helped.

Two combined classrooms at Harrisburg Christian School served for our reception. Colleagues and friends brought refreshments. We opened their practical gifts for our new home. We especially appreciated cash gifts to pay for our honeymoon expenses.

John found our first house, a small rancher on a farm near Linglestown. The house had been built by the farm owners for their son and family, who lived in it a while and then moved away. It was a quiet country location, yet close to major highways.

"Why don't you park your cars in the garage?" a friend asked us. He probably thought we had a lot of junk in it, but being newly-weds, we hadn't yet accumulated much. What we did have in our garage was an airplane—partially assembled! John and a partner were rebuilding a Piper Tri Pacer by welding together the front of a damaged plane to the back of another. Our garage was a convenient workplace as John had spare time. Only four ribs from the two wings were reusable. All the others needed repairs. I helped sometimes by sanding the wooden spars (the main structural member in the wings).

After a year in our farmhouse, our landlords told us that their son and his family wanted to come back home to the house we were renting. So, we moved to an apartment at a large complex known as Paxton Park Apartments, centrally located between our work locations and church.

At that time we had two cars. John had his 1964 Pontiac Lemans and I had "Coral Cloud." She was my beautiful '57 Dodge, with cream colored body, long coral fins at the back, and a coral hood, definitely a lady's car. But she began to have various maintenance issues. I sadly said goodbye when we traded her in, with knobs on the dash falling off as we drove her to the dealer. She was replaced by a white VW Beetle. Long and sleek to short and fat! I admit that it was kind of fun to bug around in the Beetle. Since John had the greater distance to drive to work, he usually drove the more economical VW and I drove the Pontiac.

While John gained good experience working on the planes at AMP Inc., it was probably very different than he would experience in a remote area. The planes were housed in a large high-class hangar. The aircraft maintenance team wore dress shoes, dress pants and white shirts, with a clean white work smock each day.

John's friend who worked there as a pilot, told him about a man he knew who had purchased an old antique airplane, sight unseen, from Missouri. This well-to-do businessman wanted to fly that airplane, a Cessna T50, known as a Bamboo Bomber. But unbeknown to him, it was full of major problems. John worked for him a few Saturdays. When he offered

John the option to work for him full time, John thought that would be better preparation for his future mission work. So, he accepted that opportunity.

Meanwhile the Cessna had been flown to an airport on an Island at Sunbury, PA, making it a long drive every day to work on it. John heard from friends that there was a Quonset hangar available at Capital City Airport in Harrisburg. When he told the businessman about it, he purchased the hangar. They moved the airplane to the Airport on two large tractor-trailer trucks. Then John had a much shorter commute to work.

The refurbishing was extensive, requiring a completely redesigned electrical system and major woodwork that took 14 pages of drawings for FAA approval. This was good training for the mission field where one often needed to be resourceful.

Then John went back to work for L. B. Smith Aircraft, where he overhauled a couple engines and made other major repairs for customers—more good experience.

I continued teaching at Harrisburg Christian School and John became a member of the school board. When the board decided to expand the classroom space to enable adding a grade each year, John was chosen to chair the building committee. That was a good learning experience he would use in the future. The new addition contained four more classrooms. School parents and staff raised funds to cover the cost.

Meanwhile our goal was to someday serve with JAARS, the technical arm of Wycliffe Bible Translators. What we especially appreciated was Wycliffe's priority to translate God's Word for language groups who hadn't read or heard it in their own heart language. If missionaries had to leave their country of service because of political or health reasons, that language group would still have their own resource. As was often quoted, "The greatest missionary is the Bible in the mother tongue: It never needs a furlough and is never considered a foreigner." We could serve as part of a team, using the talents/skills God had given us.

However, we needed to be debt free before joining the mission, and we both had substantial college debts. Although my salary at the Harrisburg school was better than what I'd received in Virginia, it didn't compare to public school teachers' salaries. Also, aircraft mechanics' salaries were normally less than what auto mechanics earned. That didn't seem fair considering the responsibilities involved in aviation safety. As John says,

"You can't park it by the side of the road if there's a problem." We were making slow progress to lower our debts.

We were surprised when Merrill Piper, then a recruiter with JAARS, called us asking if he could stop by for a visit. Over lunch we talked about the work of JAARS. He showed us some slides with photos of JAARS workers in various countries. The best part of Merrill's visit was the advice he gave us.

"How much are you paying on your debts?" he asked. "How long, at that rate, until you will you be debt-free?" We told him that our payments depended on how much we spent that month. I was repaying my mother as we were able with no set monthly amount, and John was slowly reducing his school balance.

"To be debt free by Wycliffe's summer training session next year, you could divide the total debt amount by the number of months, and prioritize that monthly payment," Merrill suggested.

We took that advice seriously. Such a simple plan, yet we hadn't considered it. Now we worked with a definite goal. John also steadily acquired tools recommended for JAARS aircraft mechanics. I think he was the Snap-On tool salesman's best customer!

Early summer of 1970 we headed to Norman, Oklahoma. Mom had forgiven me the last part of what I owed, and we were debt-free. We had resigned our jobs and left our apartment. John had traded in our two cars for an El Camino, in which he could transport his extensive tool collection to be used for the Technical Evaluation session. Following that we would take basic linguistic training at the Summer Institute of Linguistics (SIL) at the University of Oklahoma campus. This would help us understand Wycliffe's method of Bible translation, even though we would be in "support" roles. It also served as a candidate school. If we successfully passed, our next step would be Jungle Training Camp in southern Mexico.

(Wycliffe now has its own training institute called Dallas International University, fully accredited, at SIL's International Linguistic Center in Texas.)

John loved driving the El Camino. It was a good choice and reliable transportation for our long drive. We arrived on a really hot day at the university campus. We found our assigned room in one of the *old* dormitories with no air conditioning (known to students as the pink palaces). The bunk beds and common bathrooms reminded us of our college life.

"The Lord hath provided!" said Lester Bancroft as he joyously viewed John's tool collection. He and Ernie Rich were directing the Technical Evaluation for eight eager applicants. John had been the only one who had taken seriously the "Recommended Tool List." The other men had only a few tools. And more importantly, the staff had brought very few tools. They all were happy to use John's adequate collection for their evaluation projects. Both Lester and Ernie had pioneered mission aviation maintenance in Peru and were very knowledgeable about the field preparation needed. They gave the men the task of making some special tools for disassembling engines and to do other procedures to exhibit their skills. John passed without difficulty, and we moved on to the next phase.

Other students then arrived for the main summer sessions which were fortunately held in air-conditioned classrooms. A new curriculum for support staff included classes like phonetics, grammar, phonology, and language learning of basic Spanish needed to travel to Mexico for Jungle Training Camp.

Students, staff, and teachers all ate together in a large dining room, with Wycliffe staff manning the kitchen. Dr. Kenneth Pike, the overall SIL Program Director, was a renowned linguist who, regardless of his high status, enjoyed mixing with the students. I was in awe of him, especially when he spoke at some of our chapel services—always with a unique presentation. He loved leading the group in Wycliffe's theme song, "Faith, Mighty Faith," with words by Charles Wesley (a prolific hymn writer).

Through Orientation classes we learned the history of Wycliffe Bible Translators and the seeming impossibilities God had led the organization through—especially in the early days. Wycliffe's founder, William Cameron Townsend (also known as "Uncle Cam") had trusted God with unusual faith to open doors for Bible translators to closed areas.

As a young man Uncle Cam sold Spanish Bibles in Guatemala. Before long he realized that many Guatemalans were not interested in his Bibles because they didn't know Spanish. They spoke their indigenous Cakchiquel language. So, he began to learn their language to translate the New Testament for them.

Uncle Cam knew there were hundreds of millions of people who did not have God's Word in the language they understood best. His vision was to see individuals, communities and nations transformed through God's Word and love expressed in their language and culture. He saw the need to train young people in linguistics to prepare them for learning these languages not yet reduced to writing. In 1933 he and his friend, Leonard Livingston Legters, discussed this need. They decided to set up an intense summer course to train interested believers how to learn an unwritten language and translate Scripture into it.

The first linguistic course was held in Arkansas in 1934. It was called Camp Wycliffe, naming it after John Wycliffe who first translated the whole Bible from Latin into English. Later the course was called the Summer Institute of Linguistics.

Uncle Cam wanted to ask the government of Mexico permission for him to bring in young people to learn the indigenous languages and to translate Scripture into those languages. The Mexican government said they could not work with a religious organization, but they could work with an educational or scientific organization. At that same time there were plans to hold the summer linguistic course at the University of Oklahoma, but by state law no religious courses could be held on their campus.

So, two organizations were incorporated in 1942: Wycliffe Bible Translators (WBT) was formed to recruit and send young people to translate the Bible, and the Summer Institute of Linguistics (SIL) was incorporated as a scientific organization. The summer course continued to be called the SIL. Young people joined WBT and remained members of it but were seconded to (assigned to work under) SIL for service in other countries.

In Orientation class, this history and distinction between WBT and SIL were explained to us by Marjorie Buck from New York, who had originally told John about Wycliffe. She was a Bible translator with the Amuzgo language in Mexico and served on the Norman SIL staff each summer.

In the evenings we did homework in our hot dorm rooms. From our window we could hear cheers outside from a volleyball game which John joined occasionally. We also continued writing our Doctrinal Statement, an extensive explanation of our view of Biblical doctrines.

I felt intimidated by the brilliant students and teachers who surrounded us. Our basic linguistic classes were hard enough. Those who would translate Scripture for remote language groups had very challenging classes; they were a special breed of intellect, fortitude, and flexibility. We were privileged to be among such gifted people.

At the end of the summer session and a personal interview, we were accepted into Wycliffe Bible Translators to serve with JAARS. We drove back to Waxhaw, NC, to drop off John's tools before traveling north for deputation (later called Partnership Development).

We set up meetings in various churches to explain our work and invite people to partner with us financially and with prayer. We already had some support but needed to reach a basic monthly quota. We sent out letters to an increasing number of people explaining our progress and plans. What a lesson in humility as we learned to depend on God and His family to finance our living and ministry. We had worked for our pay checks. Now we would be working full-time for the Lord through the generosity of His people who wanted to be involved in our mission. Ironically, some "wealthy" contacts, whom we expected would support us, didn't respond. But other poor, humble people joined our support team for $5.00 or $10.00 a month. What a blessing they were to us. Some of our family also began contributing generously to our support, which greatly encouraged us!

Continuing our preparation, Jungle Training Camp was our next step. I would especially need God's help for this rugged training.

Chapter 3
Jungle Training Camp
Learning Survival Skills

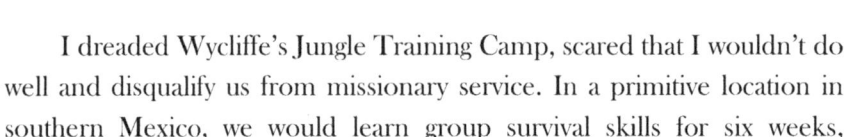

I dreaded Wycliffe's Jungle Training Camp, scared that I wouldn't do well and disqualify us from missionary service. In a primitive location in southern Mexico, we would learn group survival skills for six weeks, followed by individual living skills for six weeks. Despite my fears, I would do the best I could.

Our preliminary instructions said to bring only one duffle bag per person, packed with all we would take along: canteens, flashlights, hiking boots, cooking utensils, insect repellent, batteries, clothing, shoes, sleeping bags, and mosquito netting. We thought we would never make it all fit in. My hair curlers stayed behind. Absolutely no room for them. "Who cares what you look like in the jungle," John had said.

October 1970 found us caravanning with the Kinches and Schaefers to Mexico. They shared a vehicle, while we drove our El Camino, packed with a supply of axe heads which we had been requested to bring along for camp use. Rodney Kinch, raised in South America, spoke Spanish fluently, which helped us through the border crossing with our questionable cargo. Our prior training on tipping ethics came into play as Rodney explained our goal to help those living in remote areas. We were soon on our way after generous tips—which possibly provided meat for the agent's family that evening.

Driving through Mexico was a panorama of contrasts: colorful shops, fruit stands, narrow streets, animals along roadsides, cactus plants, cactus fences, palm trees, dry land, abundant crop land, beautiful parks, markets, even carrot juice stands with blenders. When we stopped at a gasoline station, many children and some adults tried to sell their wares. Often a person was standing by each gas pump, directing us to it. Women and children would do extra little services wanting a tip.

In Mexico City we gathered for a couple days of orientation. Then we continued driving south for two more days to Las Casas. There we left our vehicles in a special parking area and were driven to the airstrip from which MAF (Mission Aviation Fellowship) planes transported us to Jungle Camp.

As the plane lowered for the grass strip at Main Base, we had an overview of the little village of mud huts. It was called *Yaxoquintela* (Ya-sho-KEEN-tay-la), a Tzeltal Indian name meaning "a green place." We moved our duffle contents into the designated small hut which would be our home for six weeks. It had mud walls and a thatch roof. The one-and-only room had a rustic bed, a narrow table with some shelves, a couple chairs, and hooks on the walls. The outhouse was down a path, as was the jungle shower—where one carried water to pour into the bucket overhead so that it dripped through a shower head.

Our session of about 50 campers met each day for classes and began learning ways to be self-sufficient and productive in a remote area: like hanging jungle hammocks, recognizing poisonous plants, fixing kerosene lanterns, suturing wounds, giving inoculations, canoeing, swimming in a river, hair cutting, saddling mules, cooking available foods, survival skills, learning the local language, and feeding ourselves spiritually. We had many opportunities to practice our jungle camp motto: "Flexibility in the face of uncertainty and change."

Main base emphasis was on teamwork. We took turns on cooking crews, learning how to plan and prepare meals with available foods for a large group. We ate together in the group dining room, rotating tables each week so that we became well acquainted with our group of campers.

We gained endurance by taking increasingly longer hikes. Going uphill was the hardest for me. Once I became short of breath with a huge lump in

my throat. I wheezed frantically. A staff member calmly said it was my turn to be on a donkey. *(I later realized it was probably a panic attack.)*

In a basic carpentry class, my chosen project was to make a round three-legged stool with a woven seat, a badly envisioned design, as the legs collapsed. But the seat frame came in handy later for something else.

When the second session of participants arrived at Main Base, our group was ready to move to the Advance Base location, where we would individually practice what we had learned. It was a strenuous two-day hike to a newly chosen place. With a shortage of staff personnel, we had to make the long trek without staff. John, having been elected chairman of our group, was given the responsibility to lead us, with a Tzeltal Indian guide to show us the way.

"Where did the guide go?" asked John often as the light-footed Tzeltal disappeared around the curvy trail ahead. Tzeltals were used to traveling quickly through the jungle, while we "gringos" followed slowly. Our boots stuck in the mud. Our legs were splashed with muck. The midday sun and heavy backpacks exhausted us. We stopped frequently to make sure everyone was with us. The women took turns riding the three available donkeys. Once, even a donkey floundered in a deep muddy area. We made our way step by step through beautiful jungle foliage, up and down hills, on a well-worn trail.

Finally, we reached a location to spend the night. But the grove of trees upon which to hang our hammocks had been chopped down. Where would we sleep? A humble church building provided shelter for the ladies. We stretched out our sleeping bags on the backless wooden church benches and tried to sleep. The men spread their sleeping bags on the ground. At morning light, I discovered that cockroaches had invaded my belongings. I shuddered with disgust as I shook them out and stepped on some before they scurried away.

We made oatmeal in canteen cups for breakfast with milk powder, oatmeal flakes and river water purified with iodine tablets, heated over a fire. Surprise! Our oatmeal turned dark! We discovered that iodine plus starch brings color change.

We regrouped and started on our second day of hiking. Already tired from our first, our energy diminished quickly. My body rebelled, but we needed to keep hiking. I was totally exhausted. *Surely we must be almost there*, I kept thinking. *I don't know if I can go much further.* As darkness closed in, we arrived near a lake where Advanced Base Staff met us. But we weren't there yet! We had another hour to hike through more jungle in the blackest dark by flashlight. The dense jungle walls on each side and the overhead canopy of foliage gave me the sense of walking through a tunnel. I wondered what jungle creatures were observing us. Finally, we arrived at a recently constructed pavilion where the staff welcomed us with a meal. It was delicious. We had arrived!

In the next week we were to build our own *champa* (CHOM-pah). Since John wanted our jungle house to be lakeside, we ended up with the farthest location from the central pavilion. Until we built it, we slept in jungle hammocks hanging between trees. We prepared our meals over a campfire from staples brought with us. John suggested biscuits for our first supper. We'd learned how to "bake" in an iron skillet by placing hot coals on the lid. I found flour, but with no recipe, I went blank. "What's in biscuits?" I asked my worried husband. Later our Jungle Camp Cookbooks arrived, much appreciated by me—and John.

We cleared a spot to dig a hole for a latrine and stretched plastic above tied to branches for a roof. My failed stool project became our toilet seat!

Several early mornings we heard a strange noise. Was it a leopard breathing heavily? Large "cat" tracks had been spotted, so we were on guard for any dangerous encounters. (Later we recognized the same sound in hummingbird wings as they sucked moisture from laundry hanging on our clothesline.)

When the camp director checked our *champa*, he said we needed to chop down a large tree which leaned over our area. Most of the next day John worked to chop through it with his machete. However, the tree would not fall, only move slightly. It was tangled in the green canopy of branches. He labored to cut another section. Hugging the tree and pulling it this way and that, it would not come down. Finally, we moved our *champa* location away from the tree--and unfortunately further from our latrine.

The next morning when John stuck his head out of his hammock, I was shocked. He looked like a stranger! His face was puffed up, his eyes merely thin slits, and his arms red with rashes. We discovered that the big tree he chopped was called *chechen negra* (chay-CHEYN-NAY-gra), with sumac-like poison. At main base we had learned to avoid *chechen blanca*, a small poisonous plant, but were unprepared for poisonous trees.

Other campers also developed rashes. The nice straight tree trunks that many chopped to use as construction poles were poisonous. Some burned it as firewood and breathed in the smoke, causing internal irritation. John had the most serious case, with ugly rashes developing on various places of his body. The staff said he should stay in bed and discontinue activity. (We later learned that they had considered transporting him by Indian carriers for medical help.)

Fortunately, John had already built our bed frame, with a jungle hammock fastened above to serve as mosquito netting. He didn't feel sick, just weak, and extremely itchy. So, restfully recuperating, he enjoyed reading a book about Papua New Guinea from the camp library. The camp nurse checked him twice daily and gave him steroid shots.

I needed to finish the *champa* setup by myself. The next item on our construction agenda was a pole shelf area on which to store our supplies. I searched for one-inch diameter straight trees for the frame, chopped them with my machete and formed a point on one end to poke them into the ground. Next, I found smaller trees for framing and pole shelves, tying the pieces together with vines. I felt pleased with what I had accomplished. But, late in the afternoon, two Tzeltal men came by to check on my progress.

Jungle Training Camp   39

Having just helped some single ladies with their construction, they had been advised that I could also use some help.

"*Ma'ba lec!*" they exclaimed as they viewed my shelves. "It is not good!" They wobbled them to and fro showing their instability. Then they quickly began tearing down my hard work.

John saw my tears. "Don't worry," he consoled me, "They'll build you really strong shelves." One man quickly found larger poles, shoving them deep into the ground. In less than half an hour they had reconstructed solid shelving. I thanked them graciously, and they went on their way.

I continued organizing our *champa*. Mom had sewn colorful, drawstring cloth bags into which I placed bagged food staples on the shelves. After a few days John was able to build a table and a mud stove, adding a jerry can oven with aluminum foil smokestacks supported by green twigs.

We had hoped to purchase local produce, but very few people lived in this *new* camp area, leading to a limited diet. (Camp locations were moved frequently since campers depleted the natural jungle resources to construct *champas*.) For meat, we only had a couple cans of tuna and spam that we had brought in. Locally acquired vegetables were kept in a storeroom called the *bodega* (bow-DAY-gah) and divided among the campers. To distribute these, the message was called loudly from *champa* to *champa*, "Bodega . . . Bodega!" One time, responding to the call, our share was three string beans! To supplement our diet, MAF planes dropped food items in the lake. The first drop was hard-to-retrieve broken pieces of cooking bananas but later we enjoyed canned hams.

With *champas* completed, we resumed classes in the central pavilion. We each had a turn to share our basic life stories and where we hoped to serve, helping us understand and appreciate our fellow campers. For our devotional singing, we used the InterVarsity Hymnbook with new songs for us. One was especially meaningful to me:

> May the mind of Christ, my Savior, live in me from day to day,
> by his love and power controlling all I do and say.
> May the love of Jesus fill me as the waters fill the sea;
> him exalting, self abasing, this is victory.

Because of our limited meat supply, we were all excited when a live bull was brought into camp for butchering. To our dismay the bull escaped during the night! Some men found him and killed him on the spot. After butchering lessons, we each received a portion of beef. We canned some on our mud stove. The rest we stored in our pressure cooker bringing it up to pressure each day so that it would last several days.

Before we realized, it was Christmas time. We celebrated a meal together with the strangest assortment of potluck dishes I had ever seen. Spread out on tree-branch benches, metal camping dishes held inventive mixtures made from dried tortillas, flour, sugar, other ingredients, and some vegetables. And they tasted good! I marveled at our ladies' creativity. Someone decorated what looked like a Charlie Brown Christmas tree. Later that day, alone in our *champa*, John and I decided to have a time of prayer for our family and friends back home. Tears came unbidden as we realized we wouldn't see these dear people for long periods of time in years to come.

We knew our big survival trip was soon to come. But, like the rapture, we didn't know when. We were to be ready at any time for this exercise of surviving by ourselves alone in the jungle. One day in class, our director said, "Today is the day our ladies will begin their survival hike. We're going to allow them to go back to their *champa* to grab a bag of s'nuf, a machete, canteen on survival belt, and matches. Please be back here in 15 minutes ready to go." With my heart beating fast, I hurried down the trail to our distant *champa* and gathered my supplies. *(S'nuf was a survival food which was a mixture of crumbled dried tortillas, dried oats, brown sugar, dry milk powder, nuts, and raisins. Similar to granola, s'nuf was short for "it's enough." It could be eaten dry or mixed with water and cooked.)*

A staff man led us out a jungle trail, then gave us his instructions. We were to imagine ourselves in a scenario where a plane crashed in the jungle. One group would be the survivors, hoping to be rescued. Our group needed to locate the survivors.

But first, we would spend the night, each alone in the jungle. The leader spaced us out and left us. I looked for two trees the right distance apart to build my shelter. I made a sleeping platform from thin trees and twigs, cut to length with my machete. Then I tied them together and made a slanting overhang. I also gathered three large, dry logs and arranged them toward a center point for a fire to provide warmth for the cool jungle night and to deter wild animals. My plan was to move the logs toward the center as they burned during the night.

Jungle Training Camp 41

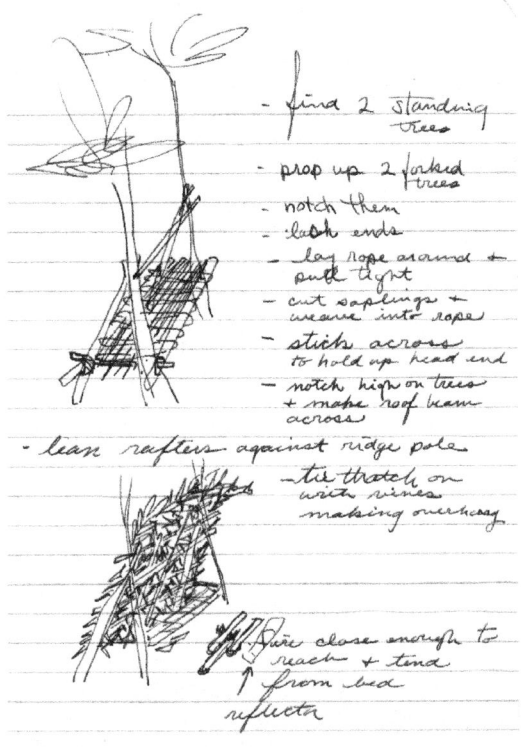

I ate some of my s'nuf. I didn't spot edible plants, but along the lake's edge there were things that looked like snails. Balancing carefully on a log, I gathered them into my canteen cup with some lake water. I started a fire to boil my snails, carefully placing my canteen cup on top. Unfortunately, the twigs shifted and tipped the cup, spilling some water into the fire. *Oh no! My fire!* It sizzled and faded. I held my breath as it came back to life.

About that time, I was surprised to see the staff man coming by to check on me.

"How's it going?" he asked.

"Well, I found some snails and I'm trying to cook them, but I'm not sure if I want to eat them."

"No, I don't think you will," he said with a slight grin. "All you have there are empty snail shells." He looked around. "Where's your firewood? It's a long night, you know."

What I thought was an adequate supply apparently wasn't enough. He disappeared and returned with several logs to add to my collection. I was very grateful since jungle darkness from 6 p.m. to 6 a.m. awaited me!

At nightfall I spread my space blanket over me on my jungle bed. While it was easy to carry and store, the blanket made a crinkle sound each time I moved. And I moved frequently to get comfortable, as well as to climb out to adjust logs to keep the fire burning. At daybreak, I was thankful to have survived the night, although I hadn't slept much.

Then our group of gals gathered to plan how to find the "survivors" from a downed plane. We discussed which direction we should head?

Some suggestions were offered. "I think I heard voices in the night coming from that way," said one of us.

"OK, let's go that way," agreed another. After hiking for some time without success, we headed in another direction, then another. As the day wore on with no success, we realized we needed to stop and set up our sleeping accommodations for another night. Someone suggested making one large fire around which to build our sleeping platforms. The community fire was nice, but not close enough to our beds for warmth. Another cold night under my crinkly blanket wasn't pleasant, but it did provide warmth.

The following day we hiked again, looking for survivors. Unbeknown to us, the staff man followed at a distance to observe our survival skills. Then he joined us for a review of our training. "Do you remember what you need to do when looking for people? How do you know if they're nearby?"

Then we remembered we were supposed to call out and listen for a response. So, we began to practice that as we hiked on.

Finally, the staff man said, "OK, the exercise is over. You didn't find the survivors. Let's return to camp." We must have seemed to him like a silly group of girls. Actually,

My boots that survived jungle camp

we had fun. Joyce, an MK, had grown up in the Peruvian jungle, so this was easy for her. Her comfort zone encouraged us all. Back at camp we debriefed and discovered that we had been close to the survivors, but since we hadn't called out, we missed them. At least we all survived reasonably well.

The men's survival exercise was different. They were allowed to take only their survival belts. They hiked for several hours when the leader stopped them. He chose five to follow him, while the remaining men followed another leader. John was one of the five to be "lost" while the other group needed to find them. The "lost" group hiked until they found a small lake surrounded by dense jungle. They were to camp there.

John built a shelter between a couple trees and found firewood. By that time, it was getting late in the day. His friend was having trouble building his shelter and asked John if he could sleep under his. "I don't think the staff would appreciate that," John said. "But I'll help you build yours."

The next morning the five, as they had been taught, marked trails from the campsite in the four cardinal compass settings. If someone found a marked trail with little machete cuts on tree trunks, they could follow the trail to the "lost ones." Since John was still recovering from *chechen*, they chose him to stay close to camp, with the other four marking trails. While waiting, John took fishhooks and string to catch fish. He took a wrapper from his *chechen* medicine, placed it on the hook and caught a little fish quickly. He cut open that fish to use the innards for bait, and he pulled in a dozen small fish. Suddenly he heard shouting behind him. The other campers had already found the marked trails that led to the "lost ones." They had done a much better job than the girls.

Then the staff had the men make a stretcher from sticks and twigs to transport any wounded or sick person. With the exercise completed, they headed back to the main camp.

As daylight faded, they needed to hurry. When they could barely see, they arrived at the outskirts of camp. I was surprised to see John arriving so soon and carrying his fish trophies. Although very tired, he enjoyed a fish-fry for supper.

Just one last big challenge was the Village Visit. Each family was assigned to spend a week with a local Tzeltal family. Joyce Powlison joined John and me for our visit at the Ruiz's humble home. They kindly gave up their sleeping hut, where we placed our sleeping bags on the packed mud floor. Down the path, a one-seated community outhouse was available. A trough, rather than a hole underneath, fed hungry pigs! We were embarrassed when pigs came running to clean up after us!

In their cooking hut, we made our best efforts to communicate in Tzeltal. We helped with some daily chores: grinding coffee beans, then grinding corn to make tortilla dough. Patting out flat round tortillas was not as easy as it looked. Joyce and I accompanied the ladies to the river to wash clothing. They laughed at our attempts and then showed us how to stand in the water to rub the clothing on a washboard. John went with the older married son to pick corn, beans and *chayotes* (a type of green pear-shaped squash with a cucumber-potato taste). The children shared the workload: sweeping, caring for younger siblings, and washing clothes. Boys found firewood to cut into slivers which they lit to light the dark paths.

We loved their fiesta when girls wore colorful wrap skirts and ribbon-decorated blouses. They recited poems in their church and formed a procession to the airstrip. They chanted, played drums, flutes, violin, and guitar, then ignited fireworks. At midnight we went to bed, but the festivities continued through the night and next day and night at a different location, climaxing with marimba music and fireworks and occasional yelling. Sleep was limited!

Saturday was for coffee shelling. The men poured beans through a machine which loosened some shells and removed others. Then throughout the day, the rest of the family, including children, picked out the remaining shells by hand.

We enjoyed two meals daily, mostly black beans and tortillas. One day they also served little red peppers. Eagerly I took a bite, which was so spicy hot, my eyes filled with tears. They laughed hilariously. For a special meal, they killed a chicken and served it with rice. Delicious! They threw many scraps on the mud floor: eggshells, banana peelings, corn cobs, whatever, to be eaten by chickens or dogs. They swept the floor once a day. After the meal, we usually played with the children.

Our time in the village was a dose of reality to the way many humble people lived. Our training helped us value the villagers' creativity and culture. We appreciated that they had allowed us to visit and learn.

With Jungle Camp training completed, we had our closing interview with the Director. We had "passed" Jungle Camp! Mostly, I think we learned that with the skills we had acquired, we could survive in the worst of situations. It took away the fear of the unknown.

We were eager to head home. Since the men, for one of their projects, had cleared land for an airstrip, we only hiked a short distance. John and I were among the first to fly out by MAF to a small town where we caught a bus to Las Casas. There we enjoyed a restaurant supper with Rodney and Pam. The *lomo fino* dish (like filet mignon), for the equivalent of $1.00 U.S., tasted so good! "I could eat another one of those," said both Rodney and John. So they, and also Pam, ordered another meal! I would have enjoyed more but was too embarrassed to ask. John had lost a lot of weight and had become quite slim, but at that rate he would gain it back quickly.

We picked up our vehicles, caravanned north with Rodney and Pam to the Mexico City SIL Center, then drove on alone to Pennsylvania.

We compiled a Jungle Camp slide presentation, with narration and music. After visiting churches and some time with family, we headed next to the JAARS Center in Waxhaw, North Carolina.

There we attended JAARS Orientation Sessions along with some fellow campers and other new members. We learned about the services JAARS provided for the Wycliffe team worldwide. We were honored to stay in the walk-out basement apartment in Cameron and Elaine Townsend's new home there.

Each of us helped with JAARS maintenance projects on Saturday mornings. John helped Uncle Cam by clearing remnants of their house construction, installing a light fixture on a pole, and other miscellaneous chores.

I helped Elaine with various projects. When she hosted dinner guests upstairs, I helped with set-up, preparation, and serving. One dinner was for JAARS field representatives who had traveled to JAARS for meetings, another for local businessmen. Once we prepared a JAARS Board dinner. I tried to work quickly, and when placing small glasses of tomato juice on the beautifully set table, one spilled on the white linen tablecloth. In a panic I tried to wipe it up. "Oh, it happens to the best of us," Elaine consoled me. "We'll cover it with a napkin and rearrange the name tags." I learned some hostess tips from Elaine. She also held a weekly Bible study in her home for JAARS ladies. Sometimes John and I helped stuff envelopes for the Townsend's mailings. Elaine complimented John frequently on how fast he worked.

Finishing Orientation, we worked at the JAARS Center. They needed aviation maintenance staff in the hangar and requested new aviation mechanics to serve there a year before a field assignment. John readied planes for field usage, installing radios, communication and navigational equipment, and making sure that the aircraft were mechanically ready. He worked alongside premier JAARS aviation mechanics, Ernie Rich and Les Bancroft, who had led the Technical Evaluation at Norman SIL, and had served in Peru. Not only were they experienced, knowledgeable men, but they also had a zest for life and for serving the Lord in their special roles. And they weren't opposed to having fun or pulling pranks on others—like placing an airplane to look like it had crashed into someone's house while they were away on a trip. Or blasting the recorded roar of a plane taking off near a friend's bedroom during the night.

I worked with Marge Bancroft preparing promotional flyers and ethnic stationery. I helped her prepare for several JAARS fund-raising banquets around North Carolina, which supplied a good part of the JAARS yearly budget in those days.

Marge looked for opportunities to promote JAARS in the local area. So we participated in a "Festival in the Park" event. Since this was basically an art festival, Marge suggested that I paint a large picture of Tariri, a Peruvian Candoshi Indian Chief, inspired by a mural in a Wycliffe display at the New York World Fair. Uncle Cam had befriended Tariri who helped greatly in the Scripture translation for their people. He had said, "We were sick of killing, but we could only be safe by keeping on killing. Then people were afraid of us." The painting included a broken spear he no longer used after becoming a Christian. In our tent we also had Bible displays and literature available for the people who stopped by.

John and I also helped in a dedication ceremony in Myrtle Beach of a refurbished airplane ready for service in Brazil. It would be ferried there by Bob Dix, a JAARS pilot whom John had known as a student at LeTourneau. Those who had helped fund the project, along with other dignitaries were invited. A Tzeltal Indian from Mexico, with his young son, also participated. They had learned some English from Jungle Camp staff. The boy was amazed seeing so many planes at the busy airport. When a large one took off with a huge roar, he yelled, "Wow, he musta eaten a lota chickens!"

We tried to keep open to where the Lord might lead us for a field assignment. It seemed the staff had Nepal in mind for us. Earlier John had been interested in Alaska, but JAARS didn't do aviation service there. When Jim Rainsberger, Chief Pilot from the Bolivia Branch, visited the JAARS Center, he was looking for a mechanic familiar with Cessnas, since they were purchasing one to serve there. After talking with Jim, it seemed like a good fit for our skills. We prayed about it and were assigned to the Bolivia Branch. Excused from the required full year at JAARS, we prepared for departure.

After a final round of visits to family and local churches, and 90% of our monthly support promised, we were permitted to leave. Pastor Burtner held a commissioning service at Brookfield Bible Church, with an encouraging send-off by people whom we had come to know well.

In Bolivia we would study Spanish for three months, then finally begin our "hands-on" service.

Chapter 4
Bolivia (1972-1976)
Life in the Jungle

———————————✈

Going to Bolivia

It seemed like we had been preparing forever, but finally we were ready to head to Bolivia—our field of service. However, before serving at the Jungle Center, we needed to study Spanish in the city of Cochabamba.

Saying goodbye to family was going to be difficult. We expected it would be four years until we would see them again.

Unfortunately, our February departure in 1972 became a hectic affair. A dangerous winter storm paralyzed our area, so my parents offered to drive us to Pittsburgh a day early to assure our reserved flight departure.

My grandmother joined us for Sunday dinner at my parent's home, after which we carried our luggage to the car. Grandma's health was failing, so she couldn't walk outside to wave goodbye. As I leaned to give her a farewell hug, she began to sob. I knew she was happy we were serving the Lord, but our being so far away was hard. I tried to cheer her up and thanked her for her prayers for our work. Perhaps she sensed that she might not see us again this side of heaven.

Thankful for a safe drive through the snow, Dad and Mom dropped us off at a motel close to the airport to catch the next day's flight.

Eastern's 727 flight took us to Miami. Upon arrival there, we called staff at the Wycliffe warehouse. The friendly host couple picked us up and drove us to tour the facilities where we had sent our barrels to be shipped to Bolivia.

At Wycliffe's guesthouse, we got a little sleep. At 1:00 a.m. our *Aerolineas Argentinas* flight left Miami. We were too excited to sleep on the plane. On a brief stopover in Lima, Peru, we saw their nice coastal airport set amidst brown flatlands strewn with adobe homes. A few hours later we stepped from the plane into the thin air of La Paz, Bolivia.

La Paz, located on Bolivia's western side, is almost 12,000 feet above sea level. It sits in a "bowl" surrounded by the high mountains of the *altiplano* (high plane). Buildings fill the bottom of the bowl, up the sides, and on top, where the airport is located. A story is told of how on one of the first flights to that airport, oxygen masks deployed automatically because of the extremely thin air.

David Farah, SIL Bolivia Government Relations Representative, met us and reminded us to take it easy in the high altitude. He guided us adeptly through airport customs and visa procurement. After retrieving our luggage, we felt short of breath, especially John as he carried a big suitcase. We realized that Dave was quite popular as many friends greeted him. He drove us to the La Paz SIL Group House, where they lived. Dave's wife Gloria served as hostess and showed us to a nice guest room with a panoramic view of houses, busy streets, and rocky slopes. Quechua Indians dressed in brightly-colored clothing moved among others in western-style clothing.

After a short rest, we joined other guests at the supper table. John said, "This looks and smells so good." But, after a prayer of thanks, John suddenly felt sick. He excused himself and returned to our room. It was altitude sickness, which often occurs when you first arrive to an extremely high altitude. I felt fine and enjoyed the meal with the others. Then afterwards Gloria kindly took John some coca tea, which helped him recover for the next day.

Spanish Study

After finishing paperwork in La Paz, our final flight was on *Lloyd Aereo Boliviano* to Cochabamba for language-learning. Our Group House host and hostess met us and drove us through heavily bicycled streets to our new home for three months.

Cochabamba, a busy city in central Bolivia, is located in the Cochabamba Valley in the 8,000 feet high Andes Mountain Range. Bolivia's fourth largest city, it is named from a compound of two Quechua words: *qucha* "lake" and *pampa* "open plain." Because of year-round spring-like temperatures, it has been called the "City of Eternal Spring." It was largely populated by Quechua people, Aymaras, and about 30% mestizos (having mixed European and indigenous ancestry). Beautiful Spanish-style houses contrasted with adjoining mud hovels. Some main roads were paved, others were dirt with rocks. Downtown traffic was almost all one-way. Traffic lights served a few main corners, otherwise you honked during the day, and flashed lights at night for the right of way.

We got settled in a second-floor apartment above the printshop at the small SIL complex. We were thankful to make ourselves at home, using a furloughing colleague's household items. From our windows, we could observe Cochabamba culture on the dirt street below, like animals being driven by young children, or a peddler passing by and calling out to sell his wares.

Some Wycliffe families lived in private homes across the street. Translation and literacy personnel served in mountain villages and returned to this Center to recoup, process their work, and handle personal needs. We ate lunch and supper in the dining room of the Group House, enjoying new quinoa dishes and peanut soup. Cochabamba's dry fall season combined warm sunshine with cool breezes for a perfect study climate.

Hank Spenst, the language-learner coordinator, shared a change of plans for us. "Your scheduled language school has just closed down," he said. "So, we arranged for classes at another school, just ten blocks away." He recommended that we get bicycles to ride back and forth to school.

Our new schedule fell into place. During morning hours, we listened to Spanish tapes trying to hear, remember, and speak strange new sounds. After lunch, we biked up a busy street to our classes, huffing and puffing in the thin, high-altitude air. John and I had Spanish grammar class together, then individual Spanish dialogue classes at 3:00, 4:00 and 5:00 p.m., with more study after supper. Once a week all the students gathered to sing Spanish songs. Our heads were swimming with vocabulary and verb tenses. Teachers pushed us as fast as we could go through the lessons. We could have assimilated more at a slower pace, but we did the best we could.

⸺ We ventured out to purchase food items in local markets. When John saw good-looking sausages, he forgot the word for half, so bought a whole kilo! Oh well, we ate them all.

We became friends with fellow students from another mission, Ron and Carolyn Stansel, who were studying Aymara. One Saturday we joined them for a relaxing outing with a picnic lunch. Heading out to the country in their truck, we traveled along a narrow road with a drop-off of several feet on both sides. Trucks piled high with produce were coming in for market day. People perched high on top of the produce while others hung tightly to the truck sides.

Up ahead suddenly there was a big commotion as a truck went off the side of the road, tumbling people and produce everywhere in a cloud of dust. As we came alongside, we stopped to help the Quechua people who were moaning and screaming loudly. Ron and John tried to help lift the truck so some people underneath could be pulled out, but the people were pulling in different directions and could not be coordinated.

We loaded some of the injured people in the truck to take them to a hospital. Back in town, we got snarled in the market day traffic, just inching along with people and carts everywhere. Finally arriving at the hospital, they would only take a couple of the injured and sent us across town to another hospital. But the traffic was hardly moving. With our passengers moaning in pain, we felt frustrated with the urgent need to get them to care. When we saw a policeman, Ron told him our situation. He kindly provided us with a police escort with blaring siren, which enabled us to go a little faster. The other hospital staff hesitantly accepted the injured. Rather than a pleasant picnic excursion, we returned home totally exhausted.

During class break, we made a quick trip in the JAARS Cessna 206 to our Jungle Center, Tumi Chucua (TOO-me CHU-kwa), to check on future housing possibilities and other needs. Through high mountain passes, cloudy turbulence, and over dense jungle, we finally arrived near the northern edge of Bolivia's tropical world. We landed on the grass strip and taxied to the open-ended hangar where our future colleagues came to greet us.

This tropical setting, rich with foliage and palm trees, was where we would live and serve. The Jungle Center was located a short flight (or long boat ride) from the jungle town of Riberalta and along Lake Tumi Chucua (hence the name). Houses were like summer cottages, mostly constructed of wood and resting on pillars that raised them about 18 inches above the ground. They had corrugated aluminum roofs and screened windows rather than glass. A few larger buildings served other needs.

At this Jungle Center, Bible translators, literacy workers, and support personnel worked together doing the many tasks essential to provide God's Word in the heart language of thirteen different language groups. We would be part of a team, each contributing our God-given abilities and skills to serve God from this remote spot of the world.

During our short visit, we bought a small jungle house, recently built for short-term volunteers. They would be leaving just before we were scheduled to arrive there.

The house was along the "back path" which ran parallel to houses lined along the lake on the "front path." Although the 20 x 24 foot house was small, it was cleverly compact, cute, and cozy for two. A 10 x 20 foot screened-in porch provided extra space.

Back in Cochabamba, we continued language learning, although John was now anxious to discard books and get to the airplanes. He focused on some Spanish technical terms to take the needed Bolivian aircraft mechanics license exam. In May John took the exam in La Paz with a designated interpreter for complex Spanish questions. He passed successfully and was officially licensed to maintain aircraft in Bolivia.

We made some purchases in Cochabamba for our jungle house. We ordered foam for a mattress and purchased a gas cylinder and an Argentine-made apartment-size stove. (That would replace the two kerosene burners sitting on a cupboard for cooking, which we had observed in our new jungle house.) While our new stove had no pilot light, that would save on gas usage. We'd use matches to start the burners and would light the oven by turning a knob for gas and then pushing a button to rub two stones together. We also bought curtain fabric for our living room windows. These purchases we placed in storage to be flown out on a weekly supply flight to the Jungle Center, as space became available.

Three months was not long enough to master Spanish, but at the Jungle Center we would interact with our co-workers in English most of the time. We would use our Spanish to communicate with Bolivian workers on the Center and local people, and hopefully continue to grow in our ability to speak in real situations.

Jungle Life

On June 3rd we were happy to fly again to Tumi Chucua, this time to live and work there.

To serve the translators, various facilities had been developed, including the hangar, radio communications shack, clinic, a school for missionary children, commissary, group dining room, maintenance shop, mail room, classrooms, and offices. People serving in each of these areas formed a great team. The larger main building housed a laundry area, finance office and library downstairs, with a small apartment and an open-air auditorium upstairs where we met for Sunday services, Wednesday prayer meetings, school assemblies, and other events.

After being on the move for several years, we were extremely grateful for the cute little house nestled among mango trees, banana palms and pineapple plants. Its cedar-like wood and corrugated aluminum roof were a special treat compared to our *champa* during Jungle Training. We knew that training helped us in this transition.

We unpacked our belongings we had brought with us and found places for them, reminded of God's faithful provisions for us. While we had a flush-toilet, older houses used outhouses. We were thankful for a shower stall, although with unheated water. The three-quarter size electric refrigerator defrosted naturally when the JAARS workers turned off the generator supplying electricity each night. We placed an electric fan to pull air through the house from the abundant screened windows. For occasional cooler weather, wooden frames held stretched clear plastic for each window. The porch housed plastic laundry tubs and a wringer washer. We could dry clothes on lines strung between posts behind the house.

While we were getting settled, different families at the Center invited us for meals. We got acquainted and learned practical ideas for successful jungle living. Meals were made completely from scratch. At one home, a quick rain shower rudely dripped through their roof onto our waiting dessert—a lemon meringue pie! We assured our hostess, hesitant to serve it, that it was no problem.

Due to importation complications, our barrels of supplies had not arrived from the States. We bought pans and essential kitchenware at someone's yard sale (redistribution sale, they called it).

After our first Sunday evening service John and I relaxed in our new home, when suddenly there was a loud explosion. I thought it must be our new gas stove John had just installed. When John laughed, I was confused! That's when I learned about "acetylene bombs" which the JAARS guys used to initiate newcomers, or to celebrate a special event. (Welding gas was pumped into a balloon, then wrapped in newspaper with a long-twisted end which served as a fuse to light with a match!)

The explosion was followed by a stream of people coming down the path singing, "There's a welcome here . . . There's a Christian welcome here." Each carried a can of food or some item for our pantry. Together we celebrated in our house as I showed them our new stove, thankfully intact!

About 70 Wycliffe/SIL personnel, plus children, lived at the Jungle Center. It was a daily buzz of activity. Motorcycles (*motos* they called them) and bicycles passed up and down the two main paths as personnel went about their various responsibilities. Others pursued their activities on foot. John began his work in the hangar with lots to do. I began working as a typist at our Technical Services Department (TSD)—not my first choice, but possibly a good place for me.

Slowly we adjusted to Jungle Center living. The abundance of fruit was a great asset to meal planning. Locals sold garden produce in a nearby thatched-roof pavilion. The center's commissary opened for business during certain hours twice weekly. We could pre-order available meat cuts retrieved from a walk-in refrigerator or freezer. While variety was minimal, we were happy for what was available.

Some ladies asked if I wanted a maid to help with housework. To me that seemed like a high-society luxury. I opted out until—after the first weeks of learning to cook from scratch with available foods, soaking fresh vegetables in iodine water to avoid amoebic dysentery, boiling water to sterilize dishes, washing and drying clothes, cleaning the house—I was exhausted. At 9:00 p.m. one evening after finally finishing my duties, tears flowed. How could I do all this and have time for productive ministry here?

I conceded! I needed a helper! Doña Victoria worked for us weekday mornings for a locally appropriate salary which proved to be within our financial budget. I practiced Spanish with her, and she didn't laugh when I asked her to hang *me* on the clothesline! She washed clothes and hung them to dry, swept and dusted, and soaked fresh vegetables in iodine water. She cleaned the half-plucked chickens for us, and I was happy for her to take home the head and feet for her family's soup. I taught her simple recipes which she could prepare for our lunch. After she learned to light and regulate our oven, we enjoyed the bread she prepared and baked weekly. She roasted our fresh coffee beans over her home fire, which we later ground in the community grinder. Our dear maid truly enabled me to survive!

One day, walking by the commissary, John and I saw several children with dark things climbing on their hands and arms. Upon closer inspection, we were shocked to see that they were young tarantulas. "Do your parents know what you are playing with?" we asked.

"Oh, they won't hurt us as long as we don't hurt them," they responded casually. Life growing up in the jungle was fun for the children, running barefoot in the safety of our Jungle Center, creating their own games, and swimming like fish in the lake.

Most people migrated to the lake's swimming area in the late afternoons. This was bath time for those who brought soap. There were pirañas in the lake, but we learned that they were naturally well fed and would only bother people if there was blood or an open sore. John and I usually chose to shower at our house. Being so hot, a cold shower refreshed us after the initial shiver. Some days we even took more than one shower to cool off. A really hot day we dubbed as a "three-shower day" (the opposite of a three-dog night).

For potable drinking water, several houses shared a "burn barrel," a 55-gallon barrel fastened horizontally over a fire box, with a spigot at one end. Every few days, a huge fire was set to boil water in the barrel. Then families collected water in buckets and cooled it in their homes. A series of cooling containers, poured off from the top (leaving sediment in the bottom) one after the other, resulted in cool, clean water, to be refrigerated for drinking.

We got our water from our neighbor's barrel, but John decided there must be a way to pipe water into our house. He designed and had built a high brick base for a barrel, which included a fire box that could also serve as a BBQ grilling area. Then he installed pipe from the barrel to our kitchen sink. When the boiled water cooled a little, John opened a drain valve at the base to remove sediment. Then  he opened another valve to gravity feed water into our house as needed. We had safe, potable water from the faucet in our kitchen!

I got so thirsty in the heat, and nothing would quench my thirst, even when I felt bloated with all the water I had drunk. I craved Pepsi Cola, my drink of choice in hot weather, but that was not available. I think I went through withdrawal! With local lemons available, I made lemonade. So, that became my substitute—more satisfying than water, if not better than Pepsi.

With no dairy products in our area, we used milk powder. The milk had to be really cold to taste OK for drinking. It worked well for cooking. Once a year we could order dried food items from the States: big containers of mixed vegetables, dried peas, powdered eggs, and milk. The powdered eggs worked fine for baking, but unpleasant for scrambled eggs. We were blessed when Leon Moyer arrived to do community development, setting up chicken projects in jungle villages and at our Center. Real, fresh eggs tasted wonderful!

People told us we would love the mangoes when they came into season. We tasted our first one with great anticipation. But it tasted like kerosene to me, and the stringy flesh stuck between my teeth. "I think mangoes are over-rated," I told John. Then friends steered us from the "common" mango to better varieties of that fruit, which really were delicious and abundantly available.

Cooking from scratch was a challenge for me. In the States I had relied heavily on pre-packaged mixes, especially helpful for our busy early marriage schedules. Now I missed cake mixes, Hamburger Helper, and cereals. We made our own granola. If I wanted to make potato salad, I had to first make the mayo, a tricky procedure for me.

Some ladies were great cooks, one of whom served us a delicious mock pumpkin pie, made from green mangoes, or was it papaya? I decided to try it for myself to make a dessert for a couple we had invited for supper. But I neglected to get the recipe. Oh well, I just put in a lot of spices and sugar, which made sense to me. When I served the pie, our guests started eating while I was away from the table. I heard a loud "Yuk!" I was crestfallen. I tasted the pie for myself, and it wasn't that bad . . . whoops! The aftertaste, so utterly bitter, made my head swim. I apologized and told them not to eat it. Although a challenge, our healthy meals without preservatives were good for us.

Young pineapple plants grew in our yard, taking three years until pineapples were produced. In our second year we began to harvest the fresh, tasty fruit. Banana palms behind the house often had several ripe stalks at the same time. That's when all possible banana recipes came into use. John learned to cut the stalk and hang it inside our screened porch to protect the almost ripe fruit from the birds.

John cleared some jungle growth behind our house to make a yuca (YOU-kah) garden. He just stuck some cuttings from other plants into the ground, and new sprouts grew. Their roots produced a tasty underground tuber. Cutting away its thick skin and tough center, I boiled chunks in water as a potato substitute, and sometimes deep-fried strips.

John noticed a visitor in our yuca patch—a *hoachi*. Like a large rabbit with short ears, it liked to eat yuca. John thought we might like to eat him. Sometimes John took his gun to the yuca patch, and one day he successfully killed the intruder and provided some nice meat for us.

Our seasons were different from the four seasons we had been accustomed to. Mostly, we had two seasons, rainy and dry. But it was almost always hot in the 90s with high humidity. Around November, following months of little rain and much dust, frequent showers and thunderstorms began to produce green grass and thick undergrowth. Then, family garden plots were cleared and burned to plant corn and yuca. Slash and burn agriculture served to replenish soil which was regularly drained of nutrients by the rain.

During rainy season, it was difficult to get our laundry dry. Twice a week Doña Victoria washed several loads and hung the clothes on the clothesline. I took them down later in the day. But often as we ate our lunch, we heard in the distance a sound like soda fizzing in a glass. It was rain falling at the far end of the lake. Both John and I would run to the clothesline to take down the clothes as fast as we could. The sound of rain increased as it approached our area, coming closer and closer. Sometimes we and our bundled clothes were well sprinkled before we crashed back into the house, just before the tropical downpour.

On rare occasions a cool breeze from the south, reminiscent of Pennsylvania autumns, refreshed us. If the wind was strong, we covered the windows with the protective plastic frames. Refreshed, we had more energy to work.

Our Work

In the hangar John was glad to be at the task of maintaining aircraft for the Lord's work. He sensed anew the responsibility of flawless upkeep as daily precious lives were flown here and there over the dense jungles.

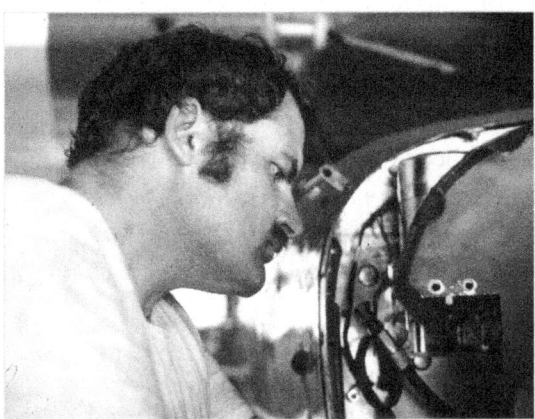

Two capable local mechanics helped John. In the open-air hangar, they serviced the new Cessna TU206 as well as two Helio Courier 295s. There were also at that time two Helio Courier 391s which were being retired from service. An early project for John was to get them into good shape to be flown back to the U.S. to be sold.

John's daily work varied, but here is a sample of an especially busy day from John's perspective, on October 3, 1972:

6:00   The alarm sounds, followed by devotions and breakfast.

6:55   I wonder if there's mail and radio messages for pickup today.

7:00   Planning for the day: Inspection due on the Cessna. Landing gear shock struts need inflating on one Helio. I'll show Miguel how to do that. Also, ready the flight for Jim to leave at 8:00 with 40 gallons of fuel. I'll fill that up after Helio six-three-zero leaves since it's parked next to the pump.

7:45   One flight off. Windows cleaned and oil checked for the next flight. Sounds like the battery isn't turning the engine over properly. The battery solenoid is stuck. Maybe the battery is low.

8:10   Now the engine starts up fine, and the flight is off.

8:30   Back to the inspection. Sounds like Jim is coming back. The voltage regulator won't work? Let's check those points. Yes, here's the trouble; that point is dirty.

8:50   He's off again.

11:30   The inspection's coming along well, but I'm glad we have two days to do it. Maybe we can get some extra work done on that plane.

12:10	Good! Here comes six-three-zero. I'll help square it away before lunch.
12:45	I'll head back to the hangar as Jim is due in shortly and needs to go right back out. I'll stop at radio to find out his location. Oh, a message says he's having trouble again and will cancel his second flight. But Don will still be going in the other plane.
4:00	Glad to see Don back with six-three-zero. He'll still be able to make his three six-minute flights to Portachuala for bilingual school students. The survey has been rescheduled for tomorrow morning, so we'll need to finish that inspection this afternoon.
6:30	Inspection's done. Time to go home for supper.
10:00	Time to hit the hay. With the survey flight scheduled for a 7:00 a.m. takeoff, it'll be another long day tomorrow.

Not all days were that hectic, but when busy times came, we were grateful to the Lord for safety. We were reminded from Proverbs 21:31 (KJV) that *"The horse is prepared against the day of battle: but safety is of the Lord."*

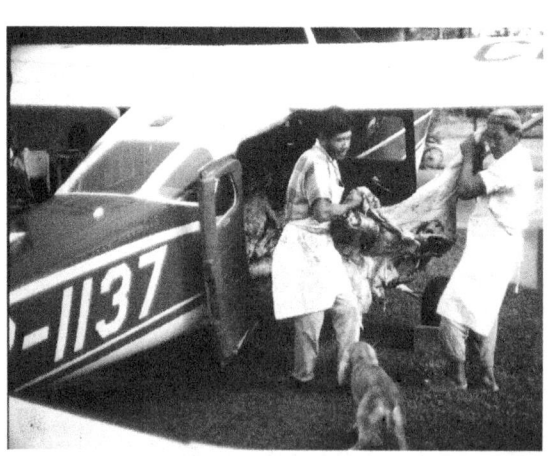

Meat has arrived!

The JAARS airplanes carried our translators, their families and equipment, to and from isolated tribal locations inaccessible by road. They transported our personnel between our Center and the nearest large city (Cochabamba, 350 miles away) and brought in food and supplies to the Center. They brought language helpers to the Center to work on translation and village teachers to attend bilingual teacher training. Occasionally they transported local folks, which helped subsidize costs of translator's flights. They transported our personnel for dental work, medical attention, and movement of children attending schools away from home. Emergency flights saved lives. Surveys were made in isolated areas for possible new tribal contacts. These flights not only helped with our personnel needs, they made Bible translation possible.

Area missions often helped each other. On one occasion a pilot from Andes Evangelical Mission brought their small Maule aircraft to our hangar where he and John worked together to do an engine overhaul—no easy task in the jungle with limited facilities.

John was quite pleased when the Helio Courier he had been working on flew again after ten months offline. It had been grounded for a major change on the wing attachment, and other complications. The addition of a seat in the Cessna made room for a child or small person.

Normally only small aircraft used our jungle airstrip. When we initiated DC-3 service for supply flights between Cochabamba and Tumi Chucua, the larger plane got stuck in the mud. Even the Bolivian President's plane got stuck when visiting the Center.

So, it was decided to regrade our airstrip. Getting a tractor-bulldozer there to do the work involved numerous steps:
- Over mountains by truck to river port
- Two-week launch trip down river
- A 40-mile overland drive (ouch!)
- A two-week wait
- River barge to nearby port
- Arrived at Tumi Chucua Center in July of 1974
- Airstrip too solid to be workable (dry season)
- Damage discovered in the tractor's tracks (from overland travel)
- Waiting for parts to arrive and for soil to soften.

Following land survey and drainage preparation, they put the tractor-bulldozer to work. After the grading was done, the airstrip was safe for the larger planes to land in rainy season.

------ꙮ------

My work assignment turned out differently than I had anticipated. Since the school for the MKs (missionary kids) on the Center was well-staffed for the upcoming school year, I had instead been asked to serve as a typist in the Technical Services Department (TSD). Here the Associate Director for Field Operations had his office. He supervised translation programs, giving motivation and direction to 13 translation teams, arranging finances for Scripture publications, overseeing community development, and the bilingual teacher training programs. I worked with his assistant, Martha Garrard.

I felt disappointed that my training as a teacher would not be used. I thought, *I came all the way to Bolivia to type?* But, as I became involved in preparing projects for press, I slowly realized that I was prepared for this job. I would be using tools in my "tool chest." I'd had experience typing with my government job. My teaching experience had given me good background for arranging words and pictures on pages for reading books and literacy materials in ways that would be attractive for learners. Preparing Scriptures for press was an honor and a joy.

This office was air-conditioned to protect our equipment against humidity—something few others enjoyed! Martha knew the procedures well and trained me on how things were done. We worked within a weekly deadline to send projects to our printshop in Cochabamba on the return supply flight. I enjoyed the work a lot and felt that God had led me to my niche, best suited to my gifts and abilities This was the launch of my new career for years to come in Wycliffe.

We prepared the Scripture books on the latest equipment, an ITEL Word Processor with a Selectric typewriter moving ball which held the engraved letters. As we typed, we could punch a paper tape on an attachment on the machine's right side. A series of eight holes in different configurations recorded each keystroke on the tape as we typed. On the left side we could fasten a prepared tape and start the reader. The machine typed automatically until we stopped it.

After a translator checked the typed manuscript marking corrections or changes, we ran the tape again, stopping it to make corrections, and at the same time punching an edited tape with the new

changes. Later we ran that new tape for an error-free automatic typing. We stored the tapes in a cupboard with a section for each language.

This equipment facilitated our work completely within Bolivia, avoiding long delays from the time Scripture was translated until it was printed. It circumvented having to send revised materials back and forth to another country for processing. We sent camera-ready pages for printing to our Cochabamba printshop.

Typing in different languages (which we didn't know) involved careful work. Sometimes we typed from hand-written copy. When frequent words became familiar, our slow speed increased. When a project was completed, we started on a different language. Each language required some letter (font) configurations uncommon to English, representing sounds unknown in English. Specially made balls for the various languages were exchanged on the machine as needed. Certain letters might have diacritical markings, such as an accent mark or diereses (í è é ä ū) for which we used a "dead key" position on the keyboard to place the mark in the same position as the letter. Other unique letters were engraved on the ball (ñ ŋ œ ṇ ɨ).

Martha had devised a great apparatus to help us keep our eyes on the line we were reading from as we typed. Because, if we looked away—like at the keyboard—we might look back to the same word in another line. Without knowing the language, we didn't realize if we skipped a line or section or repeated a phrase. We clipped the manuscript on the device at eye level, then lowered a line marker bar with a foot pedal. It served us very well.

In those days, we also formatted, typed, and printed prayer letters for our colleagues, usually from their handwritten copy. We prepared forms and items needed by the various offices and staff as well as reading and health books in the different languages. There was never a lack of projects. Our office also housed the only copy machine on our Center.

One evening each week, Center personnel met for share and prayer in groups, each supporting one of the 13 jungle translation projects. We joined the Ignaciano (Ig-NAH-see-ON-oh) group, with translators Willis and Becky Ott. They had begun their work in 1956, finding a few believers to whom evangelical missionaries and national evangelists had witnessed, who were eager to have Scriptures in their heart language. The Otts learned the language, gathered text, created an alphabet, and analyzed the grammar, with medical work as an extra. They first translated Mark's Gospel and made picture story books on the Life of Christ. Medical clinics held in villages opened the door for the Ott family to move to the village of Argentina. There they found new believers and others with an awakened interest in Bible truths as they met together to study the Word, sing, and pray in the Ignaciano language. In our weekly prayer group meetings, we learned more about the Ott's ministry and prayed for their work.

Two Araona wives share a hut.

One weekend, John and I had an opportunity to visit the Araona (Ah-rra-OWN-ah) location along with pilots Jim Rainsberger and Don Evans and their wives, Carole and Gail. Translators Don and Mary Pitman, being away, had made arrangements for the Araona people to welcome us. We landed at a remote airstrip where three Araona men met us. I had memorized greetings in their language, which they appreciated, but when they continued to speak, I couldn't understand anything. The men led us to a canoe, paddled us downriver to their village, and showed us the house where we would overnight. We enjoyed interacting with the Araona people.

Bilingual Teacher Training

Our MK school followed the U.S. school year. However, Bolivian schools had their summer vacation during the U.S. winter (November-January). In preparation for a three-month bilingual summer teacher training course for indigenous teachers, there was a flurry of activity on our Center: preparing student housing, furniture construction, adding study rooms, preparing teaching materials, and flights to bring the teacher trainees in from villages far and near.

SIL provided this service in cooperation with the Bolivian Department of Education, which appreciated our helpful service to their country. SIL literacy staff trained the teachers, while the teachers' salaries were paid for by the government. We were thus able to encourage literacy among the communities where we had Bible translation projects. People could then read the Scriptures in their language.

Our personnel helped establish bilingual schools in ethnic communities for children to learn initially in their own language, rather than being overwhelmed in Spanish-only schools. Most bilingual schools were located where there had been no previous fiscal schools, in remote locations where Spanish speaking teachers would not want to go. Many bilingual teachers had first learned to read through SIL literacy workers serving alongside the Bible translators in the villages. Some newly literate teachers were just steps ahead of those they taught, so the summer training was vital. Training sessions were in Spanish, a stretch for many teacher trainees who themselves were learning Spanish. For many of the students this was the first time for them to interact with other groups. A few felt insecure at first and had reservations about associating with the others. Most adapted well, made friends, and later found it difficult to say goodbye.

Along with the training, each language group held devotions and Bible classes in their own language. Some student teachers learned for the first time that salvation was offered through Christ, and decided to follow Him as Lord and Savior. In the 1972 session, 26 students from seven ethnic groups made this decision. When someone shared Christ with a group of four, they responded, "That's why we came—to find out." Soon three made personal commitments. Manuel too, wanted to belong to the Lord, and Demetrio, a new babe in Christ, explained the way.

Our literacy personnel developed schoolbooks in the various languages for the community schools: graded reading books, health books, and others. They also held writing workshops other times of the year where participants wrote stories about the history of their people, folklore stories, and personal observations. These were printed by a simple ditto machine process, so the participants could return to their communities with their printed stories. These booklets helped provide a body of literature in their language for reading practice, so that translated Scriptures could be read and understood as they were produced.

Annual Conference

Once a year Wycliffe/SIL members in Bolivia gathered for an Annual Conference at our Jungle Center. For several days a special invited speaker encouraged us spiritually. Bolivia Branch business sessions and elections for our field leaders were held. As translators reported their year's activities, we were blessed to hear of translations progressing in various language groups, with new believers and growing village churches. We joined in prayer for overcoming challenges in bringing God's Word to those hearing it for the first time.

Business sessions at the Conference included reports from each of the departments, discussions on current priorities, and presentation of work papers related to completing "The Task" in Bolivia. Objectives listed in our 1973 Conference were:

- Basic Goal: For each of our language projects, the translated Scriptures in use by a growing body of believers with indigenous leadership relating to other Bolivian believers.
- Translation: To translate the entire New Testament and Old Testament background material into each of these languages.
- Linguistics: To analyze and assimilate each language, enabling the creation of a phonology, grammar, lexicon, vernacular literature, and Scripture translation.

- Literacy: To develop a core of indigenous readers and writers producing literature.
- Leadership: To stimulate indigenous leadership enabling the group to interact successfully among themselves and other Bolivians.

To show determination for completing the task, termination dates were targeted: January 1, 1984, to finish all our work in Bolivia, with completion projections for each language:

 70-71 – Guaraní;
 72-73 – Sirionó;
 74-75 – Chipaya, Guaraní II, Ignaciano, Quechua;
 76-77 – Araona, Aymara, Chácabo, Ese Ejja, Guarayo, Tacana;
 78-79 – Chiquitano;
 80-81 – Cavineña

(Remaining Bolivian language groups were being handled by New Tribes Mission, South America Mission, and American Bible Society.) Our leaders challenged us to the urgency of completing translations as soon as possible without sacrificing accuracy.

We also heard reports of spiritual interest growing across Bolivia. Some bookstores ran out of Bibles. Our Government Relations colleague held Bible studies with high government officials in La Paz.

Tools for Transportation

The Cessna TU206 had been purchased in 1971 to serve in the higher altitude areas. Its turbocharged engine used the flow of exhaust gasses to compress the intake gas, forcing more air into the engine to produce more power. Translation teams also appreciated the added weight allowances that plane provided.

Ron and Fran Olson, who worked in the high mountain Chipaya (Chi-PIE-yah) area really appreciated the Cessna. Fran wrote about the difference it meant for them in traveling to that area:

August 1961—

Ron had gone ahead to check on housing in Chipaya, but this was my first trip to our tribal location.

First day:

Missionary friends in Cochabamba helped me catch the 7 a.m. train, putting baby bottles, diapers, lunch, and extra warm clothes where they would be handy during the 9-hour trip over the mountains. Debbie, 2½ months old, missed her bed and didn't like cold milk. Every time I dozed, she cried. Ron and Dave Farah met us in Oruro in the middle of a cold sandstorm. We spent the night with missionaries there.

Second day:

Up early to pack the jeep and head for Chipaya. This high plateau (12,000 feet) is flat but not smooth. Often the best driving was off the "road." The ruts and sand challenged our ingenuity. We crossed the first river by bridge, the second by raft, and the rest as best we could. All went well until sundown when we sank in spongy sand in the Lauca River. Dave stayed with the jeep while Ron and I walked an hour in the dark to the next town. Some men with a truck agreed to pull out the jeep. The river was freezing over by the time they got the jeep out. Ron and Dave were thoroughly chilled, and their feet were numb and aching from the icy water. The schoolteacher graciously shared his small house with us.

Third day:

We were only ten miles from Chipaya but had to wait until afternoon for the last river to thaw so we could cross it. A carload of officials we met in the village wanted to accompany us to Chipaya but changed their mind after spending two hours trying to get their car out of drifted sand. So we went on alone, finally reaching Chipaya about 4:30 p.m., tired but glad to be there among the people to whom the Lord had sent us.

October 1972–
    Ron had gone ahead to Chipaya to re-roof our house.
    Pilot Jim Rainsberger loaded the plane for our 7:00 a.m. flight. Fresh bread, eggs, and extra warm clothes were close at hand. Amy, 2 ½ years old, was excited about going to see her dad. (Her three older sisters were at boarding school.)
    Leaving the valley (9,000 feet) we climbed to 17,000 feet to cross the mountains. Forty minutes later we passed Oruro and leveled off over the plateau—high above its ruts, rivers, and sand dunes. In another forty minutes we landed in Chipaya where Ron met us with the motorcycle. As Jim headed back to Cochabamba, we rode into Chipaya for an 8:30 breakfast.

Realizing the valuable service the Cessna provided for the highland location of Chipaya as well as Cochabamba and La Paz, the Aviation Department decided that another Cessna should be added. In June of 1973 a second Cessna joined the fleet, a TU210, which could fly faster because of retractable landing gear.

New Experiences

    Tumi Chucua was an isolated village, basically only accessible by plane in those days. Not being able to get out and go places could give one a sense of claustrophobia. One of the gals coined a phrase which described this feeling well. She called the ailment a "grand mall seizure" with anxiety symptoms of inability to go shopping at a mall, mostly affecting women. However, the nearby jungle town of Riberalta provided occasional shopping options when several girls scheduled a five-minute flight, sharing the cost. On my first trip there, my companions coached me on how things worked. Landing on the gravel *pista* (runway) at the little airport on the edge of the town, we were not yet close to any shops. Our transport arrived quickly in the form of *moto taxies,* local men on motorcycles—one for each of us to sit behind the man and be driven to the plaza. The seats didn't look designed for much more than one person. "How do you keep from falling off?" I asked the gals.
    "Just put your arms around the guy and hold on tight," one said grinning. "And you need to sit side-saddle. Only bad girls straddle the seat."

70 What's in Your Hand?

I positioned myself, barely on the seat, and held on tightly to my driver—hugging a man I didn't even know as we drove through the local streets. Then I observed that the other girls were *not* holding onto their drivers but rather to some obscure part of the motorcycle. I quickly learned that going around a corner required the passenger to lean, counteracting the centrifugal force. Arriving at the plaza, we each paid our taxi driver. The gals were laughing at me, having embarrassed me into hugging the poor driver. "You'll get the hang of it," they said.

Around the central plaza several shops offered their wares. A drug store sold Swiss Tobler chocolate bars. A fabric store offered mostly colorful cotton selections. Other shops had a limited variety of canned goods, which they retrieved for us from shelves behind the counter. After we had made our rounds on the plaza, we walked a few blocks to a local hospital to visit nurses whom the gals knew. Then we caught a ride back to the *pista* on the *moto taxies*. This time I balanced without holding onto the driver, opting for a gentle hold to the motorcycle to keep from falling. The pilot landed at the prescribed time and flew us back to Tumi Chucua. I appreciated having been able to make a few purchases and to receive some cultural lessons from my new friends.

One day, we saw hundreds of small ants coming right through the screens onto the cement floor of our porch. We were being invaded. We had heard that the best thing to do was just let them come through and clean out any crumbs or debris. So, we vacated the house and watched as they wandered right through and out the other end. I was so glad we knew what to expect, or I might have freaked out.

On another occasion we were surprised to see that leaf cutter ants had stripped a bush in front of our house. These industrious critters could chew off a section of leaf a half inch or more in diameter and carry it to their home. Sometimes we saw a winding tunnel built on the ground through which ants carried their treasures.

Of course, there were many other insects in the jungle. Mosquitoes seemed to especially enjoy tasting newcomers to their territory. One evening as I sat near a window in our house and rested my arm on the windowsill against the screen, they brazenly reached right through the screen to bite me. One day I felt a strange sensation between two toes. A sand flea had burrowed into my skin to lay eggs, creating a swollen, dark spot. Our jungle remedy was to cut it out, a painful procedure. Other nicer insects included beautiful butterflies.

While we were in Bolivia, we started our long-held affection for cocker spaniel dogs when we bought a cute puppy. Coco was a fun and loyal companion. Dogs could run free at our Center. Unfortunately, he contracted a bad case of mange. We tried various treatments—even covering him with used motor oil—but nothing helped. He was completely miserable. We sadly had to put him down. Later we got another cocker, Rusty, who fared much better. Not having children, we showered our love on our dogs, and quite possibly spoiled them.

One day one of the ladies on the Center asked John if he could fix her refrigerator. John was puzzled at the request. "The last aviation mechanic did that for us," she told him with expectation. John was able to help, even though he'd never had training for that. *(Which prompted him to get such training during our next time at home—another "tool" added.)*

Importation restrictions continued for a couple years as we waited for our barrels to arrive from the States. John requested our Miami Shipping office to open one of our barrels and send some of our items along with personnel traveling from Miami to Bolivia if they had room. Little by little some of our supplies arrived. Then, when importation permissions were granted, our final barrel came. By that time some items weren't necessary as we had found substitutes at redistribution sales. (Next time we would limit what we brought from the States.)

On several occasions we received goodie packages from Mom or a church group, often arriving in battered boxes. We loved receiving chocolate chip packets, cake mixes, flavor packets, cans of cranberry sauce and other treats, which we called "morale boosters." One large box that

Mom sent us for Christmas was held up in a shipment that sat out on a dock for some time. It arrived with holes in the cardboard, and items falling out. I found a single bedspread in it. *Why would Mom send us a single bedspread?* I wrote, thanking her and asking about the bedspread. It took two weeks for our letter to get to her and another two weeks for an answer. Mom asked how we liked the dress she had made for me and the shirt for John. Sadly, we let her know that her nice gifts were pilfered enroute. Later we learned that a colleague had received only one single bedspread when she expected two. Apparently, thieves got confused when stuffing unwanted items back in the boxes. We were happy to give the missing, matching bedspread to the one intended to receive it.

Delayed mail meant we were behind with news. In May of 1973, we received a letter telling of my grandmother's death. She was already buried before we even knew it. I remembered her sad goodbye when we left home for Bolivia. She had been a special person in my life. I knew we would miss her faithful prayers.

During that time, John's college friend from LeTourneau, Howard Moore, was serving as an Aviation Mechanic for our Brazil Branch. He and Marilyn were located at Puerto Vello, which wasn't that far from Tumi Chucua, so we decided to visit them. We chartered a Cessna flight to Gyara-Merin and crossed a river into Brazil by boat.

A nice bus took us to Belém where the Moores met us and drove us to Puerto Velho. Their Center was like ours, yet unique. Howard and Marilyn, with their five children, had just moved into their almost finished, newly built jungle house. We were their very first guests, and John helped Howard with some finishing work. A Wycliffe Associates work crew was at their Center constructing several houses and buildings. We watched in awe as the work leader directed lengths of wood to be cut in certain sizes, then taken directly to men who quickly nailed them into place, in assembly-line fashion. An efficient, capable crew! We met translators and support personnel there who worked together to provide Scriptures for their area of the huge country of Brazil.

— Then we crossed back into Bolivia. In Gyara-Merin, we caught *moto taxies* to take us to the airstrip. By this time, I felt that I had mastered the art of sitting side-saddle on the back edge of the seat, holding lightly to the motorcycle, balancing, and leaning just the right amount around corners. I was feeling proud of myself until, right in the central plaza, my purse strap slipped off my shoulder and my specially tooled leather purse dragged on the road. I leaned to pull it up, lost my balance, and sprawled ungracefully on the road. The driver stopped to rescue me. *"Senora, lo siento. Está bien?"* I was just scraped up a bit, but mostly embarrassed. Meanwhile John's driver took him on around the plaza (one way traffic) and caught up with us as I climbed gingerly back on the motorcycle, and we went on our way. Back at our Jungle Center I mused over the fact that some cultural lessons had to be learned the hard way.

Sometimes we supplemented our food with fish John caught in the lake. He enjoyed going out in a canoe with John Ottaviano (translator for the Tacanas) for some fellowship and fishing. If they caught *piraña*, which were mostly bones, they threw them back in the water or used them for bait. Often they caught nice sized *tucunaré* or catfish. The more exciting canoe trips were at night when the guys hunted alligators (actually caiman). Shining a flashlight in their beady eyes would momentarily stun them, enabling a good shot. Quickly they hooked it with a gaff, pulling it into the canoe before it sank. We marinated the tail meat in milk to tenderize it, and deep-fried breaded bite-sized pieces.

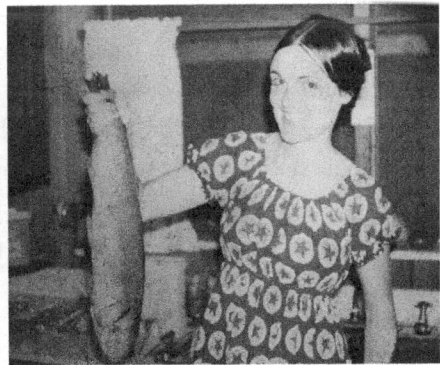

Sometimes I accompanied John on a fishing trip. I even had my own pole. John taught me how to drag the line and then reel in a fish. One time I caught a big salmon. My catch was bigger than John's.

Flying over the extensive Bolivian jungle challenged our pilots, with limited places to land and no GPS in those days. The aviation team worked very hard to follow safety standards. Shortly after our Annual Conference in 1975 we got word that one of our Cessnas had suffered an accident. As we waited for information, I prayed that the cause was not a maintenance issue. My friend, the pilot's wife, prayed it wasn't her husband's fault. As details came to us, we praised the Lord that there were no serious injuries to passengers or pilot. It was determined that a traveler in the front passenger seat had grabbed the dual steering system used for training, having been scared as the plane descended. We now needed another Cessna to resolve the drastically curtailed flight program.

(Later, on furlough presentations, John told this story to illustrate our need to let God steer our life, not grabbing control.)

Guaraní New Testament

Although we missed family and friends back home, we became part of the "family" of co-workers. Together we worked, lived, worshiped, laughed, and sometimes cried. But it was a group often in transition. When my office colleague Martha went on furlough, I was thankful that recently returned colleague, Jeanne East, could help process and prepare Scriptures for printing. At that time, we were working on at least 17 individual Scripture books in various languages.

Then we got a big project. The entire New Testament in Guaraní (Gwah-rda-NEE) was ready for the final edit and perfect camera-ready copy for printing. It would be printed at the Wycliffe printshop in Guatemala since our Bolivia shop wasn't prepared to handle such a large job. We received specifications for page size, large chapter numbers, subtitles in italics, and a list of illustrations with their captions to be placed with the appropriate text.

Back in June of 1973 Martha had begun typing the manuscript and punching tapes for each of the books. Sections of the work had been flown by JAARS to Cochabamba and forwarded out by various means to Cuaraguatarenda. There Guaraní literacy workers, Kay Weick and Rosemary Gingory, along with local language helpers, checked painstakingly to make sure that the text was correct and consistent in spelling, punctuation, word order, etc. Jeanne and I followed a similar procedure with the camera-ready pages, sending out carbon copies for proofreading in the village.

If Kay and Rosemary found a complex discrepancy involving a large change, we'd have to redo that page, and then also re-run the following pages to re-page the text. If it was a small correction, we used an interesting technique—makeshift by today's standards. We used correction tape in a unique way. We pulled off strips of the sticky white tape, which was the width of a line of type, and stuck it to waxed paper. We rolled the waxed paper into the typewriter, carefully positioned it, and typed the correction on the tape. Then we cut the tape to the correct length and carefully stuck it onto the camera-ready page. We hand-pasted large chapter numbers, cut from old calendars, since our Selectric font balls were made only in 12-point or 10-point sizes (elite or pica, as they were known). Later, as technology evolved, I was to learn easier ways to prepare Scripture for press, but that's how we did it back in the early 70s.

Martha returned near the end of the project, and she also ran some of the pages. As our deadline approached, we sometimes worked evenings. One night, Jeanne and I were so tired we were silly. We joked about using the ball with the barred I so much that we called it the "barred I ball." Jean said, "My own *eyeballs* are seeing bars." We typed a row of barred I's (i̶ i̶ i̶ i̶ i̶ i̶ i̶ i̶ i̶ i̶) on some correction tape and stuck it to our eyelids for a photo—with our "barred eyeballs."

For the final weeks of preparation, Kay and Rosemary joined us at Tumi Chucua. They meticulously went over every detail, and we made final corrections. When the JAARS DC-3 left Tumi Chucua on April 4, 1974, Kay and Rosemary were on board carrying two inconspicuous packages wrapped in brown paper. The camera-ready copy of the Guaraní New Testament was on the first leg of the journey to our Guatemala Printshop. Jungle families who may have seen the large plane passing overhead had no idea of the joy of the two who carried these parcels, nor of the years of work which had preceded their going.

This New Testament had been in progress since 1956 when translator Harry Rosbottom began learning the language. Reading primers, the Gospel of Mark, Acts, and various Bible stories had been published. They awaited the day when the various parts would be available all in one volume.

The Guaraní New Testament was a significant milestone for the Bolivia Branch, the first one completed through its efforts, although over the years many Bible stories and individual books of Scripture had been printed in separate editions.

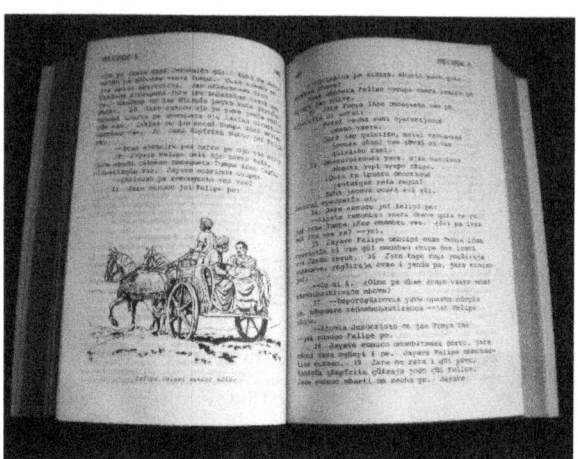

After printing, the 2,000 copies of the 900-page New Testament were transported to the Guaraní people. They now had God's Word in their very own language to read for themselves of Christ's sacrifice for the sins of the world, to grow in their knowledge of Him and in the joy of living a life for Him.

Machu Picchu

Since John was especially interested in the ancient civilizations of the Aztecs of Mexico and the Incas of Peru, we made a very special trip to the world-famous Inca ruins of Machu Picchu. Traveling together with Lynn & Betty Eby, we crossed Lake Titicaca into Peru in an old British steamer. This lake was known as the highest navigable lake in the world, with its famous reed boats. After a nice supper on board, we retired to our rooms, fortunately upgraded from the communal bunks below. We gently rocked all night and disembarked the next morning in Peru.

We flew to Cuzco, where we met Hugo, our tour guide recommended by friends. In the high altitude we took it easy the first day. We toured a wonderful market, where we bought some special pottery. We saw buildings where immensely huge stones formed the base of ancient walls whose tops had been destroyed by an earthquake and later rebuilt. The stones had been meticulously fitted together, even one with twelve angles. Still a mystery today are the methods used to carve, move, and fit these massive stones together.

Then we traveled by train, descending from 11,000 to near 8,000 feet to the base of the Machu Picchu ruins. In a minibus, we snaked up many switchbacks to the top.

It was an amazing fortress, perched high atop the mountain, with the remains of many buildings. One tall stone was precisely placed to form a sundial. We climbed up, down, and around exploring the various areas. As the others left to catch the train back, we stayed to enjoy a nice supper and an overnight in the hotel there.

The following morning, we climbed the nearby Huayna Picchu mountain, for a higher view of Machu Picchu. But the clouds hung over the mountain, and as we ascended the trail, we lost our view. This was probably good, as the trail lacked handrails, and had we seen the distance we could have fallen with a misstep, we might have been very fearful. But we made it to the top and back down. The rest of the day we explored Machu Picchu more leisurely. I even sat at a high point and sketched some of the ruins. We had seen an amazing historical, ancient site.

Scaling Back

At each annual conference our leaders led discussions, shared plans to complete the translation projects, and evaluated a closing date for our Jungle Center. Although this was difficult for some who had lived at Tumi Chucua for years, Wycliffe's priority was Bible translation. Having God's Word, the indigenous churches could continue to grow and reach out to their neighbors without outsider direction. Also, other area missions encouraged their growth and training.

As translation projects were completed, the flight program would scale down. When our furlough time came near, the new director suggested that in our next term, John serve half-time in aviation maintenance and half time with Center maintenance. We struggled, knowing the needs in other places for aviation mechanics. John felt that we should not plan to return to Bolivia.

So, instead of packing up for furlough, we packed to leave. We put together a "redistribution sale," gave away some belongings, and packed what we would take. A special veterinarian clearance paper for Rusty, our dog, enabled us to take him with us. Another couple would occupy our house. Since I had learned to be comfortable in the jungle situation and happy with my work contribution, I was sad. I didn't look forward to more change.

Our departure was timed to catch one of the DC-3 supply flights to the U.S. which left right from Tumi Chucua on September 10, 1976. We would have our dog Rusty with us in the cabin.

With about ten in all, counting the crew, the DC-3 lifted off heading to Colombia for an overnight. On the flight, Rusty became agitated. We let him walk in the aisle on his leash. Then, right in the aisle, he left his deposit. The aroma filled the plane. The pilot opened the cockpit door and rolled his eyes. John cleaned it up the best he could. A Bolivian passenger, rather a cultured lady, shook her head. We couldn't do more!

Landing in Barranquilla, Colombia, we caught a taxi to a hotel. The next day we flew on to Miami, arriving in the afternoon. In the airport, an agent yelled at me. "You can't bring a dog on a leash in here. He must be in a dog crate."

John said, "You stand here, watch our suitcases, and hold the dog. I'll find a crate." I felt illegal as people scurried past in all directions. My arms ached with Rusty's weight. Finally, John returned carrying a small crate, into which we placed Rusty. We could then check in.

We overnighted at our group guest facility in Miami, and the following day we flew via Eastern, then a smaller Eastern Commuter to Harrisburg, PA. By then I was exhausted and disheveled as we disembarked. We were soon encouraged by a huge welcoming party from Brookfield Bible Church and Harrisburg Christian School. Friends from the church had a lovely car for us to borrow, and we drove on to my folks' home in Bellwood, arriving just in time to help them celebrate their 35th wedding anniversary.

Looking back, it had been a good three and a half years for us in Bolivia. I felt like we had contributed to the program there. We would now enjoy reconnecting with and thanking family, friends, and partners. Then we would head to the JAARS Center at Waxhaw, NC, to serve there until our next field assignment.

Chapter 5
Peru (1978-1979)
To Another Country

———————————✈

Are You Willing?

We were getting used to living in the States again and were involved in meaningful work at the JAARS Center. At the hangar John inventoried and reorganized aircraft parts, did purchasing of aviation parts, and directed maintenance in the fixed wing single engine program. I served again in the Publicity Office to help prepare literature, prayer letters, brochures and displays, and a regular JAARS newsletter called the "Connecting Rod." John led the weekly AWANA Club for the JAARS Center children as well as community children. Incredibly, we had been able to build a new house for us at the JAARS Center with the help of friends and family. We had also plugged into a local church.

One day the Aviation Director dropped by to talk with John. "They need you in Peru," he said.

SIL work in Peru had almost been terminated. All expatriate organizations had received orders to leave Peru. But the Lord had miraculously reversed an expulsion order for our mission. The translation work could continue after all! Our colleagues there had been working around the clock to complete as much as possible before their expected departure date. They had continued past their scheduled furlough dates and now needed a break. An aircraft mechanic was needed to fill in during that time. It would be an 18-month assignment to begin January 1978.

I wasn't quite ready to hear this news. It would mean rearranging our focus in a short timetable. But we strongly felt the priority of the field needs. If God didn't hinder us, then we should fulfill this need. We wouldn't have to prepare so much for a shorter field term. And just the other day I had said, "I'm trying not to get too soft enjoying the conveniences of U.S. living."

So, we dusted off our Spanish textbooks and finished details to make our house rentable. John prepared storage space above one end of the garage ceiling and moved our personal items there. We visited supporting churches, friends and family and found renters for our house.

To remember our new home while in Peru, I staged and photographed various rooms. Our camera at that time had a flash attachment, using flash bulbs. When we opened the package from the photo shop, we could barely discern the dark objects in the photos. Apparently, the flash attachment had not been in sync with the camera. I was disappointed. But the Lord seemed to say, "Elsie, leave this house in My hands. Go serve in Peru and forget what you leave behind."

Off to Peru

Packing time again! We made a list and carefully packed only essential items in one barrel. John had diligently built up his aircraft tool supply with the motto, "The right tool for the right job." But for this short term, he limited his essential supply to one small toolbox. In October 1977, a couple months before our departure, we sent the barrel and toolbox ahead to our Miami office to be included with a shipment almost ready to go. Other personal items we would pack in suitcases. We felt organized and prepared. If we had known the future, we might have packed differently.

Once again, winter weather challenged our January departure. A serious snow and ice storm coming from the north, was predicted to blanket our east coast area. John decided to leave Friday evening rather than Saturday morning. We were just ahead of the storm as we drove south.

Our flight left Miami at 1:45 a.m. on the 18th of January. Spending a couple days in Lima, John began work on getting our visas and his Peruvian mechanic's license. Then, on to Pucallpa (Poo-CALL-pah), where a friend with a truck met us. We drove on dusty, bumpy roads through the city, and then along roads lined with mud houses with aluminum roofs. Finally, we arrived at the Yarinacocha (Yah-REE-nah-COACH-uh) Jungle Center, located along a beautiful lake (*cocha*).

Similar, but much larger than our Tumi Chucua Bolivia Center, this Center housed a commissary, clinic, maintenance shop, carpentry shop, cattle farm, auditorium, offices, print shop, school buildings, radio communications, airstrip, and the hangar (of course). Then there were many jungle houses where the Wycliffe/SIL staff lived.

Arrangements had been made for us to stay in the Sifert's house while they were on furlough. Located alongside the lake, it had a beautiful view with breezes from across the water. Kind neighbors brought us orchids, fresh pineapple, home-made breads, rolls, cookies, and jams to welcome us, while others invited us to their homes for meals.

It was neat to see the united spirit of helpfulness as the team served together in ministering to about 35 various language groups. There was a celebratory spirit as translators Gerhard and Ruby Fast had just finished the rough draft translation of the Achuar New Testament.

As this house had been vacant for a month, cockroaches, frogs, and a lizard had moved in. The lizard contributed to his board by removing small flying insects. Frogs ate insects too, but they startled me by jumping out of

unpredictable places. John removed them to outside duty. I made the old cockroach remedy of corn meal, sugar, and boric acid placed out in jar lids for their banqueting.

Because of a delay in the shipment from Miami, our barrel and John's toolbox had not arrived. We had to do without even the limited items we had sent ahead. Staff also eagerly awaited new SPEED computerized typewriters to process Scriptures. We didn't realize how long it would be for shipments to come through.

We were eager to get some wheels to get around the Center. John ordered a Honda 125 motorcycle from our Lima buyer and negotiated with a pilot there for a smaller second-hand Honda 50 for me. That was especially helpful for hauling groceries from the commissary.

The Peru Branch also had prayer groups organized around helping the various language projects. John and I were happy to join the Sharanahua (Sha-rra-NOW-ah) group with translators, Gene and Marie Scott. Marie's father, Rev. Herzog, had pastored the Olivet Baptist Church our family had attended when I was young. I remembered Marie, her sister, and two brothers playing trumpet/horn specials, during their visits from college. The church had prayed for Marie and Gene (known as Scottie) when they were married in Bolivia and then served in Peru. My mother thought we were true missionaries now, serving alongside the Scotts.

The Center buzzed with activity. Being the "summer" school break in Peru, there were 113 bilingual schoolteachers, representing 16 language groups studying in the 26th annual teacher training course. Simultaneous training courses were being conducted in four other communities for teachers from those areas. Two teams of MK high school students were working on an airstrip in the Pajonal Campa area. A third team helped build a corral and fence a pasture for the Pichis Campa cattle project.

Back to Work

John knew that the flight program would have some interesting challenges in Peru because of its geography. There were three distinct areas. A narrow desert-like coastline hugged the Pacific Ocean. Then, rising very rapidly, was a narrow mountain range (the Andes Mountains). East of that was the tropical jungle.

The Andes soared over 21,000 feet, with the main road over the Andes reaching 17,000 feet. The mountains fell off very rapidly. Most of the storms on the eastern sides of the Andes came in from Brazil across the vast jungle. When they ran up across the mountains, they dumped their rain which ran off rapidly.

So, rivers rose and fell very quickly. Because of that, our Peru Aviation program ruled that if float planes were out overnight, they should not stay

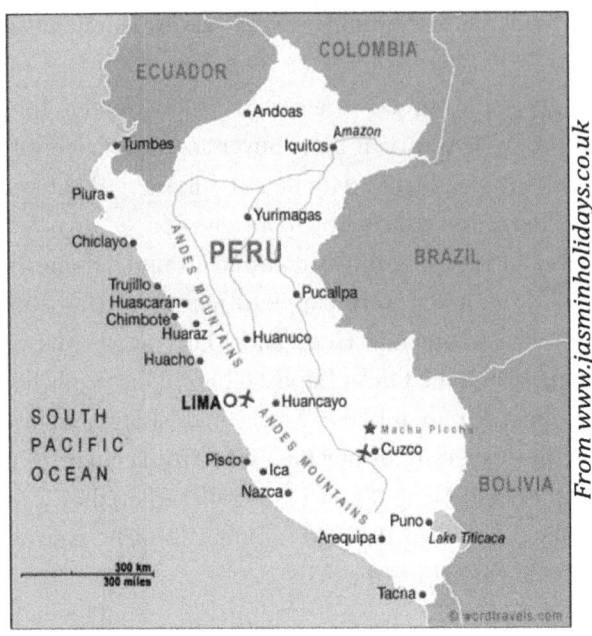

on a river. If a pilot had no choice but to leave the plane on a river at night, he should sleep in it to be ready for any emergency. In fact, previously a pilot overnighting at an Indian village had tied up the plane on a river. When the water rose during the night, the plane broke loose and was almost destroyed. The pilots knew that on an overnight trip, they needed to fly to a lake or some stable place to protect the airplane and themselves.

The Jungle Center was located along Lake Yarinacocha, which was about a mile across and nine miles long. Rains sometimes rapidly swelled the rivers which flowed into the lake, raising its level by 15 or 20 feet. Aviation staff had to be on their guard during rainy season to safeguard the float planes.

John was named the Superintendent of Maintenance and had responsibility for four planes at that time—two Helio Couriers on wheels, one on floats, and an Evangel. Maintenance according to high FAA standards was essential because of challenging flying conditions and few landing areas in the dense jungle. Two trained Peruvian mechanics helped.

He began work on major overhauls of two engines—a challenge without his tools. He had purchased a few basic ones in Lima, but the cost was almost prohibitive, with limited availability. When a traveler finally brought John's toolbox from Miami, they progressed much faster. Aircraft stock supplies on order for months were still held up, which could take some planes off flying status. The importation permissions were part of our mission's renewal contract which would allow our work to continue in Peru. The contract had been revised but was waiting to be signed by the government.

I had hoped to work in the Print Shop office where items were prepared for press. It would have been a natural follow up of my experience in Bolivia. But they had staff there and someone was needed in the hangar office, so that's where I was assigned. I had never really worked in that type of environment. John knew airplanes; I knew other things. I figured that the Lord had in mind for me to learn more about John's work. First lesson: That thing that gives power to fly the plane is not called a motor but an engine!

The Flight Office was situated in one corner of the hangar. An adjacent building blocked the lakeside breezes. It seemed that the walls sucked in and held the heat. As I tried to concentrate on the work, the nagging thought seemed to never leave me: *It is so hot here!* But that was life in the jungle that you just had to deal with. So, I did the best I could in a slot that I didn't feel I was especially suited for, but where I was needed.

A small sectioned-off corner of the office contained radio equipment for the Flight Coordinator. On the outside wall of his cubicle a huge map of Peru hung, with marked locations of frequent flight destinations. We served passengers from a counter, and my big wooden desk sat in the middle of the room. Built in-shelves stored cargo and equipment. A large scale served to weigh boxes, bags, and items to be flown somewhere.

Most mornings, planes were being loaded for the day's flights. The Flight Coordinator weighed the cargo on the scale and carefully calculated the weight allowance for each plane load. I had a "top secret" card file containing each person's weight in kilos, which was part of the total weight allowed. Safety was primary, so weight limits were strictly adhered to, as well as weight distribution for balance. One day when two lady translators were flying to a village for several months, they brought many items: boxes of basic foods, clothing, personal toiletries, typewriters, books, literacy materials for the villagers, and more. But being way overweight, only about 70 percent of it could be taken. They painstakingly sorted and repacked, selecting only the most necessary items. Their primitive living situation would be difficult without all they had hoped to take along. I felt their pain.

I answered phone calls on our Center's system. I needed to be aware of the activity around me to give correct information to callers. One day someone needed to get in touch with one of the pilots and I couldn't locate him. After some time, I remembered that he was out on a multiple-day flight and not available.

Although math was not my strong point, I tracked flight costs to do the billing. Prices based on the U.S. dollar for hours flown needed to be changed to Peruvian *soles*, with the exchange rate fluctuating frequently. Peruvians suffered each time the *sol* was devalued, resulting in higher prices. Some could hardly afford to buy basic food. Teachers went on strike for higher wages, and there were many protest demonstrations.

On one occasion we were surprised when a local plane, much larger than ours, landed on our airstrip with the landing gear up! Sliding down the grass runway, it came to a stop with little harm to the plane

except for bent propeller tips. As the pilot couldn't take off without the landing gear, he was stuck at our Center for several days, staying in our humble guest house. John and his crew found a way to lift the plane, and surprisingly the switch dropped the landing gear into place without a problem. I calculated the pilot's charges for work and accommodations, which he paid. We held our breath as he took off. Using the full length of the strip, he zoomed out over the lake just in time. After he had gone, I realized that I had charged him double for the accommodations because I was used to doubling charges for two people. The Flight Coordinator said not to worry about it, as our charge was probably much less than he would pay elsewhere.

One day my friend Marsha was a passenger. Dressed in her specially made *cushma* for her tribal visit, Marsha was ready for her flight. Leaving her family and regular duties as our Center Post-lady, she would accompany Allene Heitzman for several weeks with the Campa people. As a temporary partner, Marsha would cook, keep house, and take care of various details to enable Allene to concentrate on her linguistic work.

After helping with pre-flight paperwork, I decided to accompany the passengers out to the plane to see Marsha off. After the cargo was tied in place and just before the passengers got in, the pilot said, "Let's have a word of prayer." As heads bowed in a circle beside the plane, we asked the Lord's guidance for a safe and fruitful trip. With misty eyes I headed back to the Flight Office thanking the Lord that what we were doing was for Him. So many details had to come together to make each flight possible, and I had a part in it along with many others. The plane sped loudly down the runway and then quietly off into the distance.

In June, one of our Helio Courier aircraft was involved in a landing accident at Quitepampani, a challenging jungle airstrip 225 miles southeast of Yarinacocha where translators worked with the Caquinte Campas. On approach, there was "an optical illusion, and an indefinite horizon due to foothills surrounding the airstrip." Strong winds pushed the plane below the normal glide path approaching the high riverbank at the end of the airstrip. There was only enough power to get the main wheels over the bank and onto the runway. The tail section hit the sharp bank and separated from the main fuselage. The front part of the plane made one complete forward somersault down the runway coming to rest in an upright position. Though the plane was severely damaged, amazingly there were no injuries, thanks to the Lord's goodness and the strong tubular steel frame of the cabin! It was unfortunate though, that many dozens of smashed eggs littered the interior.

John coordinated efforts for a major rebuild on the much-needed plane, fondly referred to by its registration numbers as "951." Parts of the wrecked plane were brought to our Center on return legs of subsequent supply flights for translators at Quitepampani. A Peruvian Army helicopter and crew helped bring back the wings and fuselage.

With a stock inventory below bare minimum, John's team faced challenges. Meanwhile, they arranged to borrow a Helio Courier which was programmed to go to Liberia in a few months. At the same time, the twin engine Evangel plane was out of service while the crew did an engine change and other maintenance. With only two planes flying during that time, scheduling was tight, and some translators' plans were delayed.

We thanked God when government permission was granted to bring some aircraft supplies, computerized typewriters and other high priority items from shipments waiting in Miami. Perhaps restrictions were loosening up, but personal items would have to wait for the government's official signing of the contract.

For a needed break, John and I went to Lima in September for two weeks. John was able to pick up his Peruvian mechanics license and apply for a Type I Certificate which equaled the Authorization Inspection (AI) rating he had earned in the States. This would enable him to sign off more aircraft inspections at our Center, rather than having to bring in a Peruvian official to do it. We also enjoyed shopping and fellowship at the Wycliffe Group House. Refreshed, we returned to the Center with renewed enthusiasm to continue our work.

Then the loaner plane arrived—flown all the way from Waxhaw to Yarinacocha by Willis Baughman, accompanied by Stuart Shephard (both JAARS Center administrators). This plane would keep our flight program going while the damaged Helio was being rebuilt. Their cargo was a load of specially ordered aircraft parts for the rebuild. Official release of the plane was delayed for many days while John anxiously awaited access to the needed parts. Finally, the plane was liberated just in time to make a flight that could not have been made without it.

A work crew soon arrived to help for several weeks on the extensive aircraft rebuild: Jim Miller and Ken Stolsfous of Missionary Maintenance Services, and Army civilian worker Roy Zimmerman. Jim and Roy were our house guests, and we enjoyed their fellowship. Later Jim Metzler arrived with his wife to stay for the duration of the rebuild. The repairs progressed rapidly, and the plane began to take shape again before our eyes.

The continued challenge meanwhile was to keep the flight program going with hardly the supplies to do it. They came up with the idea of putting the run-out engine on the loaner plane, which was going back to Waxhaw. They saved just enough time on that engine for the ferry flight back. "Robbing" the "new" engine from the borrowed plane, they put it on the rebuilt Helio, and the engine originally overhauled for 951 was installed on the float plane to keep that plane on the flight line after its engine time was up.

Roy Zimmerman especially enjoyed his time getting to know the local people. He had a tender heart for their needs. By the time he was ready to head home, he had given away much of what he had brought with him. In fact, as he was dressing to depart to the airport, he came to John with a sheepish grin. "Uh, John, Could I have back one of those shirts I gave you? I don't seem to have one left to wear home." *(We kept up our friendship with Roy and his wife Bev through the years, and they even became financial partners with us.)*

A retired Braniff pilot, Orville Rogers (with his wife) came to ferry the loaner plane back to Waxhaw.

We heard that the shipment of work supplies from Miami was on its way. It had been contracted to be delivered to nearby Pucallpa, but for some reason was off-loaded in Iquitos, Ecuador, where it was exposed to the weather. When it finally arrived in Pucallpa, many departments were encouraged. John spent several happy days logging in and placing into stock various nuts, bolts, and parts. He still lacked a few essential items to complete the Helio rebuild. Hopefully they could be hand-carried soon.

We were thankful for personal items from our barrel in Miami, brought to us by travelling friends. Also, permission was granted to ship additional work supplies. Especially important to John was a new propeller and landing gear legs.

On April 1, 1979, Helio 951 flew for the first time after the extensive rebuild—a good test flight ten months to the day since the accident. The Lord had provided workers and parts just when needed. To celebrate, a group of us rode our motorcycles into Pucallpa to a Chinese (*Chifa*) restaurant.

Then John had to write up a report in Spanish (with some help) listing all the steps they had taken in the rebuild of the plane. An inspector came from Lima to check everything and give permission to put the plane into service again. After a few minor adjustments it was back on the flight line again. One pilot said, "It flies better now than it ever did."

Then John started work on our twin engine Evangel airplane. This unique aircraft had short take-off and landing capability and had been fabricated especially for mission work. One of only seven ever built, it had flown nearly 2,000 hours in Peru.

It was time to change the engine and do a second 1000-hour inspection. This included an extensive inspection on the airframe. They completely flushed out and resealed the integral fuel tanks and removed the entire landing gear system for rework. Then they moved on system by system to check and evaluate the condition of components and their future serviceability. Finally, they reworked the engine cowling and touched-up painting on the leading edges of the wings and tail surfaces. Sandwiched in between these projects, they did normal inspections on the other planes.

A telegram arrived in October. No one knew how long it had taken to get to Yarinacocha. The request was for a flight to Achuar territory to bring a sick person to our Center. Achuar translators, Gerhard and Ruby Fast, felt led to send out a plane even though the long flight could be in vain.

Upon arrival, the JAARS pilot found a young man gravely ill with high fever and barely conscious. It was Israel, a Peruvian Christian, who had been ministering to the Achuar people

with a sincere desire to help them know his Lord. Israel had given of himself unselfishly to help the Achuares, trekking through the jungle on survey trips with the Fast's sons, helping in community development projects, teaching literacy classes, and preaching.

Back at the Yarinacocha Center, our clinic staff treated Israel, and continued his care at the Fasts' home.

A week later another telegram arrived. This one had been sent on Israel's behalf, while the first telegram instead referred to Israel's brother, Elias, who had injured his back. Elias was better by the time the plane arrived, but the first telegram's response saved Israel's life. With limited communications, God's timing and care were perfectly programmed!

After serving in Peru one year, the Peru Branch administration requested that we continue in the work there. We enjoyed being close to the "front lines" witnessing the effectiveness of the programs. The JAARS administration and Wycliffe headquarters approved this decision. We revised our plans since we had only prepared for an 18-month stay. It seemed good to stay two years, then have a short furlough to settle our affairs back home.

I had been doing my best to work in the Flight Office, but, when another lady became available to serve there, God granted my desire to work in the print shop's publications office. I was thankful to God for the opportunity to do what I loved, as well as enjoy air-conditioning which protected equipment from harmful humidity.

Two other ladies worked in the office preparing the Scriptures. I first worked preparing camera-ready copy for beginning reading books (primers) in different languages. Using a typewriter, I carefully arranged short stories, word exercises in charts, artwork, and hand-writing exercises on the pages. The books had been planned by the tribal folks themselves in a workshop.

I had the joy to type camera-ready copy for many of the books. You wouldn't find Dick, Jane, Sally, or Spot in those stories. More likely Cosi, Yuma, or Miquini; and culturally appropriate stories like "Father hunts the monkey. Mother roasts the monkey over the fire. Everybody eats. It tastes good!" And for languages like Machiguenga, with words like *ikenavagetapinitira* (he always went to hunt), learning to read wasn't easy.

I, myself, love to read. I can have access to millions of books in English! For each language we worked with, we aimed to publish: 8-10 reading books, 3-6 health books, a hymnal, the New Testament, Old Testament portions, and a dictionary. A lot of books? Yes and no. An avid reader could finish the library quickly. So, literacy workers held workshops where tribal people learned to write and produce their own literature to supplement this basic library, and to give practice in language skills. More practice made better readers, who hopefully then could understand abstract portions of Scripture as well as the easier-to-read historical passages.

House Hopping

So far, we had changed houses several times at Yarinacocha. In June of 1978, we had moved from Sifert's house to the Lyons's home while they were on furlough. It was a large jungle house, well suited for their government relations work, as they hosted many guests. It included a well-trained maid, a dog, a cat, and a parrot. (Thankfully, their pet boa constrictor snake was with another family.) John loved Tex, the parrot, and Tex loved John. Tex lived on a perch by the back door. His clipped wings prevented him from flying away. But he coasted down from his perch when he heard John arrive home on his *moto*. Then he climbed up John's leg to his shoulder for a *moto* ride. He screeched for joy into John's ear as he enjoyed the breeze and scenery. Sometimes he pecked holes in John's shirt collar.

When we let him into the house, he often crawled up to nestle into the cozy bend of John's arm, making little cooing sounds. He had learned some words: "I'm a jay bird," a questioning "What?", the dog's name "Sarge", and he could mimic a roomful of people talking. One evening, shortly before the Lyons returned from furlough, we heard Tex squawking frantically in the undergrowth of the side yard. When John ran to find him, he had been injured, probably by some animal. Later that night he died. We were so sad. The Lyons would be devastated to lose him.

For a couple months we lived in a small house of a single lady Bible translator. Being empty for a while, large cockroaches made their home there. When they flopped around at night, I couldn't sleep, imagining one landing on me. We aggressively put out boric acid snacks, diminishing the population, but not completely.

When that lady returned, we were between houses as there were none then available. So, we stayed in a room of the *Quinta Rosa* guest house, where the bathroom was down the hall, and we ate our meals in the group dining room. Life was a little complicated until we moved to the home of translators Lambert and Doris Anderson after they left for a lengthy village stay. Lambert was happy to return to Cushillacocha with the Ticunas (Ti-KOO-nahs) after serving three years as Peru Branch Director. They hoped to finalize checking of the Ticuna New Testament, and then return to the States for a year's furlough. We happily moved to their nice jungle house during their long absence.

I can't imagine many places where people shared their homes so generously. Coming on a short assignment there, it was a blessing to us.

Anderson's house came with their German Shepherd dog—Kaiser Wilhelm. While there, John's co-worker in the hangar, Larry Schatz, surprised us with a little female Cocker Spaniel pup from Lima. We named her Peanut. The two dogs became great buddies. John walked them each day. One day they passed another German Shepherd, running alongside his master's motorcycle. The two Shepherds got into a vicious tangle. John intervened, but a severe bite almost severed his thumb. He rushed to the clinic, and they stitched it up, but several days later infection set in, and they had to remove the stitches. Healing was slow and John ended up with a permanently misshapen thumb nail. He received lots of advice on how *not* to stop dog fights.

Translation Progress

At that time ten New Testament translations were in final stages! The Amuesha was being printed in Dallas. Chayahuita, Huitoto-Murui, and Capanahua were receiving final proofreading prior to printing. Cashibo and Candoshi-Shapra were being processed by computer at the SIL Dallas Linguistic Center. And Achuar, Shipibo, Bora, and Nomatsiguenga Campa were in final revision stages. The results of years of work were coming to fruition.

The Amuesha New Testament was chosen to represent the 100th translation completed by Wycliffe/SIL, with a dedication scheduled for mid-July 1979. Besides being a significant milestone, it encouraged us to expect to see 100 more New Testament translations in use before long. Through many faithful servants, countless numbers of tribal peoples in remote corners of the earth were coming to know Christ as Lord and Savior.

One afternoon, the big old Mercedes Benz truck from Lima rolled in. (It made the trip about twice a month bringing us supplies—a four-day round trip.) First, at the hanger, the men unloaded ten drums of aviation fuel. Then, John followed the truck to the commissary to help unload some special cargo. Many of the Chayahuita and Huitoto New Testaments had arrived! They unloaded box after box of these New Testaments that each represented over 20 years of team effort. These two groups would soon have the whole New Testament in their own language. A thrill beyond words!

Linguists often scheduled workshops, meeting with translation helpers to work together on certain books of Scripture. Sometimes several language groups met together, sharing meaningful ways to translate various portions. In September of 1979 five groups met at our Center to translate Hebrews. Before and during the session, they faced many challenges: One language helper was unable to come. One translator felt ill and worked with the pressure of furlough preparations as his family would leave for the States immediately following the workshop. Two other language helpers started enthusiastically but grew restless in the final weeks and wanted to get back to their village. Another translator was delayed beginning the workshop having taken a young Culina boy to Lima for emergency care from a shooting accident. And the Scotts, our prayer partners, had three sick Indians in their care, two Sharanahuas at the local hospital (one in a liquor-induced coma and the other having gall bladder surgery), plus an old Mastanahua chief, from a related language group, who lay near death at our Center Clinic.

Workshop leader, Bryan Burtch, led the group through to the finish as best he could. As a result, Hebrews was soon available to speakers of five more groups. But that wasn't the only good which came from this challenging time. The Culina boy was able to forgive his friend who had shot him accidentally (much better than revenge killing as was customary). The Mastanahua chief asked God to be his Owner before being flown back to his people. Just before his surgery, the Sharanahua man accepted the Lord, praying a beautiful prayer which Gene Scott described as like going through the Four Spiritual Laws, though they hadn't been presented to him as such.

No doubt there were other good results that only God knew. Through difficult circumstances He can bring beautiful results.

At an adult Sunday School class, discussing II Peter 1:15 (NIV), we decided that this was a translator's challenge: *"And I will make every effort to see that after my departure, you will always be able to remember these things."* When a translator, for whatever reason, is "long-gone" from the tribal village, the people can continue to be reminded of God's truths by reading Scriptures in their very own language, just as I have God's Word in my language, long since Peter has gone, in a language Peter didn't speak.

Bad News

While we rejoiced in progress in Peru, sometimes our personal news wasn't good.

April 19, 1978 – John's sister Karen sent us a radio message that their sister Joette's husband had passed away after battling congestive heart failure. Although we talked with Joette by a radio sked, family seemed far away.

May 1979 – We were saddened to hear of John's stepmother's death of cancer in New York. Though John had been raised by his grandparents without close contact with his father, we felt for him in this loss and prayed he would be drawn to the Lord through the experience. Some months later he started opening up to us and wrote us letters—something he had never done before.

In early July 1979 we heard via ham radio that my father had suffered a severe heart attack and was in critical condition. John immediately made arrangements so that I could leave. Our Lima Office personnel went out of their way to get reservations to the States on an Ecuatoriana flight out of Lima the next morning. If I couldn't make that, it would be another week before a seat was available. A friend got me a ticket for that night to Lima despite a general strike in nearby Pucallpa. Wycliffe friends in Miami arranged tickets from there the rest of the way to Altoona, PA. Since I was used to John handling everything on trips, this was a scary situation traveling by myself. The plane got into Miami late, and I missed my connecting flight. What to do? Fortunately, I had a phone number to call colleagues there who graciously picked me up and took me to their home overnight. That was a blessing as I really needed that rest. I got on a flight the next day to complete my trip.

I arrived home the 4th of July to visit with Dad. He had improved slightly and was sitting up. We were encouraged, but we learned that part of Dad's heart was permanently damaged. A few days later his temperature rose as his body fought infection. I was thankful to be with my family during the difficult days when we alternately hoped for Dad's recovery or expected his home-going. Unfortunately, on July 10th Dad passed away. I consoled myself with the thought that if Dad had survived, he might have been an invalid, a difficult challenge for my mother. A viewing and the funeral brought closure, while Uncle Ralph, as executor, handled legal matters. I stayed several weeks to help and then needed to get back to Peru.

John fared well in my absence, with many supper invitations, and he's a pretty good cook himself. After things settled down, I found myself feeling Dad's death more than I had back home. It hardly seemed possible that he was gone so quickly, being only 60 years old. I regretted not being closer to Dad, but he had been there when I needed him. Mom was now on her own. Years of separation from family was a sacrifice to serve overseas, both for us and for them.

Never a Dull Moment

John had been busy in the hangar, completing many projects with summer helpers. The MK school shop teacher, Dennis James, had directed workers in carpentry projects around the hangar, sprucing up areas showing their age. They fixed up a system for aviation gas to pump from barrels, a great time saver. They also replaced rusty pipes to the gas tank with new ones, raising them on cement pillars, aqueduct-style, across a swamp to prevent rusting.

In August John flew to Iquitos, to weld an engine mount for the Peruvian Army—part of a working agreement between the Peruvian Army's aviation program and our Flight Program. We helped provide maintenance for their jungle-area planes, and they in turn gave us an allowance of fuel each month, dropping off fuel barrels when they were at various jungle outposts. This created good will and friendships. John completed the project quickly and returned the next morning on a stand-by ticket.

"The New Testaments are coming apart," someone said, and the word passed around our Jungle Center. Advance copies of newly printed Scriptures had been sent from the States to Peru ahead of the slower big shipments. After a few months of exposure to jungle humidity, the glue holding the bindings seemed to be disintegrating. Further investigation revealed that the bindery had failed to use the specifically contracted glue on about 10,000 books of five New Testament editions printed that year!

With the Chayahuita dedication and distribution scheduled for just weeks away, and others soon to follow, arrangements were made by ham radio to have new glue, fly leafs, and necessary supplies hand-carried by travelers returning from the States. People volunteered for the painful task of tearing apart the new books and rubbing off the bad glue. Then, forming an assembly line, they began the slow process of re-gluing new bindings by hand.

For the Chayahuita dedication, we also needed the Evangel plane back in service, again held up waiting for parts. This plane and the other two land planes were necessary to fly the translators, special guests, and the Scriptures out to the village. After much prayer and hard work, the Lord enabled all the planes to be ready and sufficient New Testaments repaired in time.

John and pilot Doug Deming load New Testaments for a flight.

God also held back rains at just the times needed to safely fly to several Chayahuita villages. Many New Testaments were sold—in one village all of those allotted for that location.

This to us was another battle against "principalities and powers." We felt that Satan had made a last-ditch effort to hinder the translated Word from reaching the people. Satan is strong, but God is stronger!

98   What's in Your Hand?

One of the required projects for each of our translation teams was to create a published dictionary for the language in which they worked. This was usually a monumental project. But an eye for humor helped one of our co-workers as she typed a multi-dialectical Campa dictionary on a new "SPEED" computerized typewriter. Several entries provided by the Campas brightened her tedious task:

> baker – one who burns bread
> coin – the money's egg
> easy – we don't make a mistake
> Indian – person from India; somebody else (not me)
> mind – our thinking thing
> minute – what one delays.
> moral – what is difficult for us; we marry her
> neighbor – a poor man
> oven – the thing that burns bread

It's hard to imagine a jungle being dry. But 1979's dry season was especially dry, along with 95-degree temperatures. The dirt roads going into town became so dusty with traffic that on some days it was difficult to see very far ahead. We didn't even consider going to town on John's motorcycle as it was hard to get good tire traction in loose dirt. It was also "*chakra*" planting time when jungle folks slashed and burned new areas for their gardens. Our pilots reported seeing up to 50 fires burning at one time as they overflew some areas. Sometimes we awoke to our house full of "smog" that came in through the screened windows. Dusty air was unhealthy to breathe. Dryness caused many of the fires to continue burning over extensive areas.

Even 60 acres of pasture at our Center Farm were lost by fires. The farm program developed cattle herds for various language communities. After calves were weaned, and before they were too large, they were flown to villages to help start their cattle programs. John had a special wooden container built to carry tranquilized calves in the planes. Otherwise, if a calf should wake up during flight and get active, that would not be a good situation!

Two Wycliffe Associates (WA) construction managers visited our Center to evaluate possible projects for us. (In those days WA's main function was providing volunteer work crews.) After checking our situation, they decided that we really didn't need their help. But John said, "Wait a minute. What about a hangar project?" The Aviation team had been wishing to build an extension on the hangar to provide protection for all the planes and make them more accessible for maintenance and loading. One of the pilots, Tom Brewington, sketched out a design idea on some scrap paper, and they showed it to the men.

"We could do that. A great project!" they said. So, they arranged for a volunteer group from a church in Longview, WA, to come and build a hangar addition, and donate the funds for it.

In preparation John hired a work crew to put in a cement floor. They borrowed small mixers, but the first day both mixers broke down. How John wished he could have called a cement company to come and make a dump.

The Washington volunteers were an enthusiastic group and we enjoyed having three of them stay with us. The men were experienced and worked hard on the project. They laughed together about the very hard *espingo* wood posts and beams and the need to soap the nails to be able to drive them into the wood. The ladies helped cook meals for their team and learned about local foods. In just a few weeks they completed the expanded hangar space.

John and I became good friends with the team, and we kept in touch afterward. Two of them even became financial partners of ours. What a blessing!

One Monday morning, it was time to gas up the float plane before a flight to Tigre Playa and the upper Marañon River. But no gas was coming from the pump. The tanks had just been checked two weeks earlier with an ample supply of 5,000 gallons. How could that aviation gas just disappear? Could there be a leak? But the pipeline from the tanks through the swamp to the pumps had been replaced with new pipe raised on cement pillars just that summer. A visual check didn't reveal any leakage. Could someone be stealing it during the cover of night?

Then, a little digging close to the pumps revealed some smelly soil. After a heavy rain and more digging, the men found rusted pipes in the underground connection with the pumps! Five thousand gallons, gone! Worth over $11,000. *Lord, in a time of gas shortage and rising prices, how could something like this have happened to us?* More repairs insured it wouldn't happen again.

After that, we were happy for some good news. The Peruvian Minister of Education, Prime Minister, and others had signed the contract for SIL to serve in Peru, good for another ten years. The previous contract had expired in 1976, when SIL, along with most expatriate organizations, had been asked to leave the country. After God had miraculously turned things around, SIL had been able to stay under provisional authorizations with some limitations and a feeling of insecurity, until now. Still, our security was in the Lord, as governments came and went. The new contract also loosened shipment restrictions, hopefully relieving John's challenge to maintain aircraft without sufficient supplies.

Preparing for the Long Run

We were glad to learn that Elmer Ash, an experienced aircraft mechanic, could come from JAARS to replace John from January through March of 1980, so that we could get our short furlough.

During our two years in Peru, we had moved five times. Since we now planned a long assignment in Peru, we hoped to do that in one house. Several Jungle Center houses were available for sale. We purchased one close to the hangar. The house had been emptied of furnishings, so we would deal with that upon our return. I did measure windows, hoping to find nice fabric for curtains when in the U.S.

We left on December 14 and arrived in Bellwood, PA, several days later. It was good to be with Mom who was now alone since Dad's death in July. After the holidays with the family, we headed to the JAARS Center. It felt strange not to stay in our house while there, but we rented a mobile home. We were happy with the renters in our house and stopped by to handle some maintenance problems for them. We found useful items in our storage that we could use. We took care of other things to enable a long-term stay in Peru.

In the JAARS hangar, a crew was finishing up the rebuild of an Army surplus Helio Courier airplane to add to Peru's fleet. John was so glad to see what a good job they had done. This plane would be put on floats to relieve our other float plane's heavy load, making locations along the waterways more accessible. John worked on some special projects. He welded seats to be carried to Peru in the new plane for use in one of our other planes. He also ran some tests on fire-resistant sleeving for oil and hydraulic lines inside engine compartments.

We then made a road trip to visit friends, relatives and churches in Arkansas, Kentucky, Ohio, New York, and back in Pennsylvania.

While in Corning, NY, John was invited to speak to a men's meeting at his home church, North Baptist. John sat down next to a man he didn't know to get acquainted, "And how was your day today?" he asked.

"Terrible!" was his surprising response. "I teach music at the high school to kids with no appreciation or interest. It's a completely frustrating job. And my principal doesn't support me."

Moving to another subject, John asked, "What do you do in your spare time?" He learned that Arthur Scott loved to do woodworking in his well-equipped basement shop. John mentioned that when we returned to Peru, we would need to build furniture for our newly acquired empty house.

"I can come and build furniture for you," Arthur responded enthusiastically. "When do you return? I'm ready to go as soon as school is out." And so, Arthur, with his wife Martha, planned to go to Peru and do some practical missionary service.

After our travels we packed up again to head back to Peru, better prepared for a longer stay, and with an added blessing. We were excited that my mother planned to accompany us for several months in Peru. She would see first-hand where we served.

Chapter 6
Peru (1980-1983)
Frustrations and Blessings

———————————➤

Our Own House

I could hardly believe my mother was traveling to Peru with us. It was for a stay just short of three months (maximum time allowed by the visitor's visa). We hoped that it would be a neat experience for her to see our work, meet our friends and to have more time with us.

Mom travelled well, with just a little culture shock at the Lima airport. "*Everyone's* speaking Spanish," she said. The next couple days we signed out one of the available vehicles to show Mom around Lima, and we purchased some items for our house.

Arriving in Yarinacocha, we were so thankful to have our own home. Mom had kindly loaned us funds to help make the purchase. Located near the hangar, we had our own private path to get there.

We gathered our stored possessions, but we had no furniture. We borrowed a stove, beds, and a table with chairs until we could get our own. With fabric we brought back with us, Mom sewed curtains for the windows on our sewing machine.

John and I rode our motorcycles to get around the Center, but Mom was afraid to do that. After several days of walking in the heat and humidity, she was willing to try riding behind John on his cycle. "You'll be safe," we told her, "Hold onto John." And she did—tightly! She admitted that it was a better choice. Mom was having all kinds of new experiences.

In those days we couldn't just purchase furniture in a Pucallpa store. Carpenter friend, Dennis James, helped John start a new hobby: building furniture. John made a solid wooden base on which to mount his skill saw upside-down to make a "table saw." His first projects were a couch and chairs. For cushions, we bought a three-inch thick foam mattress in Pucallpa and cut it into needed sizes. Mom sewed covers with fabric we brought back. Soon our new friend Arthur Scott was coming from New York to make a table and chairs. *(In his spare time, John later continued to make other furniture: end tables, coffee table, lamp bases, and a desk.)*

While we had been on furlough, the Candoshi-Shapra New Testament had been dedicated and distributed. At the celebration in his village, Chief Tariri demonstrated leading a war challenge as in past years. "We don't want to forget what life was like before God changed us," he said. Chief Tariri had become well known since a book was written about him. *(This was the man whose likeness I had painted for the art fair some years earlier.)* At a celebration in another village, one of the men spoke representing his people: "Our village is dedicated to God now that His true Word has come to us."

Back to Work

The new Helio Courier rebuilt at JAARS had arrived. John and the team installed floats on it and put a repaired second float dock in the water for its use. After an inspection by a Peruvian inspector from Lima and registration paperwork, it was placed into service. Having a second float plane in operation greatly added to the versatility of the flight program. The fleet now numbered five.

John appreciated extra help that summer. Mark Ott, son of translators in Bolivia, came for experience after finishing his aircraft maintenance training at LeTourneau, and before heading for another year of studies at Columbia Bible College. *(Later, Mark served full time on our maintenance staff.)* Other help came from Jim Dolgner, a maintenance instructor from Moody Aviation in Tennessee. He and his family saw first-hand the need and blessing of safe air travel to remote areas, which better equipped Jim to prepare students for mission service. Both men were a real asset to our program.

John also served as Fire Chief for our Center that summer. With little rain for several months, grassy areas turned brown, with dry leaves on the ground. When local people burned areas for their gardens, there was always the danger of it spreading. He also needed to keep the ancient fire truck in running order. When a fire was spotted, the Center alarm whistle called together the volunteer fire crew to speed to the needed place.

I was glad to be back working at the Print Shop. I enjoyed typing the camera-ready pages for the *Rapa Nui* Reader No. 2, between other "quick" jobs. This was for a language group who lived on Easter Island, a territory of Chile, served by our Peru Branch. Most of our Peruvian print shop workers didn't work in July because of a general strike in Pucallpa. But our office kept on with preparations.

Mom also worked. John found a good job for her since she liked to sew. They needed new upholstered coverings for airplane seats. Using a durable machine, Mom happily sewed in the upstairs hangar space, with a fan keeping her cool.

Mom's three months with us quickly passed. Near the end of her time with us, we had plans for a special excursion.

The Tour Guide

We decided to combine a trip to Machu Picchu at the end of Mom's time with us, to coincide with Arthur and Martha Scott's arrival. With John unable to come, I was the tour guide for our little group. Having been to Machu Picchu previously, I thought I could handle it. I made reservations through Hugo, our previous tour contact.

When it was time for Mom and me to fly from Pucallpa, the political situation was serious. There had been a country-wide mail strike for several weeks. Now, other strikes created unrest around our area. People protested local resource funds being funneled to develop other areas, while Pucallpa had only a small section of paved road.

Merchants closed their stores. Protesters closed roads and slashed tires on vehicles of those who ventured out. If we didn't reach the Pucallpa Airport to fly to Lima, Mom's tourist visa would expire. A staff member contacted local police who gave us a special permission placard for our vehicle for safe passage. Mom was very uneasy. "Elsie, don't you want to come home with me," she said, "and get out of here?" We prayed and held our breath on the drive to the airport, being watchful for any problems, and thankfully made it without incident.

Mom and I arrived safely in Lima and stayed in our guest house. Arthur and Martha Scott soon arrived on schedule. We thought we were all set to fly together to Cusco, but our tickets were for two different flights. Not a great start for a tour guide. I was unable to make changes. So, Mom and I left on our flight, and told the Scotts we'd meet them at the Cusco Airport several hours later.

In Cusco, our friend Hugo met us. "Don't worry," he said. "I'll take you to my house, and when we hear that plane come in, we'll return to meet the Scotts." He settled us in the living room of his home and went about his work as we waited. His wife kindly served us cups of hot coca tea, helpful to avoid altitude sickness. Meanwhile, in the distance we could hear planes coming and going. At just the right time Hugo reappeared and took us to the airport. With our party reunited, Hugo dropped us all off at a hotel.

At breakfast next morning, I warned them to avoid the fresh-squeezed orange juice. (Fresh fruits and vegetables often gave travelers amoebic dysentery.) But the juice looked so refreshingly delicious that the Scotts opted to have some anyway—big, tall glasses. Thankfully they were fine. We toured Cusco, and the next day rode the train, then the bus up the switchbacks to walk around the amazing ruins. We completed the trip without serious problems.

The Scotts flew on out to our Jungle Center, and I stayed in Lima with Mom another day to see her off to the States. On our last evening, I wanted to take Mom out to the rotating restaurant on top of a tall building. We planned to take a taxi. I knew it probably wouldn't open until 7:00 p.m. Then I realized I couldn't remember the restaurant's name and didn't know where it was. The others had already finished their supper at the group dining room, and I couldn't find anyone to ask. I felt uneasy for us *gringa* ladies to go out on our own at night. And I lost my confidence. With great disappointment and a few tears on my part, Mom and I, dressed in our finest, raided the group kitchen fridge for some leftovers to eat. I knew for sure that my days as a tour guide were over!

The next day Mom was on her way. But her travel challenges weren't over. We had so hoped that someone from our group going that direction could accompany her. But she had to go by herself, with a stop in Iquitos. In Miami the plane connection didn't work, so she spent the whole night waiting in the airport for another flight. Not a nice experience for a novice traveler. Hopefully the difficulties of the last week didn't ruin the special time we had enjoyed together as she saw firsthand our lives and work in Peru.

When I got back to the Jungle Center, Arthur and Martha were busily involved, and John had taken good care of them as our house guests. Our new dining table and chairs were taking shape.

One evening we talked about Arthur's unpleasant teaching situation. I think the Lord prompted me to share an idea with him. "Maybe you could invite the principal and his wife to your home for supper and share your concerns."

(Months later we learned that they did that. When the principal saw Arthur's shop and realized his woodworking expertise, he set up a woodworking class for Arthur to teach at his high school.

We loved the furniture that Arthur made for us so much that some years later we shipped the table back to the States and still use it to this day.)

Unusual Air Strip

John hoped for an opportunity to work on airstrip improvement. Of special concern was the marginal airstrip at Chequitavo (CHECK-ee-TA-vo) where two ladies worked on translation for the Pajonal Campas. Two hills with a dip between them made landing dangerous. If the tops of the hills could be carved off and moved to fill in the dip, it could be a good airstrip. Our Bobcat tractor 310 (a small front-end loader) was the perfect tool for the job—if we could somehow get it out to Chequitavo.

With our mutually beneficial relationship with the Peruvian Army, we asked if they could carry out the Bobcat in their large helicopter. Later permission was granted. One of our planes would lead their helicopter to this very remote spot. (This was before we had GPS in the planes.)

John rode in the helicopter along with the loaded Bobcat and four barrels of fuel. Doug Deming, piloting the single-engine Helio Courier, banked into a steep turn and wagged his wings to signal the landing spot for the helicopter following him. Then Doug flew off to his own destination.

Flattening tall grass with its powerful rotor blast, the "whirly bird" settled down on top of a grassy hill and cut the engines. The Peruvian crew and John, glad to get down through the rapidly accumulating clouds, surveyed the scene.

The pilot stepped up to John. *"Y dónde está la pista?* (And where is the airstrip?)" he asked.

John pointed to the slope which disappeared over the grassy edge. "This is it," he said with a smile.

The pilot looked at the undulating terrain. "You land planes on this?"

"Yes, that's why we asked you to bring this tractor," John explained. "Looks like there's lots of work to be done!"

Local Campa Indians helped set up a ramp from the cargo door to the ground with six-inch thick tree trunks they had prepared. When John drove the Bobcat tractor down the makeshift ramp, timber started cracking. John quickly accelerated and landed with a thump, a little sooner than expected. That could have ended badly, but no harm was done.

As they offloaded the drums of gasoline, rain clouds closed in. Translator Allene Heitzman and literacy specialist Linda Potter invited everybody to shelter at their jungle house to wait out the storm.

Damp and tired after the 20-minute hike through the Indian village and up a steep hillside, they enjoyed beans and rice that Allene and Linda warmed on their Coleman stove. No doubt the Peruvian crew marveled at these two ladies living in such a simple thatched-roofed, split-wood, mud-floored dwelling in an almost forgotten section of their country.

Then, in the following days, John rode the Bobcat like a bronco! Curious Campas watched in fascination as it swiveled this way and that, scooping up enough dirt to fill two wheelbarrows, then scooting over to the low spot to dump the load, and pack it down. Some Campas, along with Linda, also hauled wheelbarrow loads of dirt.

John drove the tractor perpendicular to the edges to pack the dirt. One day he thought it might be quicker to drive parallel to the edge. Bad idea. The Bobcat tumbled over on its side. John thankfully only suffered a sore arm. Since there was no way he could roll the tractor back by himself, he tried giving a super loud yell across the way to the village to see if some Campas might come to help. Several slight ladies came running. *Oh dear,* John sighed to himself. *I wish some men had come.* But to his amazement those ladies grabbed the Bobcat and quickly set it upright. John thanked them profusely and went back to work.

One of his challenges was to keep the tractor going without maintenance resources. After a week's hard work, the tractor was as tired as John.

Meanwhile, at the Jungle Center, I checked with the doctor there about a bothering breast lump. He advised me to get a biopsy in Lima as soon as possible. I hoped we could delay until John returned. But since the tractor had problems, they brought John in when they flew parts out, along with aviation maintenance colleague, Larry Schatz, to work on the airstrip for a week.

This enabled John to fly with me to Lima, to the Anglo-American Clinic where I occupied their last hospital bed. An open biopsy, via a freeze section, showed that the lump was benign, with no trace of cancer. I was so thankful that John had been able to come to Lima with me.

After returning to the Center, John flew back to the airstrip along with Dave Scott, the college-age son of our prayer partners. This time they set up a tent at the end of the runway to quickly shelter in a rainstorm. They worked from dawn to dusk, taking turns, one on the tractor while the other rested in the tent. Two weeks later, John returned to his responsibilities in the hangar while Dave stayed to finish the work. Despite many rainy days and tractor problems, the project was finally completed.

John was thankful for the opportunity to help develop this new location for the Pajonal Campa work. We were grateful that the Peruvian Army was willing to transport the tractor for us as we had no way to do it. We expected that when the helicopter crew returned in November to pick up the Bobcat, the pilot would say, "Oh! There's the airstrip. I see it clearly!"

Frustrations and Blessings

Daily frustrations sometimes obscured God's goodness. John had several days in a row when everything seemed to be going wrong: a flight returned after a half hour's start to replace spark plugs, another plane had a flat tire at a remote location, Peruvian hangar mechanics had to be sent home because of a surprise holiday, electricity failed at the hangar and our house, John's watch battery gave out. John joked that his biorhythmic patterns must have had joint lows. We needed to remember the ways God had blessed us.

God had protected our flight program in many dangerous situations. New believers were added to tribal groups. We were encouraged by churches, family, and friends who prayed and supported us financially. All that made the difficult days worthwhile.

The Cashinahua (Kah-she-NOW-ah) New Testament, was dedicated and distributed, being the thirteenth to be completed by Wycliffe/SIL in Peru.

We were especially thankful when a shipment finally arrived and was released from customs about seven months after our arrival. It included John's roll-away tool chest and crate of tools. Although the tool chest was damaged on several corners and tools were rusty from rain exposure, he cleaned them with elbow grease, and they served well. It was just so good to have them available.

At the Print Shop I worked on a rush job for an Achuar hymn book. Then I continued working away on schoolbooks in various languages, typing photo-ready copy. Computers were coming on the scene! The other ladies in the office, Kathy Bergman and Lydia Carlson, worked on Datapoint computers and finished editing *two* New Testaments, Achuar and Bora. Their tapes were sent to Dallas for final formatting. I took a week's mini course on the new DEC computer to evaluate its potential for preparing primers and readers.

Datapoint Computer

Our pilots often brought language helpers and their families from the villages to our Center, where translation progressed more quickly with fewer distractions. But sometimes other issues arose. On one occasion, translation helper Gustavo greatly helped Gene Scott translate I Corinthians. Gene was encouraged by Gustavo's discernment and enthusiasm to have more of God's Word available for the Sharanahuas. But one of Gustavo's children contracted whooping cough, making it impossible for them to return home to their village on their scheduled flight. This disease had previously caused deaths among many village babies, and they couldn't risk another epidemic there.

Gustavo became angry as he didn't understand an incubation period. "I'll never come here to help you again!" he told Gene and refused to translate further. As prayer partners with the Sharanahua team, we often asked God to do a special work among these changeable, difficult-to-love people. Pilots told us that they even felt Satanic oppression when flying into their area of the Purus jungles. Progress was like rowing upstream. Later, Gustavo's temper cooled, and he resumed work. But we wondered if he would continue working with the Scotts; he was by far their best translation helper. Then we reminded ourselves that we must often disappoint the Lord by our own inconsistencies. Yet He is ever-patient and ever-loving, forgiving us again and again.

The Lyons, our Public Relations team, belonged to a local Rotary Club in Pucallpa giving the Peruvians exposure to our work at the Yarinacocha Center. Recently many of those had professed Christ as Savior. A core group of about six began meeting Saturday mornings for prayer, fellowship, and growth.

Captured

We were shocked and saddened when terrorists kidnapped SIL linguist Chet Bitterman in Colombia. He was from Lancaster, PA, and we knew his family.

On January 19, 1981, seven armed M-19 guerrillas had gained entrance to SIL's Group House in Bogotá. A "policeman" knocked at the door, then others hidden from view entered the house. The 17 people there were gathered (some still in pajamas). The men were tied up with hands behind them as they lay prone on the floor. The intruders held them at gunpoint while they ransacked the house, taking radios, papers from the files, and correspondence. They were looking for SIL's Colombia Branch Director, but not finding him, they took Chet instead, who happened to be in Bogotá to have gall bladder surgery before heading to an assignment with the Carijona tribe in the Colombian jungle.

The M-19s announced their demands in the newspaper that SIL be out of Colombia by February 19th or Chet's life would be in danger, and there would be new violence against our group. Not giving in to demands, SIL leaders decided to stay as long as the Colombian government permitted them.

People around the world prayed for Chet's release. The February 19 deadline passed, and March 5 was the extended date. Meanwhile in Bogotá, the old group house and the home of an SIL family were bombed. Thankfully nobody was hurt. We heard conflicting rumors. Then 48 days after his abduction, on March 7, his body was found in a commandeered bus in the outskirts of Bogotá, having been shot in the chest and wrapped in a rebel flag.

An entry in Chet's journal written nearly two years earlier read: *"The situation in Nicaragua is getting worse. If Nicaragua falls, I guess the rest of Central America will too. Maybe this is just some kind of self-inflicted martyr complex, but I find this recurring thought that perhaps God will call me to be martyred in His service in Colombia. I am willing."* Chet's story was chronicled in the book *Called to Die*, written by Steve Estes.

We didn't know the motive of the M-19's violence. Perhaps some tribal work was close to drug traffic areas, which threatened them. Perhaps the influence of changed lives hindered their plans. They said they thought we were spying for the CIA. For whatever reason, we knew that God's work often caused persecution. *("...our present sufferings are not worth comparing with the glory that will be revealed in us." -Romans 8:18 NIV).*

We all had prayed much for Chet's release, yet we realized that God is sovereign. Since He had allowed this, we knew He would receive glory in the end. We continued on in Peru, perhaps re-evaluating our motives and how much we were willing to suffer, if needed, for the Lord's sake. Our missionary tasks were not to be taken lightly. We were in a spiritual battle.

We so appreciated the prayers of folks back home. Later there would come a time when we in Peru would face similar danger.

Bent Wing

The 1981 Bilingual School training session had been the biggest in quite some time with around 300 students attending in the facilities next to our Center. At the end of the session, our aviation team had many additional flights moving the teachers back home and bringing in other students to the Swiss Bible School just a few miles from our location.

All five planes were fully scheduled. Students who had attended the training were eager to return to their communities. Even a little bad weather could throw the schedule way off. All was going as planned until Tuesday afternoon.

Way up north, one of our pilots dropped off his next-to-last passenger in a remote area and taxied the float plane down the river for takeoff. As he approached a bend in the river, he prepared to initiate a step turn in which one float was lifted from the water to turn the plane. A southerly wind, rare to that area, surprised him causing a deviation in his direction as he accelerated for takeoff at the bend. Quickly chopping the power, he aborted takeoff, but the plane continued straight ahead toward a big leaning tree on the bank. The impact broke the right wing.

Heavy rains on Wednesday prevented a planned rescue flight, further complicating the flight schedule. On Thursday the Chief Pilot flew John, and his reliable Peruvian mechanic José, out to assess the situation, taking along equipment for possible repairs. They hoped to fly the damaged plane out after repairing the wing.

Upon arrival they realized that would be impossible. They needed to move the plane to a place where they could work on it. They roped a 2x6 board between the floats and attached a 15-horsepower outboard motor. With this, they were able to power the plane six hours downriver to an oil company base where there were floating docks from which they could work.

Then John was picked up and flown back to our Center to plan the next steps, while José stayed to guard the plane. John prayed for wisdom. That night he awoke with an idea he felt was an answer to his prayer, and he could hardly wait to get down to the hangar in the morning to try it out.

He checked the measurements of an old spare wing. It would just fit between the struts of the second float plane. They strapped it into place and did a test flight. It would work! Flying in this "pseudo biplane" they returned to the oil camp.

After solving some problems, such as how to keep the plane from tipping into the water when they removed the damaged right wing, they made the switch. With the temporary wing in place, they got the plane airborne and returned safely to Yarinacocha.

They requested a new wing from the States and made plans to have the damaged wing transported back to Yarinacocha. *(It arrived back at the Jungle Center a year later, having travelled by Army barge.)*

Meanwhile, when doing a thorough inspection on the plane, they disassembled the tail section and discovered the beginnings of corrosion on the spar of the vertical stabilizer. That corrosion could have continued until beyond repair had they not caught it in time. This minor tragedy turned out to be a long-term blessing in disguise. They could repair the airplane now and not lose it due to corrosion later. We were reminded that the Lord can bring good out of bad situations.

In addition to doing a permanent wing repair, John needed to keep the regular maintenance going. Fortunately, a young mechanic, Owen Blickensderfer, arrived to serve for a year. He was good help in time of need. In early August John was happy to return the float plane to service.

Day by Day

Back when John was in the Army, he had come to really appreciate the hymn, "Day by Day." That hymn became his favorite and a comfort in daily challenges. God could be trusted to give strength for whatever each day brought. Our life in Peru provided interesting day-by-day experiences:

John was Chairman of the Conference Planning Committee for the 1981 Peru Branch Conference. We had served on the committee the year before so were prepared for the many details that needed to be handled by various sub-committees.

John acquired another extra duty: Peru Procurement Coordinator, overseeing Peru Branch buying and shipping from the States, including liberations from customs. John asked for prayer as he searched for a good way to ship the freshly printed Achuar New Testaments from the U.S. to arrive in time for their dedication. Thankfully they arrived for the joyful event and for distribution in three jungle communities. For the dedication flights, the pilots dealt with bad weather, having to stop enroute for a jungle overnight with one load of guests, who missed the first service. Good news was that an Achuar pastor had led another 30 people to the Lord prior to the Scripture dedication.

Following that, the first copies of the Bora New Testament began arriving and would soon be presented to the Bora people.

One day John saw a snake crawl under our house. Others joined the excitement, thinking it was a bushmaster. After John shot it in the head, they decided it was non-poisonous after all. Oh well, better safe than sorry.

We knew there were "bats in our attic." They were living in the side storage areas of our upstairs. Bats were actually very helpful for keeping down the insect population. However, we didn't appreciate their occasional visits inside our house.

Amoebic dysentery was common among our colleagues, and its medicine was unpleasant. John tried a natural remedy for his frequent needs. He chewed a garlic clove each night, hoping the aroma would soon fade away. When good morning kisses were sometimes a little strong, I said, "That's better than no kisses at all."

Rainy season was so personal in the jungle. We lived in it! Everything was damp—even our clothes hanging in the closet. One day as I left our post office, I folded sheets of stamps I had purchased and placed them in my woven carrying bag. But I left them there in the bag for several days. It was a futile task to salvage $5.00 worth of stamps all stuck together. I should have remembered to put them in our hot box right away.

Mango season stretched over many months. We had five large mango trees in our yard.

- August-September— peanut-sized green fruits dropped on our aluminum roof, ping, ping.
- October-November—We got used to pong, pong and BONG, BONG, day and night.
- December-January—BLOMP, CRASH, SPLASH, large mature mangos woke us from sleep or made us jump. But we enjoyed the delicious fruit and shared it with others.

In October 1981 "Uncle Cam" Townsend, founder of WBT/SIL, and his wife Elaine helped us celebrate the 35th anniversary of translation work in Peru. At a reception at our Lima Group House, Peru's president surprised Uncle Cam with the highest award bestowed on a civilian, the *Orden del Sol*. It recognized the work of SIL in helping the Indian peoples of Peru. We thanked the Lord for the blessing and privilege to work there. *(Not long after that, on April 23, 1982, Cameron Townsend joined his Heavenly Father whom he had served so faithfully for the sake of the Bibleless tribes around the world. His challenge remained with us to "finish the task.")*

As a distemper epidemic spread through Peru, many dogs suffered, including our Peanut. She got weaker despite our care, until we had to put her down. John missed walking her by the airstrip where she would chase birds as they flew out over the lake, so that she splashed into the water full tilt. As someone said, "We should learn to love people the way a dog loves his master—unconditionally."

High Water

We relied heavily on our radio technology and communications staff. "Flight following" was vital as the planes flew over miles of jungle. Daily radio contact with linguists in tribal locations helped serve their many needs. Their weather reports were important for scheduling flights in remote areas. Technicians maintained avionics equipment, tribal radios, office equipment and anything technical.

The ringing phone woke us one night at 2:00 a.m. in March of 1982. Being part of a security crew at that time, John quickly jumped up to respond, wondering if there was an emergency.

Wes, one of our radio technicians, called to tell us that our prayer partners, Gene and Marie Scott, had radioed in from their village location, using the special emergency button on their radio which sounded an alarm in Wes's home. They requested prayer because flooding water had overrun the riverbank and was flowing rapidly under their house. Several village houses had collapsed, with water eroding dirt and sand in which stilts held their houses. Many villagers fled in canoes. For those left, no canoe was large enough to safely escape. Several neighbors sought safety in Scott's house.

We knew the Purus River was higher than usual and ate away a few inches of the bank by their village each week. The Scotts had already built a new jungle house further from the river. *"Oh Lord, please protect them,"* we prayed. *"Give them wisdom to know what to do; how to help the people."* Others who were called also prayed.

During the day, the Scotts reported water continuing to slowly rise. The water crested over knee-deep inside their house, so they with others gathered in a house on higher ground. Only a tiny circle of ground remained uncovered by water. Winds and rains prevented flights until the following day, when a float plane flew out with a load of rice. The Scotts, with a sick Sharanahua lady, returned on the plane, making less people to feed and sleep in the decimated village. Later the water level slowly receded, but the village was basically destroyed. Thankfully the Scotts had completed their translation goals ahead of schedule. *(Later the village was rebuilt on higher ground.)*

Many villages along the Purus River were severely damaged with loss of food supply. Yuca, rice, and banana crops were ruined. Our pilots flew relief foods to some areas. Cashinahua villagers had anticipated the floods and had rescued about two-thirds of their rice crop. Working together (prompted by Christian leaders) was unusual for that group who were traditional individualists. But the damp rice they harvested began to mold. One of our Center maintenance men devised a dryer system which he took out to the village along with a rice huller, enabling them to dry the rice on the spot, then hull it. World Vision aid funds enabled the purchase and distribution of that rice to nearby communities in urgent need of their main staple.

Villages and neighbors in low areas near our Center also suffered loss of their gardens when Lake Yarinacocha was extremely high. Our Community Awareness Committee helped distribute foods, medicines, and clothes, which encouraged many in need.

Most of our Center was on high ground, but the lower parts of the airstrip and hangar were partially flooded. How strange it looked when the floatplane docks were pulled up close to the Flight Office. The wheel planes used an airstrip further down the lake. Passengers and cargo were transported to and from there by canoe.

During that time, doing aircraft maintenance required creative measures—like carrying tools via canoe, fueling planes by bucket, and raising the air compressor higher. We were greatly relieved when the water level began to recede. Shallow spots filled with tadpoles, so we expected to soon see an abundance of frogs.

Saturday Surprise

On a hot Saturday afternoon, I had finished household chores and planned to relax for an hour with a good book. Propping a pillow on the arm of the couch, I stretched out to get comfortable when the phone rang.

"Hello, Is John there?"

"No, I think he's at the hangar," I replied.

"John might like to know that the president may be heading down that way."

"President of what?"

"President of Peru!"

I remembered that Peru's President Belaunde was in Pucallpa for the weekend to inaugurate the new port facility. In fact, we had postponed a flight to Huánuco that morning since local authorities requested that one of our planes be on hand at the Pucallpa airport in case it was needed to fly the presidential party locally.

That was why John was still at the hangar, to help receive the delayed flight returning from Huánuco. I called the hangar. No answer. I needed to run down and tell them. Not finding my plastic shoes quickly, and not wanting to get my other shoes muddy, I ran barefooted down our mushy shortcut path to the hangar to see if I could find John or someone there to advise.

A small group of people were waiting to greet the arrivals from Huánuco. I didn't see John but found the flight coordinator's assistant and passed on the news to him that the president might be coming. I think he thought I was joking.

Then the hangar boat, with John steering, pulled up bringing several Huánuco passengers from the nearby airstrip. I stayed to greet the arriving folks. With the boat unloaded and cargo carried to the Flight Office, John headed back for the rest of the passengers.

As the boat arrivals checked in at the Flight office, I saw a couple of Army jeeps, two motorcycles and a car driving down the dirt road toward the hangar.

"He's here!" I yelled to the flight coordinator, noticing his sweat-soaked and torn tee-shirt. He grabbed some keys, dropped them, then went quickly to unlock and open the gate. Others, intimidated by the high officials, disappeared into the hangar.

Not wanting to seem impolite, I stayed to greet the entourage. The president himself, along with officials and military personnel, got out of the vehicles and walked toward me. I frantically tried to remember the proper way to greet a president. Doing my best, I thrust out my hand and said *"Bienvenido Señor Presidente."* (Welcome Mr. President). He introduced each of his officials and I shook their hands greeting them one by one. Then they walked over to view the high-water situation in that area. John, by then, arrived in the canoe with the second boatload of passengers, but not in time to greet the officials. Within minutes the entourage was back in their vehicles and on their way.

And so it was that barefooted, perspiring, and hair askew, I met President Belaunde and gave him a not-too-royal, but very hearty welcome.

The local flood water receded enough to use our own airstrip when the bilingual teachers finished their training session. Back-to-back flights took teachers to their home communities and brought in others to attend Bible School. In fact, the 300 hours flown in March by our five pilots broke a long-standing record in our Peru program. We thanked the Lord for safety during those busy times.

After that we looked forward to some R&R.

Journal of an Unforgettable Trip

"Over the road to Lima? No, we've not done it yet, but someday, maybe," we said.

"Everyone should experience this," our friend said enthusiastically. "You see so much more than when you fly. You get a feel for the country and its people. You see the tropical foliage gradually change as you climb higher; see towns, animals, and houses along the way. Be sure to go during dry season." That advice we tucked away in our mental files to possibly explore—someday.

As vacation time approached, we planned our usual flight to Lima for a two-week stay. Then an opportunity arose. Our friends Abe and Debbie Koop were returning to Lima after their short assignment at Yarinacocha. They would rather fly than drive back in their VW, having added a new baby to their family, born in our Center Clinic. Would we like to drive their car to Lima? Perhaps the roads would improve by April when we planned to have our break. We could bring their remaining household goods that they couldn't take on the plane. It sounded like a great idea. Together we prayed, made our plans, and the Koops flew back to Lima.

Because the rainy season lasted so long, we wondered if the dirt roads would be passable. We heard about landslides and repairs. A week prior, John talked to a truck driver who had no problems driving from Lima. He said the road was better, with work currently in a section which was closed to traffic between 6:00 a.m. and 6:00 p.m. We should plan to be through San Alejandro before then to avoid a long wait. It would take 10 to 12 hours to get to Huánuco where we could overnight. John set our departure time for midnight Thursday.

That afternoon I packed a lunch of fried chicken, hard boiled eggs, carrot and celery sticks, bread, canned meat, mustard, home-made granola, milk powder, sugar, brownies, two apples, a Tupperware pitcher of water, and a thermos of coffee. John packed the car, and we went to bed by 8:00 p.m. and tried to get some sleep before leaving.

At midnight, we drove off in the loaded car after a prayer for the Lord's help. We didn't realize then how much we would need it.

120 What's in Your Hand?

We wound our way through Pucallpa and onto the Central Highway. John swerved to miss many potholes. Each time he gained speed, he had to brake for a bump. I took a Dramamine since I felt nauseated. Progress slowed on unpaved sections of dirt and mud. At 2:45 a.m. we came to a line of trucks parked alongside the road. We passed them thinking they had turned in for the night, but soon we got stuck and could go no further. We wished for a shovel. Nobody else moved. We tried to sleep a little, disappointed we couldn't make our 6:00 a.m. deadline.

At daybreak, we were surprised to see a line of trucks facing us and a line behind us. We were stuck right in the middle in the little VW. At 7:30 a.m. some men pushed us loose, but in a few hundred yards we couldn't move because trucks in both lanes waited for a tractor to help them through a bad spot. We pulled out books and read while waiting. We watched men on one truck sorting through their load of cabbages, throwing rotten leaves over the edge, making a pile on either side of them. The odor hung heavy in the damp air.

A tractor came and pushed trucks out of our lane, so we were on our way at 9:00. Proceeding cautiously, John tried to look way ahead to determine which parts of the road to choose and what speed would keep us moving. The ruts made by the trucks were further apart than the VW tires. At 9:40 we got stuck straddling a hump. In pouring rain John tried to find something to put under the wheels for traction. Rotting fence posts didn't help. Traffic was stopped in both directions. I tried the controls while John pushed, with no success. Three young men sloshed down the road towards us carrying luggage, apparently abandoning their vehicle. They tried to push us out, but our wheels only spun deeper into the soup, splashing them. They went on their way not too happily.

We pulled out a towel for John to dry. His shoes and lower slacks were coated with mud. We prayed, asking the Lord to protect Koop's car, then got out our books and read. Local people walked by saying the road ahead was bad. We considered returning, but hesitated, knowing what we had already come through. The road ahead couldn't be much worse. But we couldn't go in either direction. We ate some chicken and eggs. It continued to rain. After five long hours, a small truck came toward us. He passed, tires spinning, and got stuck 100 yards beyond. Soon a bus also bobbed along from the same direction, having good traction. He kindly stopped, got out a chain and pulled us out with little difficulty. We were *very* grateful to be moving again until we came upon a line-up in both directions waiting to get through a huge water hole that seemed to be over two feet deep. As each truck in turn got through, it backed up and pulled the next with a chain. We approached our turn apprehensively.

To our relief, some men suggested they push us along the side since the VW was small enough to make it. At 4:05 p.m. we were moving again, but only for half a kilometer to another wait with blocked vehicles. At 5:30 men motioned us through to squeeze down the side of the line of trucks coming the other way. It was now getting dark.

We got stuck again, so many times we lost count. We were still two kilometers out of San Alejandro. John talked a while with some men about our work. We snacked and waited and got sleepy. John set a few items outside the car on a spot of foliage and rearranged the load so we could stretch out a bit, John in the front and I alongside a suitcase in the back. With feet hanging out the window it was almost comfortable! We dozed a little. Then about 1:30 a.m. some men said they were going to go for it and would pull us through behind them. We quickly repacked the car and watched as they painstakingly dug out and filled in paths for each wheel, then moved through, tipping the large truck dangerously toward a drop-off on the right. We expected him to stop then and attach his tow chain, but he kept on going. Disappointed, we moved ahead as best we could, but got stuck again.

At 3:30 the driver of a tractor told us he'd been out since early that morning helping move vehicles. He borrowed a tow chain, then maneuvered cautiously to pull us out. He was heading home so helped us through several more bad spots on his way until we came to a stopped bus with a line of trucks behind it. We decided to call it a night. We had only used one half of a tank of gas in over 24 hours on the road going as fast as we could go. Really efficient, those VWs!

We tried to sleep on the front seat, but I couldn't get comfortable. We re-shifted the load, setting some things out again. But the gnats were biting, and it was too stuffy to close the windows. Neither of us slept.

At 5:45 a.m. we endeavored to make a run through the bad area ahead and progressed only 100 yards. After several more stops, we saw a nicely dressed lady digging with a shovel. When I took a photo, she laughed. We talked and she asked for a copy of the photo. We exchanged addresses. Her family was taking vegetables from Huánuco to Pucallpa. I enjoyed meeting another female in a world of mostly men. People said the road was bad for just a few more kilometers. It was beginning to sprinkle again. At another place I got out to help push the VW off a shoulder, then ran to catch up with John.

We arrived at San Alejandro at 9:30 a.m. and stopped at the road check where we had to show our papers. The gas station was out of gas. We looked for the roadblock but found none. A local man said it was OK to go through, so we continued still more hopefully onward. Our spirits lifted as we avoided "traps" and as the road conditions improved. At the next village there was no gas either. John added the gallon he had brought along in case we ran short. We passed through the town of Aguaytia at 11:45 where there was another road check. There we were able to fill the gas tank.

Then we came to the famous Boquerón, a lovely waterfall area where our Jungle Center teenagers had enjoyed camping trips. We stopped at a roadside fall where John finally removed his muddy shoes and threw away his socks. His toes were wrinkled and blue. I thought it was a fungus. "Just faded from my blue tennis shoes," he assured me. We washed mud off us and cleaned the floor mats and windows of the car. John even changed his muddy trousers and found clean socks and shoes. Refreshed, we continued without problems. We passed tea plantations, and bought gas at Tingo Maria, where they checked our papers once again.

After 42 hours on the road, we arrived at Huánuco about 6:30 p.m. and checked into the last room available at the new hotel. We were *very tired!* After a wonderful shower we went to the new Wycliffe Center to greet friends. They said folks from our Yarinacocha Center had been checking by radio, concerned that we hadn't arrived as planned. We asked to leave the car in the compound to avoid a break-in for the Koop's belongings. After walking back to the hotel, we enjoyed a nice steak. John almost fell asleep in the dining room, and I felt light-headed. Soon after crawling into bed, we were soundly asleep.

On Sunday we enjoyed Huánuco's charm: colorful Quechua and Mestizo people, the bustling city streets with adobe buildings close to the sidewalks hiding private courtyards and dwellings, the mountains rising on all sides into blue and breezy skies. We attended the Peruvian Alliance Church, had a long siesta in the afternoon, and joined our Wycliffe friends for informal evening worship and fellowship.

(The Huánuco Center was special, because for many years our linguists didn't have governmental permission to work in Peru's highlands. In recent years restrictions were lifted. This Huánuco Center was well used for translation workshops, Quechua worker orientation, computer training for Scripture adaptation to related languages, and training for Quechua co-translators.)

On Monday morning we were on the road again, climbing higher. The sun was shining! An hour out we came to a small landslide across the road being cleared by three bulldozers. Taking a photo, I realized it was the last of a 20-exposure film, rather than 36. What a shame that I'd used most of the film on the muddy roads.

We climbed higher on good roads into the Andes Mountains, passing through mining areas. Trees became smaller until there were none. Cool air refreshed us while we saw beautiful blue lakes, sheep grazing, llamas, cattle, horses, large rocks with waterfalls, and adobe houses with thatched or tiled roofs. A group of workers were busy along the road making gravel on the spot by hammering local rocks into small pieces.

Later we saw snowflakes falling. I loved it. Approaching the high point of Ticlio, over 14,000 feet, we "sniffed" oxygen from the bottle we had brought along. This helped us avoid high altitude sickness. The VW struggled as we climbed steep grades in thin air. As high as we were, mountains still loomed majestically above us. Beautiful scenes and no more film for the camera, not even for the snow caps in the distance. That part of the trip well made up for the first part. Maybe we would try it again someday—with lots of film—during dry season!

We descended in still grandiose surroundings to Lima, joining heavy traffic, a very dirty VW among clean and shiny autos. We arrived at our Lima Group House in time for supper.

John cleaned up the car and we returned it to the Koops with their belongings, hoping we hadn't done any damage to their vehicle. We enjoyed the rest of our vacation time shopping, visiting, eating, and relaxing. At the Group House Sunday evening fellowship, John shared an important lesson he had learned during the trip. He liked to feel capable of finding solutions and moving ahead. However, at times there was nothing he could do to get us out of the mud. When we come to the end of ourselves, we must wait for the Lord's solutions and timing. Our return flight to Pucallpa by air took less than an hour.

Responding to Challenges

Deadlines: Our Print Shop Office was always busy with schoolbooks in various stages. In fact, when we instituted a new priority system of first-come-first-served, over 100 waited in line. Some were simple health books or pre-primers, but others were long reading books. I worked for several weeks typing a Level 4 Reader for Campa Pajonal with over 160 pages. Also, our colleagues' prayer letters needed photo-ready typing. I tried working faster, but accuracy was important too. The other ladies worked mostly on Scripture booklets.

Preparing prayer letters for press involved many steps. After typing a letter, print shop staff made negatives of the text, often reduced to a pre-calculated percentage to fit the page, and having spaces sized to fit any photos. Half tones were made of the photos, also at sized percentages. Negatives and half tones were taped into place on a masking sheet, then openings carefully cut in the sheet to expose them. Next, any light or dark specks on the negatives were "painted  out." Then metal plates were burned, which were run on the printing press. *(A complicated process in that day has been incredibly simplified with today's technology.)*

Reaching the Parkinahuas: A primitive group of Indians remained isolated in the deep jungle. They were very illusive and dangerous having killed people, including Machiguengas, who ventured into their area. Could they be reached to give them God's Word? Up to that time our SIL team had been unable to make contact.

With the New Testament in their Machiguenga language already for several years, churches were flourishing in one area. The Snells (translators) rejoiced that 80 Machiguengas had accepted Christ recently, and four Machiguenga men were sent out by the church to reach others.

The first two Machiguenga missionaries journeyed to visit three other Machiguenga villages. The other two men went to an area where Parkinahuas had been known to live. We asked prayer for God's protection on the men and for the possibility to contact the Parkinahuas. We wondered if the Machiguengas could do it. Not on that trip, but perhaps soon.

Family needs: On Friday, August 7, 1982, we received a radio message from John's sister Karen that their dad had passed away. John decided he should go to the funeral. He quickly got tickets to Lima for Saturday night, and then out of Lima after midnight. He was able to fly to New York and on to Albany, where Karen (driving from Pennsylvania) picked him up on Sunday in good time for the Monday funeral. It would have been good to have assurance that his dad had made his peace with God while waiting many hours for help after a bad fall. He knew the way of salvation shared by John and others. Though John hadn't been close to his dad, we were thankful for better communication in the past few years. It was good that John could travel there to show his concern.

Tropical Challenges: One evening John attended a meeting with local community leaders to solve the problem of the growing amounts of *huama* (water hyacinths) on Lake Yarinacocha. Although very pretty, they had proliferated, obstructing local boat travel. Commercial traffic to the port was essential. At times wind blew the *huama* in mammoth clumps almost covering the entire width of the lake. Our float planes could barely take off and land. It seemed that we needed to be involved in some type of community action to save the lake. Someone suggested importing manatees to eat the unwanted vegetation. Weeks later God solved the problem. A big windstorm blew the plants to one end of the lake and out a river which connected to the lake during high water!

Training Challenges: That year some 250 bilingual teachers attended Teacher Training. During a weekend spiritual retreat, the teachers heard alternatives to materialistic philosophies. Some Aguaruna teachers openly criticized Christianity. On Friday nights Ted Long showed Bible films in Spanish to interested teachers. After showing one on Christ's death and resurrection, Ted talked about not having to be afraid to die when Christ is our Savior. Later the most vocal of the group came to Ted and admitted that he was very fearful of death and wanted to discuss this with him. For several Sunday evenings about 20 Aguarunas met with Ted to discuss salvation, then took the step to accept Christ as Savior. Christ changed their lives, and we prayed that these young teachers would be faithful as they returned to their respective communities, facing probable opposition.

Also, 12 chosen representatives from six communities attended a three-month Health Promoters' Course addressing health needs of the small villages. Taught by our Health Promotion team in Spanish, being the students' second language, was difficult for some. We hoped that they would have a heart for helping their people as they set up medical posts in their communities, relieving our translators' load to provide medical care. One student did come to know the Lord, and we prayed for him and others to be positive testimonies, with a new status in their communities. I helped by decorating the 12 graduation diplomas with patriotic red and white ribbon, making them culturally noteworthy.

Machiguenga ladies attended a sewing course. During personal interviews held with each participant, several came to know the Lord.

Shipping Challenges: In January of '83, John requested to be released from his Procurement Coordinator duties to concentrate on directing the aircraft maintenance. Although he enjoyed various aspects of the procurement job, he realized that his total load was just too heavy.

Fortunately, Bill Richmond, a Maintenance Specialist, agreed to take on that responsibility. In the transition process, John asked Bill to accompany him on a Procurement excursion. John used a group vehicle to drive to Pucallpa. On the way the truck's carburetor linkage broke, which they ingeniously repaired temporarily with a piece of string. In town, they first stopped at our customs agent's office to pick up long overdue, urgently needed permission paperwork to export aircraft engine parts for overhaul. The secretary told them the agent was in Lima, but surprisingly, they ran into him at the customs office! He said he'd provide paperwork very soon. Then while trying to work through the stages of import permissions, the electricity went off in the customs office. The office quickly closed. "Come back at 3:30," they were told.

John and Bill had better success at the airlines office where they picked up all 27 cartons of a shipment from the States that had been held up in Lima customs for a month and a half after its arrival. They loaded it on the truck and brought it to a storage shed at our Center. When final customs permissions on that would be granted, they could distribute the contents. That included items such as aircraft parts, medicines for the clinic, printing supplies, and light bulbs.

Sometimes the frustrations of doing our work could overshadow the joy of serving. We needed to appreciate the laid-back lifestyle which valued unhurried time with people, and to loosen up our get-things-done-quickly mentality. We should relax, trusting our Heavenly Father who knew about those unending delays. We asked prayer to overcome frustrations and Satan's discouragement. There was always *mañana* to get things done.

After several years of trying to send engines to the U.S. to be overhauled, the aviation staff decided the time lapse, shipping problems, and expense were not worth the effort. With legal restrictions on the number of hours an engine was permitted to function, a workable solution was vital. It seemed better to overhaul engines in our Peru hangar shop. Various engine components would still need to be overhauled in U.S. shops, but components were easier to transport than an entire engine. Replacement parts would still have to be ordered and received.

Meanwhile, they requested Jim Entz, JAARS engine specialist, to come to Peru to overhaul three engines, one of which was needed in a few months. The best time for Jim to come was February while his wife Bev was on a musical tour. We prayed that all the necessary "ingredients" would arrive in time for Jim to complete the overhauls.

When Jim arrived, he brought many needed parts with him. We enjoyed having Jim as our house guest and laughed when he took an after-lunch siesta on a wooden worktable in the air-conditioned parts room. He worked diligently to finish the engines in the time available. Although 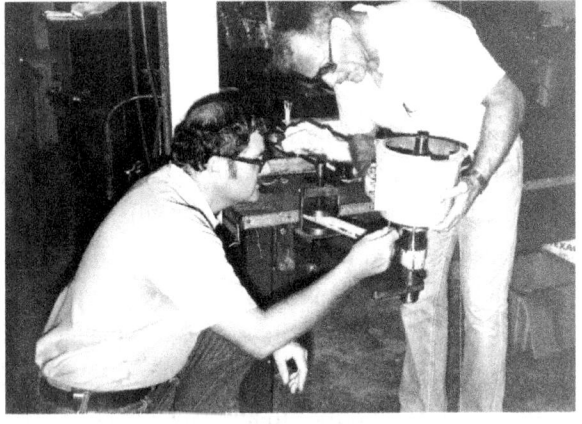 ordered much earlier, not all the needed parts arrived. But the work was mostly completed when Jim had to leave. John would finish final details later.

With our furlough departure scheduled for late June, we realized there was much to be done before we left. That included several big hangar projects and preparations for the annual inspection of hangar and all planes. Also, we needed to pack away personal items in our house and arrange for someone to stay in it and take care of our new dog, Flip. We made tentative furlough itinerary plans.

Interrupted Meditations

My devotional time on Monday, March 19, meshed with the happenings around me. I recorded my thoughts:

It was a lovely morning—a cool 72° after many unbearably hot days. Sun rays, filtered by mango leaves, slanted across the desktop and decorated my study sheet. It was nice to have a little extra time for devotions this morning. John had left earlier than usual for the hangar since it was to be a big day of flights. I concentrated on the first chapter of I Thessalonians.

> *The Thessalonian believers must have really been an encouragement to Paul. They had responded favorably to the gospel after only a short and interrupted ministry there. But Paul hadn't ministered in his own strength. It was God's doing, and it was a response of the chosen.*

The sound of an airplane engine starting up drew my mind to the hangar, just steps from our house.

> *Lord, please give them safety today and throughout this busy week.*

Soon I heard the plane take off toward the lake. Immediately another plane started its engine. It taxied out of earshot down the runway and soon it also took off over the lake.

> *They're getting a good early start on two flights.*

Then I heard a third engine rev up—this time from a float plane on the lake. I saw tribal students running down the road toward the hangar.

> *More passengers. Or perhaps they were going to say farewell to some friends.*

A few minutes later I heard the float plane moving up the lake for takeoff and craned my neck to watch from our window to catch a glimpse of it through the trees. My heart thrilled anew to know John's part in readying and maintaining the planes for such days as this. I took up my pen to write down my feelings so they would be fresh—to share in a prayer letter, and as I did, a *fourth* engine started to hum. Soon another float plane was taking off down the lake, passed my view, then doubled back and flew off in a different direction.

From this Center, Lord, just as the planes have gone to various locations this morning, so your Word is being prepared and sent out. May there be many villages tucked away in the jungle who respond as did the Thessalonians—with a work of faith, a labor of love, and patience of hope in Christ. Any successful ministry is only through Your doing.

Later, from the kitchen, I heard the roar from the fifth plane.

Our scheduled furlough was to begin late June. But John's coworker, Mark Myers, slated to take John's place, had left early in May due to serious family medical needs. Could we leave as scheduled? After exhausting possibilities, we were happy to hear that Dave Immel, with his family, could come from Waxhaw. They would arrive shortly after we left as they still needed to raise travel funds. We appreciated the JAARS Waxhaw Center releasing Dave from his responsibilities in the engine shop. His wife Patsy, a secretary, would work in the Print Shop office—a great arrangement.

Furlough plans, in addition to travel and visits, included John getting additional training in engine overhaul. We also hoped to upgrade our Spanish with a trimester of study at a Costa Rican language school.

Final days passed quickly, and we were on our way to the U.S. It had been a good field term, not without challenges, but with satisfaction of contributing to the team effort.

Chapter 7
Costa Rica and Peru (1984-1987)
Contact and Completions

---→

That furlough was the last time we would use Mom's home as our base for travels. Mom felt lonely after Dad passed, so she made the decision to rent out her house and live with my sister and family in Lebanon, PA. We helped Mom decide what she would keep, and we sold the rest in a Fire Hall auction.

My sister's family helped close out her house. It was snowing when we packed a rental truck with Mom's belongings that she would take with her. Then we said farewell to the house and to each other as Mom and the Barkers headed to Lebanon and we headed to Florida enroute to language school.

Costa Rica

For several years we had hoped for more language study. We could communicate in Spanish but were not fluent. We were thankful for the opportunity to study at the Spanish Language Institute in Costa Rica before returning to Peru.

We arrived in San Francisco de Dos Ríos, a district of Costa Rica's capital, San José. The weather was spring-like in the 70s and 80s with cooler nights. We rented a second-floor apartment from a friendly Costa Rican family who lived on the first floor. We could catch buses downtown from there, walk to school just a block and a half away and to the post office and grocery store near us.

John helped with home duties so we could both have study time. He did most of our grocery shopping, including fresh vegetables, fruits, and delicious dairy products. He even washed our laundry by hand and hung it on pulley lines stretching across the courtyard.

Students were mostly young adults from various evangelical missions preparing to serve in Central and South America. We got acquainted with Wycliffe members headed for Peru: Mark and Patti Bean (to do translation work in the mountains, Kim and Carolyn Fowler (for translation with the Parquenahuas if/when they were contacted), and Bud and Judy Giles (support workers, and our host family who helped orient us to the area.)

That trimester 200 students learned from 40 Costa Rican teachers. Classes had a maximum of six students for language activity, phonetics, conversation, and word exercises. Grammar classes were larger. Student council leadership led a daily chapel and social activities.

Since John and I had already studied Spanish and had been using it, they tested our conversation. I tended to speak cautiously, trying to use good grammar, while John conversed more naturally, not getting upset if he didn't say it perfectly. They placed us in advanced classes, but we soon realized we were in over our heads. We needed to review the basics before progressing. John requested and received a transfer to a lower level. I struggled onward. There were days when we wondered why we were doing this, and other days we were encouraged with progress.

In addition to classroom learning we had other contacts for interacting in Spanish. We attended a Central American Mission church where John helped with a work crew building a church addition. We visited a nursing home, and I attended a ladies' Bible study. Once a week I caught a bus and then walked ten blocks downtown to meet with an Argentinean lady, exchanging 1½ hours of Spanish for equal time in English. She also taught me how to drink mate (MAW-tay), made by infusing dried yerba mate leaves, a species of the holly family. It tasted like strong, bitter tea. She served it in a hollow gourd cup with a special metallic sieved drinking straw.

We took a bus trip with a family and a Costa Rican friend to a park that overlooked the central valley. We invited a Costa Rican couple for supper who were interested in joining JAARS. Also, we were invited for a meal at a Wycliffe family's home, who lived in the city and were doing Bible translation for the BriBri language.

One evening as we studied, the neighborhood was especially noisy with loud talk and yelling. It seemed that someone was having a big party. We hoped it wasn't a fight. Finally, we understood the loud and long yell: "Goooooooooooooaaaaaalllll!" They were listening to a soccer match on the radio.

As the course neared the end, John became eager to get back to airplanes. It was hard for him to focus on studies. After final exams in mid-April, we flew to Florida, then drove to Pennsylvania. At my sister's home, we packed up what we wanted to take to Peru, said good-byes and left for another term of service.

On May 16, 1984, we arrived in Peru. It was easy to move back into our house at the Yarinacocha Center as we had left our household items for a family to use in our absence. We started serving again in the hangar and the print shop, overlapping slightly with our furlough replacements for good continuity. Citrus fruit was ripe, rainy season was ending, and we enjoyed a few cool fronts lowering the temperatures into the 70s. We felt refreshed and ready to work. That was good because the future months would bring exciting challenges.

Good news was coming from the Sharanahua people. After more than 25 years of often discouraging work with this group, Gene and Marie Scott witnessed God work in their hearts during a recent tribal stay. One after another confessed sins and asked Christ to be his "Owner" (Lord). For several weeks others made decisions almost daily. We rejoiced with them that the first draft of their New Testament translation was nearly completed.

A Series of Emergencies

One day John and the hangar team watched as a commercial operator flew overhead with the engine making strange sounds. They knew the plane was in trouble. Then, to their shock, they heard it crash a short distance over the trees past the far end of our runway. Smoke rose from that spot. John and the fire crew immediately rushed with our fire truck around the bumpy dirt roads to the scene. The plane was on fire, with people inside! They helped put out the fire, but sadly, three died. Other burn victims were taken to our clinic for treatment, then to Lima for more care. The smells and sights of that traumatic experience stayed with John for a long time.

That same day, one of our float planes flew to pick up translators at an Amarakaeri village in southern Peru. Trying to locate the right river bend on which to land, the new pilot landed near where he saw a man walking. He hoped to ask him where he was, but the man ran off into the jungle. Unfortunately, hidden rocks in the river ripped a long hole in one of the plane's floats. Thankfully no one was hurt. Hearing this news, John gathered supplies and, with Peruvian employee José, was flown out to assess damage. They hoped to do temporary repairs to fly it back. Sleeping on the sandy riverbank and cooking over a fire, they worked on the repair for a week. To augment their limited food supply, meat was provided by a local man to whom they gave one shell for his gun each day. That was all he needed to come back with a dead monkey or other treat—one shot suppers!

Meanwhile a message came that a government Helio had experienced an engine failure and they requested John's assistance in the northern part of Peru. So, leaving José to guard the damaged plane, John was brought back to our Center. The next day he left for Iquitos flying commercially. In three days, that plane was flying again.

Returning to the Center, John learned of a stuck valve in our other float plane. So, the following day he was off again, this time to the village where that plane waited. With both float planes down, the flight schedule was all backed up. Thankfully, John was able to fix that one in a few hours, getting it quickly back into service.

Meanwhile, Joel Witt, our other mechanic, with some helpers, had been flown out to join José to finish the temporary float repairs. Then they moved that plane to a safe take-off area, thankful that heavy rains had elevated the river level. The Helio flew back safely to our Center and the float eventually was changed for a borrowed one.

Experience had shown us that when New Testament projects neared completion, Satan opposed us. With Ticuna, Arabela and Amarakaeri all in final stages, it wasn't surprising to face increased challenges.

New Contact!

For years Wycliffe/SIL members had been trying to contact an isolated, primitive tribe hidden in the jungles of southern Peru. Previously we called them Parkinahuas, but the name was shortened to "Nahuas"

(NOW-ahs). They had resisted outsiders and even killed people who ventured into their area, so caution was necessary.

A surprising breakthrough began when three of these basically naked tribesmen ventured out of their tribal area and attacked a camp of Peruvian lumbermen with bows and arrows. Two Nahuas were captured and taken downriver to Sepahua (Say-POW-ah), a small jungle town. They treated the Nahuas well, giving them clothing and tools, and then released them.

About a month later, the same two returned to Sepahua with two others, taking a big step into a new world. They were put in touch with a Yaminahua man who was able to communicate with them, finding their language similar to his. The four Nahuas expressed their desire to stop killing and live in peace. They said they wanted help. Some of their people were sick.

Two days later, Wayne Snell (veteran translator), with pilot Steve Ottaviano, made an unscheduled stop at Sepahua to meet with the four men. With some trepidation they greeted the Nahuas, who surprisingly seemed harmless and of shorter stature than expected.

Wayne and Steve arranged for Yaminahua translators, Lucy Eakin and Norma Faust, to fly out and do some preliminary linguistic analysis with the four men. They identified the language as a Panoan family member close to Yaminahua and Sharanahua.

Meanwhile, Kim and Carolyn Fowler, assigned to work with the Nahuas, arrived in Lima for their Orientation to Peru and Spanish Assimilation Program. They were asked to come right out to the Jungle Center. John and I were asked to be on their prayer partner team since we knew them from the Costa Rica language school.

We received word that the Nahuas were asking SIL for medical help as some of the Nahuas had died. Probably others were also very ill. As an isolated people group, they had not developed immunity to many diseases. Their ventures to the "outside world" had been made at a cost.

A quickly assembled medical team (doctor, nurse, and Lucy Eakin) willingly tackled trekking to an unknown, dangerous, primitive people group to give emergency care. (Dr. Cal Wilson, in God's providence, had come on a six-week volunteer medical trip to serve in our Center Clinic, in the absence of any doctor there at that time.) José, a Yaminahua, and Gustavo, chief and pastor of the Sharanahua people, also joined the group to help communicate with the Nahuas. On August 2, the pilot flew them to the Mishagua River. They canoed two days upriver as far as possible, marveling at the incredible beauty of the lush rain forest with colorful flocks of parrots, howler monkeys, and tall ferns. Finally, they had to leave many supplies in the canoe and continue on foot another two days, sloshing through water, over steep hills, and narrow trails, carrying medications and other essentials. The two women suggested that they travel at their own pace with Gustavo, while the doctor forged ahead with José, who knew the Nahua camp.

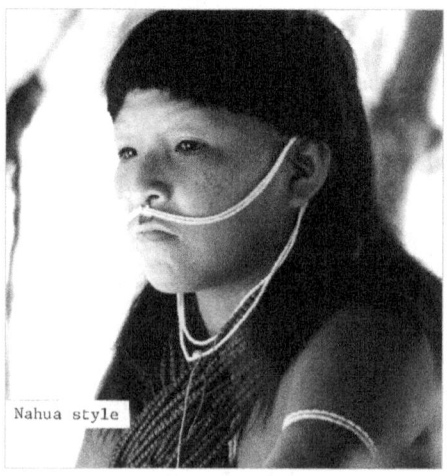

Nahua style

However, the camp was abandoned. They found the Nahuas in another area, lying in hammocks strung from trees or in crude leaf shelters, with smoky fires by each hammock. Most were extremely sick, coughing sporadically, groaning in pain, and too weak to hunt or gather food. José learned that six people had already died. Dr. Cal began a very energetic campaign to fight the sickness—basically flu and pneumonia complicated by malaria. With Jose's explanation, the Nahuas surprisingly were eager and thankful to receive shots of penicillin, rather than difficult-to-swallow, strange tasting pills.

Men simply wore a string or woven belt around their waist, some with a tuft of fibers covering their private parts. Women wore short bark cloth skirts; some wore thick strands of beads covering their breasts. Most had a string of beads under their noses and over their ears. Children wore just a string or monkey tooth belt.

In the next week, our pilots made three air drops of medicine. Soon the team on the ground was treating 85 people as more struggled into the camp, having left some along the trail, dead or too weak to continue.

Quick housing for medical team

Our prayer group prepared food and supplies to be dropped. We transferred foods (like peanut butter) to less breakable containers and wrapped items very carefully. (An earlier drop had decorated trees with cough syrup when bottles broke.)

Because of the extremely primitive conditions and the traumatic situation, the medical team was changed out twice, one time including Kim Fowler, and then the next time

Carolyn Fowler joined them. Pilots dropped medicine and supplies weekly.

The team did an extensive vaccination program. To identify people and keep records of who received what was very important! They came up with the idea to give each person a number as they received their shot, marked on their arm with a magic marker.

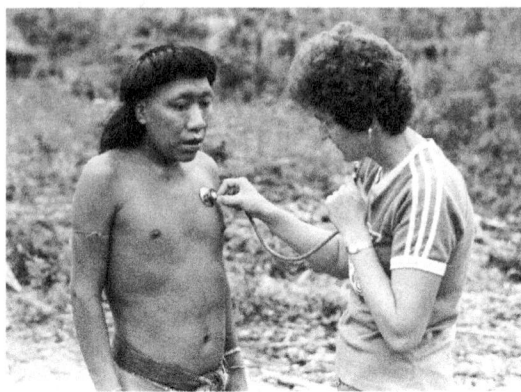

Number 66 became well known to them soon as Chaika. In all they treated about 200, with 40 or 50 having died before help reached them.

Gene Scott (linguist with the related Sharanahua language) went with one of the teams. In part of a report following his initial visit, he wrote this:

> Have you ever felt abandoned? I suppose there is no more helpless nor hopeless feeling than to feel completely abandoned. The most heartrending cry from our Lord was, "My God my God, why hast Thou forsaken me?" During the month of August and the first part of September over and over again we heard the plaintive plea, "Don't abandon us."
>
> Time after time we were asked, "Am I going to die?" When I told them, "We have come so that you can get better," they would reply, "Aicho!" (Eye-CHO), meaning "I'm delighted," their equivalent of thank you. As we went around giving out the medicines, I tried to share the Good News of Jesus' love to these who had never heard. One lady said, "That is why you have come, so that we can hear those good words!"
>
> A sweet old lady whom we called Chichi, meaning Grandmother, took hold of my hand as if to never let it go. I have never seen such affectionate people who wanted you to touch them, who wanted to know that someone cared about them. Chichi said, "Think about me (Care for me). Massage my aching muscles." As we administered injections and massaged her emaciated limbs, I repeated to her over and over again Christ's love for her. She kept saying, "Aicho! I want to hear." One night José, a Yaminahua man instrumental in getting us in contact with the Nahuas, awakened me to tell me that Chichi had died.

He said that before she died, she kept talking about the things I had been telling her about the Lord. Then she said just before she died, "I'm ready. I'm going now." I wouldn't be surprised if we all see Chichi in heaven.

Five others also prayed asking Jesus to be their "Owner."

The following account was written by Sandi Barkman (then clinic receptionist and wife of Butch Barkman, who headed up our flight program):

> Scotty (Gene Scott), Joan (nurse), and Kim and Carolyn were trying to finish up an exhausting day of immunizing some 75 Nahua Indians before sunset. The day had begun when the JAARS plane had dropped carefully wrapped vaccines by box-load down to them in their rugged surroundings. They were just about to finish up when they noticed one of the women sneak behind the crude table they had provisionally made, grab something, and run. This had become a common occurrence since their arrival. The Nahuas just didn't seem to have any sense of ownership at all. "What's yours is mine," seemed to be their way of thinking. The problem was that these four had brought the absolute essentials with them, and so when something was stolen, it made life just a bit more difficult.
>
> Back at the Center we began praying for this frustration. Some of our administration and anthropology consultants prepared a series of questions for Scotty to ask the chief of the Nahuas, to try to determine just what their philosophy was about taking things that belonged to others.
>
> One day the opportunity came. Scotty sat down beside the river with the chief and asked him, "If you had a *chakra* (field) and someone from your tribe took some of your produce without asking you, what would you think? What would you do?"
>
> "Nothing," the chief replied. "Why should I? I'm the chief."
>
> A puzzled Scotty went on. "And if you had something in your house and it was yours, and someone came into the house and took it from you without asking you for it, what would you do?"
>
> Once again, "Nothing" was his reply. "That would be only right. I am the chief."

As Scotty finished his series of questions, he realized that in this newly discovered culture, being the chief meant you are the servant of all. It meant you shared what you had with everyone.

When they hear the story of the Big Chief sharing His Son with the whole world, they will understand. He's the Chief!

After the last round of vaccinations, the team returned to the Jungle Center to recoup and regroup. Three weeks later Kim and Carolyn Fowler returned to a location on the river where the Nahuas wanted to make a new village with more game to hunt. They again found some people suffering from sickness. Then more sick ones came to that location.

With rumors of bad sickness upriver, help was again sent. Sara (a nurse) and Mary Ann (a young linguist) were flown to a landing site on a river bend where they connected with an Amuesha boatman to travel upriver. Other boat passengers were a Yaminahua man with a daughter and a Mestizo man (who would go downriver after the girls were delivered upriver). As they putted along, it began to rain so they covered up with some plastic.

After successfully passing through an area with rapids the boat got turned sideways and was swamped. People, cargo, and the boat were swept downstream! Mary Ann swam for the bank and caught a branch and then saw Sara on the other side also holding a branch. The others also ended up on Sara's side, except for the boatman who stayed with the boat. They were not in a good situation. Using jungle camp experience, the girls each made themselves a sleeping shelter, and encouraged the others to do the same. Although the night was cold and damp, there were no mosquitoes. The next day with the rain stopped and the river a little lower, Mary Ann swam across to join the others. Later they were happy to see the boatman returning from downstream poling his canoe, having lost the engine. He had retrieved some cargo, but no radio. They attempted to continue upriver poling but were very happy to see a canoe sent downstream by Kim Fowler to look for the girls since they were overdue arriving.

Sara found the sick Nahuas difficult to treat, not responding now so much to penicillin. There seemed to be a lot of malnutrition. Many were weak and not able to get out of their hammocks to get food. Others fished and killed monkeys for them. When one lady died, Carolyn and Sara talked them out of burying her children with her! The grandmother thankfully agreed to care for them.

Our prayer group sent out a supply of oatmeal for them when the girls were picked up. Sara shared in a meeting later, "Our struggles are a spiritual battle *'against principalities, . . . powers, . . . rulers of the darkness of this world . . .'" (Ephesians 6:12 KJV).*

Abandoned Child

I sent Christmassy items with the Fowlers when they returned to the Nahuas on December 20. I selected and mounted old Christmas cards that illustrated Christ's birth, adding appropriate Sharanahua Scriptures. Although the Nahuas couldn't read, they understood much of the Sharanahua language.

That trip was easier for Kim and Carolyn with no canoe capsizes, long delays, or serious medical cases. They spent more time learning the language.

Kim and Carolyn also worried about a weak little child who seemed malnourished. They started giving him some food from their limited supply. One day they saw the Nahua family leave camp with the father carrying the child on his shoulders. Several hours later the family returned without the boy. It seemed that they had abandoned this helpless child. Kim and Carolyn tried to urge the family to look for their boy, but they only made a half-hearted effort. With darkness approaching, Kim and Carolyn felt the child could not survive the night alone in the jungle with poisonous snakes, venomous insects, and wildcats who could kill a small boy.

The child's mother had died in the flu epidemic, and the father now had another wife. Apparently, the child's crying and partially crippled legs were more than they could handle. Perhaps abandoning him to the "fate of the jungle" was their cultural solution.

Three days later, just before dark, Kim and Carolyn were shocked to see the little one crawling on his bony hands and knees back to where they were camped. How he had managed to survive must have been God's protection, giving him strength and a sense of direction. He had returned!

Carolyn's heart reached out to him, and since none of the families wanted him, the Fowlers became his temporary parents. They called him

Jeremias (Heh-rra-ME-us), meaning Jeremiah. They guessed he was about three years old.

When Kim and Carolyn returned to our Jungle Center, they brought Jeremias along. A check-up in our clinic indicated that malnutrition caused many of his problems. With medication, good food and loving care, he quickly gained strength and his legs and arms filled out. He toddled wobbly about, stealing all our hearts. Later Jeremias was able to live with a Christian Sharanahua family who had recently lost their child. He received love and care in a culture much like his own.

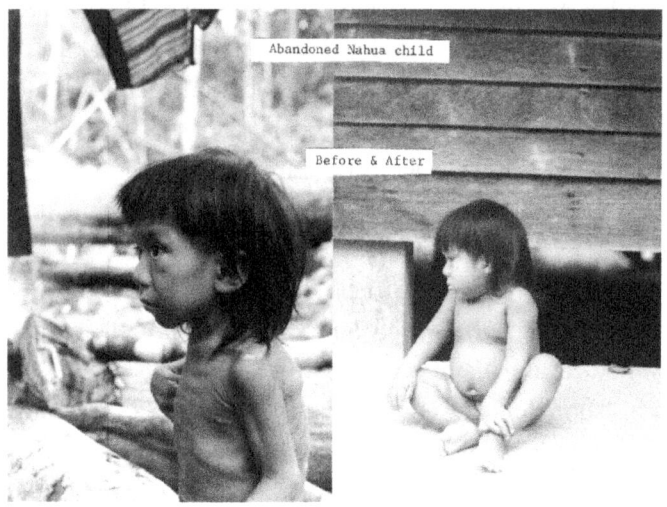

More Sickness

After an airstrip survey trip in mid-1985, Kim and Carolyn brought two Nahua men back to the Center for medical help. The men were skin and bones, suffering from pneumonia and other problems. When they were well enough to return home, the pilot heard a report that about 25 sick Nahuas had come to Sepahua. They were apparently begging and "borrowing" food from people there, with some doing some work in exchange. Kim and Carolyn had planned to get a little rest after a year of ongoing emergencies, but they quickly flew to Sepahua to assess the sickness. They found just a few actually sick. They stayed to help the Nahuas and used the time to learn more of their language, although in an uncomfortable living situation. We prayed for their strength, hoping they could later rest.

When that situation improved, Kim and Carolyn had much-needed dental work done in Lima. Delayed appointments gave them a forced vacation. Then they traveled out to be with the Nahuas for several months, and hopefully to encourage the building of an airstrip in that area.

Airstrip construction was started on a site chosen by the Nahuas and approved by government officials. The Fowlers contracted with a helpful Mestizo, to lead a work crew for clearing the land.

As months passed, events unexpectedly changed. A few at a time, the Nahuas drifted (literally) downriver to Sepahua on crudely fashioned canoes, not being "river people," and without oars or means to paddle back upstream, or money to pay a motorist to take them.

Many set up makeshift housing on the outskirts of town. Some lived and worked for town families who gave them food in exchange. But the Nahuas had not started their own *chacras* (gardens) either in Sepahua or in their old area. It seemed they were in a strange transition period, with about 70 eventually living in Sepahua. That frontier town was a mixture of Mestizos, Yaminahuas, a few Sharanahuas, Piros—and now Nahuas. What a comedown it seemed from their natural paradise.

Kim and Carolyn continued to make visits to Sepahua to treat sick ones and give a third round of vaccinations. For various reasons, they felt it would be difficult for them to work there long-term. We all hoped the Nahuas would return home.

Where is the Crew?

The Nahua airstrip construction came to a near halt over Christmas holidays when the hired workers went home. But they hadn't returned by February. So, Kim Fowler contracted with a new crew leader who promised to come with helpers, but they also were overdue arriving. Maybe *mañana*.

Meanwhile our administrators searched for any of our staff who could help. Most couldn't leave their responsibilities long enough to make a trip worthwhile. John wanted to go, but he was constantly busy keeping the planes flying.

Kim and Carolyn had been at the airstrip site working on language learning since before Christmas. They were thankful that about 25 Nahuas had settled there in an area called Putaiya (Poo-TIE-ah), having left Sepahua.

The Fowlers had minimal food sources, so our prayer group gathered and wrapped supplies for an air drop. I cooked up a hearty stew, and then froze it for the trip.

While Kim was out hunting with the Chief, he encountered ant territory and was bitten many times. When his legs and arms went numb from an allergic reaction, he was in a dangerous situation. He forced himself to keep walking until they arrived back! Antihistamine brought relief thankfully. Such is life in the jungle!

Finally, a crew came together to work on the airstrip. John was, after all, able to leave his hangar responsibilities for two weeks. Along with him were Bill Richter (our flight coordinator, with experience as a lumberman in Oregon's forests), Wayne Howlett (administrator of jungle linguists), and Carol Sagert (nurse who helped previously).

On Thursday, March 13, they landed in two float planes on an *estirón* (wide river bend). A canoe sent downstream by the Fowlers soon arrived, and they quickly loaded supplies and headed upstream. The *peque peque* engine (a nine-horsepower Briggs and Stratton) was noisy and slow as it pushed the large wooden canoe, but it was much better than paddling! John marveled at the flocks of colorful parrots flying overhead and in the trees of this isolated, beautiful tropical habitat.

After four hours they arrived at a *tambo* (temporary shelter) to camp overnight. A rainstorm that night delayed their start the next morning, but they arrived by nightfall at the airstrip site. Kim and Carolyn greeted them enthusiastically.

Saturday the rain came down steadily. Not to be deterred in their limited time, the four men worked in the rain digging trenches along the edges of the strip for drainage. At the end of that day, they dragged back to camp totally exhausted. John said later that they wouldn't have had strength to do that any other day except the first day when they were "fresh."

In constant rain, they continued to work for the first week. Their wet clothing didn't dry, and the muddy soil was difficult to move, but it wasn't all bad. The water puddles showed them where fill was needed, and the days were cooler.

Kim, Bill, John, and Wayne

With creative ingenuity they constructed a wheelbarrow with a chain saw and machete. This helped greatly. One day three Piro men (lumber workers) came to help them, and another day five more showed up.

As the weather improved, their impossible task seemed possible. They progressed, clearing 15 more meters. Bill Richter had an idea to expedite the task of cutting down tall trees for the approach on the other side of the river. Using his previous experience as a lumberman, they notched trees all along the area, then chopped down one at the end so that they all fell in domino fashion.

Carol cooks for crew.

Meanwhile Carol cooked meals for the crew over a wood fire. She carried water from the river to boil for drinking. John suggested making a system to catch rainwater to save steps. She washed dishes in a canoe down at the river, then scalded them with boiling water. She helped Carolyn with medical work and was encouraged by Chaika's prayers (number 66), displaying his continued walk with the Lord.

On Friday the 28th pilot Doug Deming landed Helio Courier 492 on the new airstrip—a momentous occasion! The Nahua chief asked if that big bird had a man in it, then was glad to officially greet the "bird man." He even put on three shirts for the occasion. Many curious Nahuas came to see the strange bird up close.

Doug flew the crew out of the new airstrip, while the Fowlers stayed longer to continue medical treatments. We thanked the Lord that the airstrip would make it so much easier to help the Nahuas.

Later Kim and Carolyn brought Chaika with them when they flew back to the Center to regain his health with better medical facilities. He became a good translation helper for them during the weeks he was there. Then they needed to rest and handle correspondence and personal business which they had neglected for months.

Costa Rica and Peru (1984-1987) 147

The next time the Fowlers flew to the Nahua village, it was just a short flight of 1½ hours until they landed happily on the new airstrip. What a difference from their previous journeys! In their absence the Chief's wife had died, as well as another friend. They were greatly concerned that Chaika had not been heard from for many weeks and was feared dead. He had become like a brother to them. He had apparently gone on a jungle excursion and just disappeared. *(Sadly, he was never heard from again.)*

In January of 1987, Sharanahua pastor Gustavo and a young man from his village, visited the Nahua community of Putaiya to share the gospel with them, using their related language. About half of the village showed interest. It was hard to know what the Nahuas understood since it was so new to them. They planted good seed and prayed it would take root and grow. Gustavo also taught them fishing techniques, since they were not fishermen.

Groups of lumbermen passed regularly through the area, and the Fowlers were concerned about possible lumber exploitation and game being depleted. Land titles were being processed, but they wondered who would enforce boundaries way out there.

In April Ivagene Shive, new linguist waiting to contact the Moronahua Indians, accompanied Carolyn Fowler to Putaiya. She had been studying other related languages in the meantime to get a head start. This trip was good preparation for Ivagene as she learned to shake poisonous spiders from her shoes before putting them on, and not to panic when the Nahuas killed 20 deadly snakes while cutting the airstrip grass with machetes.

While there, a Yaminahua couple, Juan and Sylvia, arrived for two weeks to help the Nahuas with various projects while sharing their faith in Christ. Meanwhile Kim Fowler stayed at the Jungle Center working with a Sharanahua language helper to sort comparative word lists in Sharanahua, Yaminahua, and Nahua.

Later Kim and Carolyn had an extensive stay in Putaiya (June to October) to practice and communicate well with the Nahuas. When some Nahuas suffered again with flu, Kim and Carolyn also caught it, and hoped their strength would return to normal. Also, they were concerned that there had been very few babies born since the epidemic in 1984, so they were excited when two of the ladies became pregnant, indicating a return to normalcy, as was the planting of large gardens and a good corn crop.

Perhaps soon Bible translation could proceed under more normal circumstances.

Translation Milestones

During this time, other translation projects were making good progress. It was a season of reaping from the labors of many years.

On Saturday, July 6, 1985, two blasts of the Center horn signaled us to tune to the Yarina Radio frequency for a special announcement. The Amarakaeri (Ah-mah-rra-KAY-rree) New Testament final edit pages had just come off the printer in our print shop office. Everyone was invited to come for an impromptu celebration service after lunch.

We gathered outside the print shop. The tall stack of computer print-out pages was displayed on a cement step, representing the page-by-page toil of 29 years for translator Bob Tripp. Through smiles and tears of joy, colleagues thanked God for the strength He had given the Tripps through physical illness. We prayed that the Amakaeris would hunger for His Word as they hungered after the gold they panned in their area.

(Bob and his wife Martha were practically newlyweds. Only eight years previously, *after* Martha had finished the Amuesha New Testament, these two single translators had become a married team to finish the Amarakaeri work.)

After the impromptu celebration, they traveled to Wycliffe's International Linguistic Center in Dallas where the data prepared in Peru would go through a photo type-setting process. We heard there was a waiting list of 38 New Testaments and a complete Bible being processed there! However, since their text was already paged with spacing for pictures, type styles selected, and well-checked content, we hoped they could move quickly through the bottleneck.

Adding to our excitement, the rough draft of the Culina New Testament was completed in the tribal location. Lambert and Doris Anderson also completed the revision of the downriver edition of the Ticuna New Testament with a good team of eight language helpers. Rol and Furne Rich finished proofreading the Arabela New Testament manuscript and were in the final stages of layout. After a computer transfer to tape, they too left for Dallas for the final typesetting process.

After 39 years serving the Candoshi-Shapra Indians, Beth Hinson returned to the U.S. for surgery which revealed two malignant brain tumors. In July she passed into the presence of the Lord with the assurance that the Candoshis had their own printed New Testament which they cherished for their continued use and growth. A job well done.

In August, Gene and Marie Scott finished the Sharanahua New Testament draft—the last verses of Revelation. In September seven highland Quechua Translation teams held a Matthew workshop in Huánuco to review rough copies of the Gospel of Matthew, which had been computer generated through the newly developed Computer Assisted Dialect Adaptation program (CADA).

In June of 1986, Paul and Esther Powlison finished their rough draft translation of the Yagua New Testament. Another exciting milestone. One after another, many translations neared completion. What a thrilling time!

Nazca Lines

When John was a teenager, he read about the famous Nazca lines in Peru dating to pre-Inca times. Design shaped markings on a desert plateau are only visible from the air. There are shapes of a hummingbird, condor, monkey, spider, dog (or fox), lizard, fish, flower, and plant. No one knows exactly why or how they were made. Some think they are a celestial calendar. Others think they are related to worship of mountain gods or of gods who brought water. In May 1985, John and I traveled to see them.

From a hotel in Ica, we booked a tourist flight over the Nazca lines. The small plane circled low to the ground, so we could have a close-up view of the designs. The plane's stall buzzer sounded again and again. I wondered about our safety. I began to feel dizzy, queasy, and hot. Unfortunately, I lost what little was in my stomach. John said, "Hon, look on the left. Wow!" I quickly looked and then returned to the bag, spreading an unpleasant aroma for the other plane passengers. "There's the hummingbird!" A quick look, and more for the bag. I did see some amazing sights, but not as many as John enjoyed.

Aviation Solutions

During this time, the delayed shipment saga continued. One float plane was grounded for lack of parts, so they borrowed parts from that plane to keep the others flying. Also urgently needed were computer supplies and a new computer system disc since the one in our Center system was full, with not enough room to process the Arabela New Testament. Center maintenance men waited for parts for the second generator, out of operation for eight months. Normally two generators ran dually to supply the electricity for our Center.

Finally in June 1985 the container shipment, stalled in Lima since January, was released! After worrisome delays coming over the road by truck, it arrived at our Yarinacocha Center in July. These goods were essential for our work, so we thanked God that at last they had arrived.

For some time, our aviation team had discussed the need for a turbo-charged Cessna 210 for mountain work. With more translation programs being initiated there, a plane that could fly in higher altitudes would greatly enhance the work. Mountain roads were often dangerous, with frequent landslides, coming from above, or dropping off the side of the roads. The Lord provided in an unusual way through our co-workers in the Bolivia Branch where we previously served. As they phased out their program, they donated their beautiful Cessna to our Peru Branch. Pilot Doug Deming ferried the plane from Bolivia to our Peru Jungle Center. The team was delighted to have this high-flying, speedy addition to our fleet. The inaugural flight brought the David Coombs family from Cajamarca, formerly inaccessible by our aircraft. The trip, which used to take two days driving over sometimes dangerous mountain roads, took only an hour and 40 minutes, a blessing to David who suffered with chronic back pain.

In May and June of 1986, the hangar team encountered problems with defective parts in the crank cases of three engines in our fleet. The same defects were reported from co-workers in Liberia. With three planes grounded, only the Cessna and one Helio Courier on floats were available to fly. Like the pony express, they changed pilots rather than horses. Because of the time lag to receive replacement parts, it looked like they couldn't meet translators' flight needs for many months.

As John discussed this problem via ham radio with the aviation team at Waxhaw, Jim Entz, who had helped previously, volunteered to come right away for two weeks and hand-carry supplies to rebuild engines. In the following weeks, one by one the planes were returned to service. We were glad to be part of a neat team working together to keep the planes flying.

Looking for the Moronahuas

It's difficult to fathom that there are still uncontacted people groups living in remote areas, isolated from the rest of the world. In Peru one such group, called the Moronahuas (Morr-oh-NOW-ahs), continued to elude contact with outsiders. Two young ladies were ready to translate God's Word for them, but a contact opportunity had not yet come.

In early January 1986, pilot Dave Wey was asked to divert on a return flight to fly over a seemingly uninhabited area of jungle to look for Moronahua houses. The area was covered with dense trees, occasionally intersected by small winding rivers, with no good landmarks to navigate by. The flight covering 275 miles crossed only one airstrip, Pardo Breu, near the midway point.

During the first half of the flight, Dave located a single jungle hut, possibly Moronahua, and dropped prepared gifts of machete and yuca. Heading home, as he passed over Pardo Breu, the engine began to run rough and vibrate. He decided to land, and the five Cashinahua passengers were happy to be safely on the ground. Dave discovered that an exhaust valve seat had worked loose. This was causing damage to the cylinder and piston that would have led to complete engine failure in another 15 minutes!

It seemed that Satan reacted to thwart the attempt to contact that group to give them God's Word. But God was faithful. The problem occurred over the only suitable landing site along the entire flight route! We felt the prayers of those back home for flight safety. John was flown out to replace the cylinder and piston. Upon his return to our Center, he replaced the well-used engine with another that he had just overhauled.

After that, additional jungle huts were sighted in an extremely remote area, problematic to reach. We eagerly awaited new equipment, then held in customs, an OMEGA navigation system that could pinpoint their location. That equipment had originally been ordered some time ago for use in our new Cessna to fly in dangerous mountain areas. A special technician had come from the States to install the system back in October, but when it wouldn't function, it was returned to the factory for repairs. We really hoped to have it back soon to greatly enhance flight safety.

The Sunday Sink

Each week we met with co-workers in our open-air "auditorium" for Sunday services in English. We were accustomed to distractions such as barking dogs or flying bats. But one Sunday, when calls on the auditorium phone required John and then other aviation personnel to leave quietly but quickly, even the guest speaker wondered what was happening.

The call was from a guard who told John that the float plane was sinking in the lake! As John ran to the hangar, the muddy roads were slick from recent rain. Looking over the bank, he could see the plane's tail submerged and its fuselage half flooded. The nose pointed upward at a steep angle, held by ropes tied to the floating dock.

Additional men, called from the auditorium to help, quickly unloaded the cargo, which had been preloaded Saturday for an early Monday flight.

The plane continued to sink. Some quickly defueled its tanks while others placed large inner tubes under the tail and floats. When these were inflated, the Helio slowly began rising. Another person hand-pumped water from the flooded float compartments. John positioned the hangar tractor to pull the plane onto the wheel dolly and out of the lake. Everyone was greatly relieved when the dripping plane was out of danger.

Costa Rica and Peru (1984-1987)

Apparently, as the heavily loaded plane sat low in the water, rain and waves had splashed over the floats and seeped under the access panels. Loss of sufficient buoyancy had caused the plane to begin sinking. Aside from some wet cargo, there was no real damage. Thankfully cassette players and tapes with recorded messages of translated Yagua Scriptures had not gotten wet.

Our Sunday guest speaker, graciously unoffended by the diminishing congregation, was Elaine Townsend, wife of Wycliffe's founder, Cameron Townsend. When she discovered the reason for the confusion, she led us in prayer that the plane would be rescued. Then she concluded her report of Wycliffe work around the world. We were thankful that God granted her request. Within two days the plane and its contents were dried out and ready to go again.

Special Guest Helper

We were pleased that John's sister, Karen, was now working in a new job—at the Wycliffe Regional Office in Willow Street, PA. Knowing the area well, she brought continuity to the office while many of the Wycliffe staff came and went during furloughs and transition times.

Karen was glad when one of her sons, Michael, was able to visit us in Peru during his summer vacation in 1986. Mike helped with various jobs in the hangar like welding, as well as painting interior and exterior hangar walls.

He also helped to build *casitas* (small houses) for students who came to the teacher-training sessions.

One week when there was extra room on a flight, he was able to go along on the trip. Not one to sit still, he joined the Center kids in their activities. One holiday he went with friends for an all-day canoe adventure around a river circuit that connected with the lake when the water was high.

Mike borrowed my Honda 50 to get around. One day he drove over a good-sized snake crawling in our yard. We were relieved when the neighbor boys confirmed that it was a "beautiful" rainbow boa, and harmless. Then he held it like a favorite pet. John showed him how to get rid of unwanted tarantulas: pour gasoline on them and drop a lit match. A guy thing! What could I say? We told his mom that her son liked to swim with the pirañas in the lake when someone went with him.

Progress and Challenges

Celebration: Special events marking the 40th anniversary of SIL work in Peru had three purposes: to honor the pioneers who began the work in 1946, to express gratitude to the people of Peru for their hospitality and cooperation, and to acknowledge God's leading and provision.

In April a reception was held at our Lima Group House. The same week a ceremony inaugurated a display of our work at the National Library in Lima. The Minister of Education gave a gracious address and honored our group by presenting linguist Dr. Olive Shell with the Order of *Palmas Magisteriales*, a medal of honor, for her 40 years of service to the tribespeople.

In May many local Peruvian friends attended a reception at our Jungle Center. After a program in our auditorium, we served a buffet supper in our Center Dining Room where John sliced and served meat like a master chef.

Inflation: Beginning January 1, 1986, because of high inflation, Peruvian *soles* were officially replaced by *Intis*. *Sol* is the Spanish word for sun, while the new currency was named after the Inca sun god, *Inti*. One *Inti* equaled 1,000 *soles*. That change eliminated the need to bring a wheelbarrow of cash to pay for a high-priced item.

Old bills and coins were accepted for several years since we only saw a few *inti* bills in our jungle area. Our local checks and transfers were in *Intis* or in U.S. dollars. It could be very confusing. At that time 17,300 *intis* equaled one U.S. dollar.

(By 1990, the inti had also suffered high inflation. And soon the "new sol" replaced the inti at an exchange rate of a million to one.)

As well as financial instability, there were occasional incidents of unrest. An explosive device was thrown into the yard at our Group House in Lima, resulting in broken windows, but no-one was hurt. Other U.S. connected organizations had similar incidents. It seemed that a discontented group wanted publicity, so we were not greatly concerned. We heard that the U.S. news had reported the incidents, perhaps exaggerating the events.

On another occasion when we were in Lima, there were two blackouts when terrorists bombed electrical towers. One evening while we drove back to the Group House, the traffic light ahead of us went out, causing an immediate traffic jam. We turned right using side roads to avoid traffic and were thankful to arrive safely, except that the remote wouldn't open the compound's electric gate for us to drive in. Resourcefully, John left the vehicle at our other group house. After 24 hours when the electricity returned, we put away the candles and flushed the toilets again. Compounding the danger, the police and other workers went on strike. We prayed for wisdom for the country's leaders.

Local Disaster: We often watched fishermen on Lake Yarinacocha skillfully throw out their nets and pull in a catch of fish. *Peque peques* motored up and down the lake hauling fish and produce to the docks at Pucallpa. At busy and crowded market stalls, you could purchase fresh fish and other items.

One day, the land gave way on the bank with market stalls and people crashing on top of boats in the muddy water. Word spread that 150 people were killed. When rumors settled down, the count was more like six, but hard to be certain since young orphan boys often begged food around the market. Sadly, a lot of fishing boats were destroyed, affecting the livelihood of many.

Strange Disease: Some of our co-workers had symptoms of extreme tiredness and weakness. We wondered if it was some type of rare tropical disease. Blood specimens tested negative at the Communicable Disease Control Center in Atlanta. We knew what it wasn't, but not what it was! Several suffered for over a year, with little help from medications.

(Later it was finally diagnosed as chronic fatigue syndrome. Some were hospitalized, and some never fully recovered, limiting their work ability. Others thankfully recovered slowly. We wondered why God would allow such dedicated servants to suffer.)

Empty Boxes: Opening our mailbox No. 238 in our Center Post Office was a highlight for us. We hoped that a mail strike in June would be quickly settled. But days turned into weeks of empty boxes.

The strike hurt all services in Peru as well as communication with the outside world. We felt cut off from friends and family. After a month we began to worry. We prepared emergency correspondence and some personal letters with U.S. return addresses and U.S. stamps to be carried by travelers to mail in the U.S. Occasionally a few tantalizing pieces squeezed through. After 51 days, mail service began to resume. First came letters posted in early August, then June, and after that, July. Later packages and tapes came through.

What news did we miss? A friend's serious illness, birthday greetings, a forged check, delay in a check sent to us, news that my mother was on a trip. One man was surprised to learn that his father was engaged to be married! We didn't know if all the delayed mail had arrived, but we enjoyed catching up.

We hoped the political situation would settle down after Peru's new President, Alan Garcia, was installed. This was the first peaceful transfer in 40 years from one constitutionally elected government to another.

Broken bone: When I celebrated my 45th birthday, I assured myself that I felt like 25. At a Center Picnic celebrating Peru's Independence Day on July 28, we played various games. As I ran in a relay, I fell and had such pain in my right shoulder that I knew something was wrong. Our nurse-practitioner said my shoulder was not dislocated, but we couldn't get an x-ray until the 30th because of the holidays. The x-ray did show a break in the collar bone close to the joint. They wrapped me in a sling-type bandage, then later a figure-8 harness around both shoulders. The harness was hot and sweaty.

After six weeks, when we took off the harness, I still had pain and stiffness. I continued babying the right arm. "Wrong thing to do," said a nurse friend. "Your joint has frozen from immobility." So, I began therapy-type exercises slowly gaining more "reach" as time passed. I felt more like 65 than 45! I should mention that our team did win that relay race, but I think I lost.

During our next trip to Lima, I saw a doctor who thought there wasn't a great problem. He said, "First we fix the bone, then we get the arm moving again." He suggested a pulley exercise. John set up a system attached to the top of a door frame, so when I pulled down and up with the left hand, the right arm went up and down. *(With continued exercise it took almost a year to get back to normal.)*

Ham Radio: For many years John had been interested in getting a ham radio license. That would enable us to talk more often with family and with friends, as well as allow John to serve others. A friend offered his radio equipment at half price. Another one loaned him study manuals and tapes to learn Morse code. It seemed an opportune time to do it.

We reconfigured an upstairs space in our house for the equipment. John could listen in but wasn't permitted to talk until he had his license. He hung an antenna wire over tall trees in our yard, with a brick tied onto each end to anchor the wires. When the wind blew the tree branches, the bricks floated up and down—a peculiar sight to people who saw them. It looked as if the tree grew bricks. He studied the manual and Morse Code in spare moments.

He took and passed the novice radio exam. He then applied for his U.S. license, followed by applying to receive his Peruvian equivalent license to get on the air on the 12-meter band. To upgrade his Peruvian superior license, he needed to get 100 QSL cards. This was a post card confirming a two-way radio communication between two amateur radio stations. Later,

in Lima, he took a written examination in Spanish to earn the Superior license allowing him to use the better radio bands.

In those days ham radio operators were often very helpful in transmitting information in emergency situations. This also gave us the ability to contact a ham operator near our family in PA who could connect us via a collect phone call to them.

Special Duty: In November at our Annual Conference, John was elected as an alternate to our Peru Branch Executive Committee, a special privilege and responsibility. The seven-member committee met four sessions per year, and other times as needed. It was the policy-determining body for our work in Peru. John thoroughly enjoyed the first regular session in February. He spoke highly of the committee members who really sought the Lord's wisdom for making decisions.

Those Little Critters: Amoebic dysentery sounds ominous to North American minds, but in Peru it was a common ailment. Treatment was readily available (usually Flagyl), but often with side effects worse than the nasty symptoms: diarrhea, nausea, headaches, aches and pains, and extreme tiredness. If ignored it could cause serious damage. Most of us "self-treated" as we were all too familiar with the symptoms, probably not the wisest way to handle the problem.

Amoeba, a one-celled animal, can be seen only under a microscope. It lives in humans and animals in a dormant stage when contacted. As it enters the intestinal tract, it becomes active, grows, reproduces itself, and causes an internal abscess. Fresh vegetables and fruits grown in soil with human fertilizer can cause infection. Amoeba can be contacted through uncooked foods, dishes not washed properly, or through food-handlers lacking good sanitation.

John and I had amoeba this term more often than all our other terms combined. Our clinic had checked possible sources of contamination, but it seemed that it was due to an increased population with more opportunities to spread it. It may even have floated in the dust during the dry season. Someone suggested this kitchen motto: *"It's not the food in your life, but the life in your food that counts." -M.I. Morgan.*

Artist Needed: In 1986 our Print Shop published a total of 22,497 books under 40 titles. Several long-worked-on projects were finally printed, including Matthew in Huamalies Quechua (the first Scripture publication for that group), Mark in Cajamarca Quechua (the second Scripture for them), a Piro Dictionary, and a complete 1946-1986 Peru Branch Bibliography for our 40th anniversary year. Also of interest were Huitoto and Achuar translations of the Peruvian Constitution. Complete New Testaments were prepared in our office on the computer and sent elsewhere for printing.

In past years we had a full-time Peruvian artist on staff. When he left, I took on responsibilities for some of the artwork: adapting drawings to illustrate stories in reading books, drawing lines and boxes on word exercises, making examples for writing lessons in manuscript and cursive, also layout and stripping of masking sheets. While I loved art, and had some natural ability, I hadn't had the opportunity for professional training. But I "used what was in my hand" to help keep the books progressing through their various stages.

More Precious than Gold

Many prayed for the Amarakaeri New Testament through its final edit and printing. Bob and Martha Tripp approached the New Testament dedication celebration in September with mixed emotions. Few Amarakaeris showed interest in spiritual truth and the translated Scriptures. Their goals were to become rich by panning the gold in their rivers, or at least to acquire shotguns, clothes, cooking pots, liquor, and portable radios.

In the days prior to the celebration, Amarakaeris began stopping by the Tripps' home in the village a couple at a time saying they wanted to accept Christ as Savior. One day Bob left breakfast uneaten to go pray with a man. And as Bob visited around the village, others also said they wanted to commit their lives to Christ.

John was thankful that the two float planes were able to make their scheduled flights for the celebration. At the dedication ceremony, Abram (chief translation helper) invited those who wanted to know and follow the Lord to come forward. There were 29 who responded, mostly young people who had attended Martha's reading classes during past years, as well as some older people.

It was a thrilling answer to prayer—44 new believers! Bible classes were started the day after the dedication. Meeting each day, they learned where to find passages to meet various needs.

Their theme song for the dedication was: *"Like we desire so much the gold, Let us even more desire God's Word."* May this be true for all of us.

What If We Never Came?

Anticipating the Ticuna New Testament dedication on Easter weekend, over three tons of Ticuna New Testaments were shipped by river launch to the Ticuna villages in Peru's northeast corner. Ticunas also lived in the adjacent countries of Colombia and Brazil. An adapted edition had been printed for those in Brazil. As elaborate plans were formed for the big event, translator Lambert Anderson wondered, *Will anyone come? Will people buy the Scriptures?*

(Lambert and Doris Anderson had begun work 34 years earlier with the Ticunas, who at that time were known for filing their teeth to points. Doris, gifted with music ability, had recognized that Ticuna was a five-tone language, involving complications to learn and write it. During some of those years, Lambert was called upon to serve as Peru Branch Director.)

Their prayer partners, Bill and Delores Richmond, went out to Cushillococha early to open up Anderson's village house, set up water barrels, fix steps, turn the generator on, connect the stove, etc. Traveling out on a barge, they slept on top of a load of Bibles one night.

Local Ticuna believers planned meals and housing for visitors. Aviation staff flew out 22 people from the Jungle Center, including Peruvian employees and U.S. visitors. They needed five plane loads involving about 50 hours of flying for two pilots.

And they came! From up and down the rivers, group after group arrived in canoes and river launches from 15 different villages up to 250 miles away. Many arrived singing hymns and choruses. Some Ticunas expressed to Lambert, "We heard you existed, so we have come to see you with our own eyes." One man representing 2,000 in his Brazilian village, invited Lambert to come minister to them. There were nightly meetings with 500 attending in the 1,500-square-foot church building. A floor joist broke under the extra weight!

Almost 1,000 gathered Sunday morning in a specially constructed pavilion for the main four-hour-long dedication service. They sang three national anthems, and each delegation presented a song. The message was in Ticuna. Lambert described the early days of their work. Leonardo, the main translation helper, testified to how he came to the Lord and how God took care of him and his family financially and with good health all the time they worked on the translation.

Then together, a Brazilian, a Colombian, Leonardo of Peru, and Lambert of the U.S., unveiled the cloth with the Scriptures under it. Leonardo named those who had helped on the translation, and in turn each one prayed. As Lambert officially presented a copy of the New Testament to Leonardo, 34 years flashed through his mind. Leonardo couldn't respond, but simply bowed his head and prayed.

During one part of the service, Doris Anderson looked out over the crowd and said to Lambert, "What if we never came?"

People crowded into the book sale room to buy New Testaments. The price equaled one day's wages, most of the cost being funded by the World Home Bible League. Some left with armloads. On Sunday, Monday, and Tuesday 1,000 copies were taken to various locations. Someone commented, "There are many places where the Andersons can't visit, but the Scriptures will. Lambert and Doris come and go, but the New Testament stays."

High River, Low River

Rol and Furne Rich served over 30 years with the Arabela people. Some wondered if this small group was worth their efforts. But through the years the Riches were faithful to their commitment. Each time they were flown the 450 miles to Buena Vista in northern Peru, they prayed that the

river would be high enough to land the float plane. During all those years God answered their prayers.

The Buena Vista church was a blend of three languages—Arabela, Quechua, and Spanish—with parts of their meetings in each language. Some understood all three; some understood only one of the three. For those who only understood Arabela, all the believers rejoiced on March 15 when the Arabela New Testament was dedicated to God.

Local believers had just finished constructing a new church building which they dedicated the previous evening. Crepe paper streamers hung from the ceiling as the building filled with eager, thankful people celebrating God's precious Word in their language. They recalled together with Rol and Furne the long years of work to complete the translation. Special songs in Arabela were part of the program.

The service was followed by a monkey meat feast with yuca and bananas. In a meaningful baptism service at the river, the son of a local witchdoctor joined others to demonstrate his faith in Christ.

We were disappointed that the Arabela New Testaments had not arrived in time for the dedication. But that did not deter the joy of celebration with one sole advanced copy.

Several weeks later the New Testaments arrived and were distributed. Previously the Arabelas carried a virtual library with them to their church services—various individual Bible books. Now, in one volume, they were proud to carry and use their very own Arabela New Testament!

A Vital Service

With no other reasonable way for our tribal workers to get out to the villages, our aviation team was a vital part of enabling translation and literacy work to happen. In addition to our top-notch pilots, John's maintenance team in 1987 included two other U.S. and two Peruvian aircraft mechanics. The Evangel was soon to be sold, having served us well for ten years, but no longer economically viable for us, leaving four Helios and one Cessna.

The Aviation team had been concerned about the restricted weight limits for carrying cargo in our Helio Couriers. They researched the possibilities of finding a Helio that could carry a heavier load. They learned that a South Carolina corporation had one for sale at a reasonable price. Our Executive Committee authorized Peru Branch funds to purchase it.

We were thankful to acquire that plane since Helio Couriers were no longer being produced. It was flown to JAARS headquarters to undergo a major inspection and be prepared for a ferry flight to Peru. During inspection, much was found that needed special attention. It would take considerably longer than planned to get that plane into service. Even though the Waxhaw-JAARS staff was very short of personnel at that time, they gave priority to working on our Peru Helio. If customs paperwork and details could be in order by September 12, they planned to dedicate it at a Waxhaw-JAARS Barbeque when hundreds of JAARS friends would attend. If our personal plans worked out, we also hoped to be there for that event.

Finishing Before Furlough

As our furlough approached, current goals included our present busy schedule and what we hoped to complete before our September departure.

John and the team were doing major work on Helio 951. They stripped it down to the "bones" to re-shift some weight forward, install a cargo door, redo the engine mount, replace the entire tail cone, and repaint it.

John also was serving as Acting Director of Aviation until mid-August; was checking on customs paperwork to import the Helio replacement; overseeing the packing and shipping of a container from Peru to the U.S. with aircraft parts for overhaul, departmental and some personal items; participating in Executive Committee meetings; and then turning over the Chief-of-Aviation-Maintenance responsibilities to Mark Ott.

"We pray for you every day," wrote some friends in a letter to us. Reading that, we were surprised, grateful, humbled, awed, and greatly encouraged! We remembered others who had promised regular prayers—some daily, some weekly, and some as they learned of special situations. Reflecting on this very intense term, we realized that God had been with us personally, and with our colleagues, through many challenges and victories. We had worked together as a team to bring God's Word to diverse people groups in Peru. Most were forgotten by the world, but important to God. Our frustrations paled when we witnessed results from our efforts.

We reached our goals and left on September 7, 1987. We looked forward to furlough time to reconnect with our home team, to be refreshed, and to enjoy the benefits of U.S. living for a short while.

Chapter 8
Peru (1988-1992)
Progress Through Difficulties

Ferry Flight

What great timing! John and I arrived at the JAARS Center in time for the Annual JAARS Barbeque Day and dedication of the Helio Courier for Peru! Our Peru Branch Director, Lambert Anderson, was a special speaker! Together we joyfully celebrated the JAARS team's hard work preparing the plane for the long flight to Peru. We connected with friends and visitors while enjoying the chicken barbeque, parachutists, and stunt flying. There was still customs paperwork to be done before the plane could be on its way.

Then we headed to Lebanon, PA. Through the kindness of my sister and her husband Mike, their house was now our "furlough home." They took us in as their family, as they had done with Mom. It felt good to be back with family.

We had learned upon our arrival in the States that John's younger sister, Joette, was to be married in New York the coming weekend, so we didn't want to miss that opportunity. We were glad to see Joette happily married. She had met Jerry at the Bible School she attended, and he was now in the Army. He was headed to Germany, and Joette would join him there soon. (Her first husband had died of congestive heart failure.)

During October and November, we drove 6,000 miles on various trips to reconnect with partners to show our appreciation for their support, prayers, and friendship. After enjoying the holidays with family, we headed to the JAARS Center in North Carolina for a five-month stay.

A highlight of our time there was when two Peruvian aircraft inspectors came to give their approval, according to Peruvian law, for the refurbished Helio Courier to be ferried there. With completed paperwork, a pilot and copilot were selected to make this exciting and challenging flight. We gathered early Sunday morning, January 31, to send them off to Peru.

A ferry flight in a "small" plane across the ocean was a major undertaking. Later we heard details of the long, and potentially dangerous trip:

Flying High: The two men sat snugly in the small cabin of the single engine Helio as it droned along about 120 miles per hour in the bright sunshine above the clouds. Having climbed out of bed at 2:00 a.m. that morning it was to be a long day. Looking down through breaks in the fluff, they caught glimpses of the ocean, white with winds and waves. They watched a cargo ship far below as it bounced in the blustery waters. In one instant it seemed partially submerged, and in another the bow protruded up into the air as if gathering breath for the next onslaught.

The pilot and co-pilot mechanic were glad to be "above the weather" where they felt safe and secure. Not many people, however, would have felt so secure in their situation—a single engine, six place plane, flying from Ft. Lauderdale over Cuba to Kingston, Jamaica.

At the Kingston airport a man asked why they were flying this possibly dangerous mission. "There's no way we could do it in our own strength," said pilot Fred McKennon, and explained that he and Jim Andrew were ferrying the plane to Peru where it would serve translators who were bringing God's Word to remote people in their own languages.

The man seemed pleased. "Why we're Christians too," he rejoiced and then told of God's blessing in his church there.

Fred and Jim wondered what deviations might occur in their itinerary. Approaching Havana Control 30 minutes ahead of schedule they waited for a radio response. They'd have to turn the plane around if they didn't get their verbal clearance. Just as they approached Cuban airspace, the "cleared as filed" response came.

There were other challenges on the trip: winds in Cartegena, Colombia; two hours without radio contact; an instrument takeoff out of Bogota; and following beacons through mountain passes until they saw the typical fluffy clouds over the jungle. After three more hours of paperwork in Iquitos, Peru, they headed for the Jungle Center at Yarinacocha. At 4:30 p.m. on February 4, right on schedule, they descended toward the grass strip. Looking down they saw a large crowd of people gathered to greet them. For the next days, jungle rains also welcomed them, making any more flying virtually impossible.

Later, at a JAARS Center meeting, the pilots reported on their trip. Fred said, "The Lord just put that flight together." Jim told of how at one stop he met a man he had known from previous DC-3 flights to Ecuador, who sped up the oft-delayed refueling process. Our meeting leader asked the audience, peppered with pilots, how many of them had experienced such a trip that went so closely to schedule. Not a hand was raised. "I feel they had such a good trip because so many were praying," he said.

As I thought about their flight high over the ocean, it reminded me that, with Christ as Lord of our lives, we can live above the circumstances that ruffle the waters. We can trust in God's sovereign power. In Ephesians 4:6-8 we're told that through prayer we can have the peace of God which transcends all understanding and removes anxiety. That sounds like flying above the weather! Flying high!

Back Again to Peru

We left PA on July 13, 1978, taking with us our nephew John for a six-week visit. We called him "John D" to distinguish from my husband John, after whom he was named. He was about to experience some travel challenges.

We drove first to overnight with Uncle Ralph and Aunt Martha in Virginia. (Little did we know that this would be the last time we would see Aunt Martha on this earth.) From there we flew to Miami, where John renewed his Inspectors Authorization at the FAA office, and we toured a little with John D. On to Lima, we went through customs with no problems.

On the 21st (my birthday) we went to the airport to fly out to the jungle. We waited and waited for the flight. John D was majorly bored with the long delay. He passed the time playing Digger on my new laptop computer. Finally, we learned that there was a pilot strike and that the plane was not going anywhere. Not the happiest way to spend my birthday! The next day, after switching airlines, we finally flew to Pucallpa.

Back at the Yarinacocha Jungle Center, we all got settled in our house. John and I went back to our jobs and John D helped in the hangar with various activities including painting and cargo pickup. He enjoyed joking with the guys in the hangar, and swimming in the lake. We were happy for him to see how the people on our Jungle Center served in various technical capacities to enable the common goal of Bible translation. One highlight of his time was meeting the ex-president of Peru who came for a JAARS flight to a jungle community. Now I was not the only one in our family to have shaken his hand. But I still had the distinction of having done it barefooted. John D's six-week stay passed all too quickly and he headed home.

This field term was filled with political upheaval and many challenges to keep the work moving forward. Our whole team in Peru needed God's strength to keep on despite the obstacles. Even so, God gave us special blessings along the way.

In a July 28 Independence Day speech, the new President of Peru expressed his concern over continued terrorism in the country and the 15,000 lives lost because of it. He wanted to crack down on narcotics traffickers. Yearly inflation to that date was calculated at 231% with a 34.1% increase in July alone. The people suffered with high price increases to counteract the Inti's devaluation. The minimum wage, equal to $1.00 per day, kept many in poverty.

A new contract was needed for our continued work in Peru. An 11-member governmental commission investigated our work. They required regular comprehensive reporting. We prayed that our administrators would respond wisely to their inquiries and that the commission would evaluate data fairly, regardless of their personal philosophies.

John focused on rebuilding a Cessna plane for our local government entity, which was important, as the head man was a good friend and was influential in our contract renewal process.

Turtle Egg Time

July and August were favorite months among turtle egg lovers throughout the jungles of Peru, when those delicacies could be dug from sandy beaches along rivers.

There was a good possibility that the illusive Moronahua Indians would look for turtle eggs. So, Mary Ann Lord and Ivagene Shive made plans to make camp in a remote area along the Piqueyacu (PEE-kay-YAH-koo) River in hopes that contact could be made with them.

Kim Fowler and Tom Salisbury preceded the girls into the area, chose a likely spot, and constructed a simple thatched-roof house, while keeping a keen eye open for Moronahuas during their couple weeks there.

Mary Ann and Ivagene were first flown to the Yaminahua village of Paititi. There they hired two Yaminahua boatmen/guides to take them down the Piqueyacu River. One boatman's wife and baby came along. The river was low with many fallen trees in the way so there were stretches where the large dugout canoe had to be pulled.

Insects swarmed around them whenever they stopped. Alligators they spotted along the way seemed afraid of people. On the second day out, as the canoe squeezed through two tall tree stumps, the carburetor broke from the boat motor. They waited a day and a half until a new carburetor and tools to install it could be dropped via our aviation "delivery service."

On two nights they stopped at Campa Indian settlements. The girls played a tape for them of gospel songs in a closely related Campa dialect. One morning Mary Ann read to a group of attentive Campa listeners in their own language about the death and resurrection of Jesus. It was probably the first time they had ever heard the gospel.

After five days, they reached the destination and set up camp. The boatmen built a couple small cook houses which were later occupied by their visiting relatives. And did these folks like turtle eggs? To the girls' dismay, the Yaminahuas collected the precious eggs they had been hoping would draw the Moronahuas down to their camp.

Then five Campa men came with their wives and children to give a hand clearing fallen trees from the river to enable a float plane to land when the water level would be higher. They listened to the gospel song tape many times and asked to hear it again. The Yaminahuas sang gospel songs and studied some translated Scripture in their language. Six weeks passed as they waited excitedly, expectantly. On one outing the men shot a large jaguar, but it got away.

It seemed that for this trip, Mary Ann's and Ivagene's ministry was to people other than the Moronahuas, just as the turtle eggs were enjoyed by others. Perhaps the next year it would be the Moronahuas' turn. The Lord knew, and we sought His timing for a future contact. He could do His work with or without turtle eggs.

I later asked Mary Ann how the Indians prepared turtle eggs for eating. She said they mostly boiled them in water, adding salt. Sometimes they would beat the eggs to make a soufflé effect. About the size of golf balls and with leathery shells and large yolks, they were found about 25 per nest. I would later have an opportunity to taste them for myself.

Words of Gold

In the Fall, we received news from home that my Aunt Martha had an inoperable growing tumor in her pancreas which blocked her intestines. It appeared that, short of a miracle, she would not live long. She had been a very special person in my life. At that time, I wrote a story to express my appreciation to her. I'll include part of that story here, written in 1988:

As I helped my Aunt Martha carry breakfast dishes to their cozy blue kitchen during a visit some years ago, I wished John and I could stay longer, but our schedule pushed us onward.

I remembered the times I had lived there with them in their lovely home. Memories of those days played upon rusty chords of my mind. Attractively served meals with anticipated desserts had been a delight then and became my wifely goal motivating my limited cooking abilities. Classical music from their stereo to soothe an evening of homey activities had broadened my listening tastes. Uncle Ralph reading Scripture for evening devotions and the unique loving relationship of my aunt and uncle had prompted special care in choosing my own mate. I had learned some realities of life there as I paid my monthly room and board, as Uncle Ralph instructed me in fastening chains to my car tires one snowy morning, and as I was gently reminded that I should clean hair from the sink after shampooing there.

As we needed to be on our way, I knew it was time to say goodbye. But I wanted to say some words of thanks that probably had not been said previously. I mumbled some quick words inadequately. "You know, I learned a lot during that time I lived with you." My words fell far short of what I wanted to express. "You really helped me to grow in a lot of areas."

"Oh, you had it in you all the time," Aunt Martha sweetly said to me. And suitcases were replaced in the car. "It was so good to see you again."

And so it was that during that quick overnight visit on a furlough trip in the U.S. that the special words dropped into my life—just part of a conversation that gave sustenance to me that I little realized at the time.

In 1988, while doing a Bible lesson on the impact of words, I remembered Aunt Martha's words to me: "You had it in you all the time." Those words unconsciously sustained me: *You're a worthy person. You've got good stuff in you.*

During college days, when my job schedule limited my study time as I crammed for exams, deep within me came the sustaining thought: *You have it in you. You can do this.* Over the years, when I felt inadequate to the task, from somewhere came the confidence that I could do a good job. As John and I faced new challenges in our first foreign mission experience in Bolivia, I felt that with God's help I could do what needed to be done.

Even now, those feelings of doubt sometimes creep into my mind. *Elsie, what are you doing here? This is too much for you.* But I keep going, buoyed up by friends' prayers, by God's strength, and by that inner feeling: *You have it in you; you can handle it.*

My Aunt Martha now suffers from pancreatic cancer. I realize that my special encourager won't always be here. But when she arrives in heaven, I think she'll have a grandstand view of her family on earth. She'll be cheering us on in new ways that we aren't able now to

comprehend. In some very quiet moment, I expect to hear a distant voice saying to me, "You had it in you all the time."

(Aunt Martha passed away in 1989 and has been greatly missed. After that time, Uncle Ralph continued to be a special encourager to John and me for many more years. We've been blessed and thank God for them.)

Problems and Progress

As the Director of Aviation was in the States for a month, John directed busy weeks of flying and maintenance. Mechanic Joel Witt had to leave suddenly for the States when his 14-month-old twin daughter required serious surgery. The hangar secretary (of many years) also had to leave quickly for surgery and chemotherapy. John was thankful that new pilot, Pete Lawry, had arrived in Peru with his family and would soon join the team after orientation and language assimilation in Lima. We continued to thank the Lord for flight safety. John's constant desire was that no flights for translators be delayed because of maintenance.

Our prayer partners, the Fowlers, took a short furlough in the States, then extended their time due to a split in their home church and loss of financial support. Meanwhile the two ladies, while waiting for contact to work with the Moronahuas, made two trips out to the Nahuas and were thankful to find them basically healthy. They were especially glad to see the old chief doing well as he had sugar diabetes. He had apparently been faithfully taking medicine on his own—although he was ahead of schedule on his tablets. It was hard to tell if he had taken more than specified, or perhaps had shared some with others. (A chief shares!)

That reminded me of another Nahua who had learned to take medicine. The previous year when Kim and Carolyn were treating Isadahua (Ee-sah-DOW-ah) at Putaiya, it became apparent that he needed more special attention, so they brought him to our Center. He was so weak that Kim had to carry him into the clinic from the car for each appointment. He was anemic and jaundiced, with an amoebic abscess on his liver. With medicine for amoeba and a blood transfusion he began to feel better but complained of hip pain. A bad infection in his hip joint had developed into osteomyelitis. That usually required surgery, but by then Isadahua was feeling a lot better and anxious to go home. A hospital stay in Lima would have been a traumatic cultural shock to him. Kim and Carolyn agonized over his need, trying to also balance the many needs of the other Nahuas.

They decided to return him to Putaiya with antibiotics and pray for a miracle. Over and over, they explained to him how to take his medicine. "Take one pill in the morning when the sun comes up. Take another one when the sun is high in the sky, and one when the sun goes down." He seemed to understand.

Six weeks later when the Fowlers returned to Putaiya they found him feeling well, with lots more energy. His draining hip wound was almost completely healed over. He even helped cut the airstrip. It was a miracle—but not the only one. During that time Isadahua had asked God to be his Owner! He explained to the Fowlers: "You know, I pray to Father God every day. I pray in the morning when the sun comes up. I pray at noon when the sun is high in the sky, and I pray at night when the sun goes down—just like I took my medicine. And I pray as I walk along too."

Church attendance had grown in Anatico, a Pastaza Quechua community previously disinterested in the gospel. It began the previous summer when Abel (a-BELL) came to Yarinacocha to take a technical course which didn't pan out. Charlotte Zahn, Quechua linguist, offered to hire him as a language helper to work with her at our Center. During that time, he came to know the Lord, was discipled by one of our pilots, and attended a local Spanish-speaking church. Then two elders from that church traveled to Anatico with Abel to do evangelistic work. God blessed their efforts, and 18 made decisions to follow the Lord, while 18 others rededicated their lives to Him. Abel continued there as a church leader.

During the past year people in the Yaminahua community of Paititi gathered each afternoon at 4:00 to hear the Word of God and to pray and sing praises. This group was started by leader Juan, who, while helping linguist Lucy Eakin translate Scriptures in Lima, observed the enthusiasm of people attending the large Christian & Missionary Alliance Church there. When he returned home, he gathered the people and told them they were going to meet regularly to learn the Word of God. When Lucy and partner Norma later were at Paititi, they were surprised to hear various people pray out loud at the meetings, something they hadn't done before. Another man told them he was now a believer also. That motivated Norma and Lucy to accelerate their translation of more Scriptures as the Yaminahuas would soon finish studying what they had available.

Three Bible studies for Spanish-speaking ladies in the Pucallpa area had recently held weekend retreats. Highlights of those were several new believers, spiritual growth in others and presentations of certificates for those who had read the New Testament through in 1988. Many were wives of local leaders and businessmen who were also sensitive to spiritual needs in difficult times.

I was excited about an opportunity to go out to a Yaminahua village in May of 1989 to be a temporary partner for two weeks. But at the last minute, plans changed. Sincere attempts denote a willing heart, right? We all knew that I would never be "Jane of the Jungle," however this was the third time I had volunteered and been scheduled to be a temporary partner to a lone lady linguist for a village stint. Perhaps I needed to just "stay with the stuff" in my office.

When my IBM 65 Electronic typewriter broke down, it prompted getting a computer for me, and a Ventura Publishing program to prepare camera-ready copy. This high-end program was also used to prepare New Testaments for printing. A thick paperback entitled *Ventura Tips & Tricks* became my favorite book as I read it from cover to cover.

(*Some years later this program was bought out by Corel and with changes became Corel Ventura Publishing. Later Adobe InDesign became the program of choice for publishing New Testaments.*)

When our printshop manager and his family needed to leave quickly for the States, we were on our own. Then a literacy worker was diverted to manage our shop temporarily. Finally, Bill Pinch, an experienced printshop owner from Phoenix, AZ, volunteered to come and help. Even without

Spanish, he led us well. Later, his wife Pat joined him and helped with layout and keyboarding. Together they blessed us greatly until a new permanent manager, Rich Reed, arrived.

Dangerous Times

Peruvians suffered one of the most difficult economic periods of their history. Official inflation figures for 1988 were 1,722%. In January '89, prices increased on controlled food commodities and gasoline. A prior good wage would now barely purchase essentials. The bilingual teachers were receiving the current equivalent of about $15 a month. The exchange rate for us fluctuated.

Meanwhile, another concern was the increasing unrest in Peru. Subversive groups continued to gain control of more areas, limiting access of translators to language communities. It appeared that intimidated authorities with limited resources were unable to stop the groups. Each week we heard of more incidents—killings, bombings, extortion, forced indoctrination, conscription of youth. In Puerto Callao, about a mile from our Center, the police station and an educational office were burned down. Later the mayor was shot and killed while he was at the port receiving lumber for a project.

We didn't seem to be a target at that time. Yet we moved around with a lot more caution. We did have an emergency bag packed in case we needed to flee on quick notice. But we realized that our safety was truly in the Lord. I did feel concern as John was asked to oversee security for our Jungle Center from May through July (in addition to his other responsibilities). We had hoped to have nephew Tom Hackman with us that summer, but our leaders felt it was not a safe time to bring visitors to our Center.

Subversive activity in the mountain areas was sporadic. Translators Bruce and Jan Benson had wanted to go to a village to show films of a Luke series in Spanish on the life of Christ. In May of '89, during a period that seemed to be quieter, they made the trip and had a wonderful time in two communities with Quechua pastors. However, driving home on the morning of May 29, they were stopped on the road at gunpoint by subversives of the Shining Path Movement in a commandeered truck.

Bruce and Jan, their 14-year-old son Bryan, a Quechua co-translator, and a local pastor with them, were all taken captive and separated. They had no idea what their fate would be. That same week two Catholic nuns were captured and killed. Amazingly, the Benson group was unharmed and soon released to find their own way home. The subversives confiscated their vehicle with supplies. Bensons were able to get safely to Lima a day and a half later. They gratefully thanked God for His presence and protection through that traumatic encounter.

Then we learned more. The Benson's stolen cargo included a generator and film projector. Bruce had asked if they would also like the six Spanish films. We prayed that God would use those films. A year later, Bensons heard from a friend in Huánuco telling of the remarkable change of one of the young comrades in that subversive group. After that, the Bensons met Jorge (HOR-hay), and heard his story.

The projector and films had been taken to a large encampment in the jungle. One day when they were bored, the troops had decided to check out the films, thinking they would see *Rambo* or some "Yankee imperialist" movie. Instead, they saw the entire Luke series! Many were deeply moved and wanted to lay down their arms. A top leader visited the camp and discussed the film content. He told them that Jesus was a good man, a true historical figure, and a revolutionary just like them, opposing the powerful Roman government of his day. But he warned them against believing in the resurrection of Christ which he said was an imperialist lie to keep people oppressed. He suggested that the troops not watch the films again as they would plant wrong ideas in their minds. But, after the leader left, the films were shown at least seven more times to about 700 comrades!

Jorge had later found himself in jail, bound and expecting to die as fellow prisoners had. When his blindfold miraculously fell off, he read graffiti on the cell wall: "Jesus is coming soon, prepare!" Amazingly he was released! Walking along a jungle trail, he met a blind pastor who sensed his deep need and led him to the Lord.

Jorge told Bensons about his previous activities and intense hatred of Christians. He told of how the group had planned to kill them, but for some reason their leaders couldn't agree on it. With tears in his eyes, he asked the Bensons to forgive him for his part in their trauma.

(After that time, Jorge grew in the Lord and proceeded to make a new life for himself. God provided in special ways when he had no money or work. He studied at a small Bible Institute in another country and shared his faith and testimony freely, seeing many people come to Christ.)

What a beautiful reminder of how God can take even the worst of events and use them for His glory. We don't always see the good results, so we thanked God for allowing us to know about Jorge and be encouraged to keep praying for others like him.

During the busy summer John was the only gringo aviation mechanic for several weeks. However, he continued his policy to always have the Cessna ready for any emergency. This proved wise when they needed to fly teenager Bryan Benson, with acute appendicitis, from Huánuco to Lima, since local doctors were on strike. Although his appendix burst during the flight, Bryan soon received good medical attention at a clinic in Lima. That was the second time God protected Bryan in a serious situation.

The Fowlers returned to Yarinacocha in May, thankful for new supporters. They were eager to use the new airstrip in Putaiya to check on the Nahuas. A couple groups of Nahuas poled up the river from Sepahua, making about 60 in the village, but bringing some sickness with them again. Fowlers were glad to help this fragile group. By July the population had grown to about 70 when a Yaminahua man, Segundo, with his family, visited them to share about the Lord. Translation work progressed slowly. By August both Kim and Carolyn had symptoms of chronic fatigue syndrome. Kim often slept 20 hours a day! They went to Lima for tests. By October Kim was officially diagnosed with chronic fatigue, but had gained about 70% of his strength. Carolyn was doing better.

Cutting the Grass

Kim and Carolyn Fowler's tribal house had an unusually big yard. Actually, it wasn't a yard. John called it "the little house on the *pista* (PEE-stuh)." Their house was alongside the airstrip of grass that needed to be cut frequently so planes could land on it.

Cutting their airstrip was not easy. The Nahua people, while glad for the planes that came, weren't yet into taking on the responsibility for its maintenance, though they would help cut with machetes while someone else was working. Cutters had to be alert in case they surprised a poisonous snake enjoying the green cover. Kim, who continued with symptoms of chronic fatigue, needed to pace himself carefully, especially in the hot sun. The Fowlers figured six weeks between cuttings was a maximum time interval during rainy season.

Kim and Carolyn wondered how the grass would be cut in March 1990 when they were in Lima, taking computer training to adapt Yaminahua Scriptures to Nahua. John felt he could get together a crew to cut the grass, allowing Fowlers to continue in their important work. John and two other men in our prayer group got permission to be away for a three-day work trip. Dave Wey doubled as pilot and crew member. Larry Sagert and John were known to the Nahuas from their time doing airstrip construction.

We three wives prepared and packed food and cooking gear as the men would be on their own for meal preparation. They also carried two gas-powered lawnmowers, sleeping bags, mosquito nets, bug repellant, minimal clothing, boots, some drinking water, medicines, trade goods for the Nahuas and a stun gun (useful for treating snakebites). The plane was full. (That was how the Fowlers traveled each time they went out, as they didn't yet have a safe place to store supplies in the village.) The men also squeezed in one more very important item that didn't weigh much—a card with useful Nahua phrases to help them communicate.

When the plane landed in Putaiya, they got right to work, as takeoff was impossible in the high grass. On the second day some Nahua hunters brought in three big monkeys which ladies boiled for a tasty soup with cooking bananas.

Dave became the medicine dispenser. He discovered that when he gave pills to one person, others quickly developed aches and pains and wanted some too.

Nahuas visited until dark, watching them do everything. (Lack of privacy is something most translation personnel learn to live with.) The men played some cassette tapes for the Nahuas with a greeting from Kim and Carolyn as well as Yaminahua Scripture and choruses.

They worked hard in the hot sun to finish in three days. They had to take time to boil water for drinking as they needed liquid. Meals, though simple, took time to prepare. Sleep wasn't easy in Fowler's jungle house with unfamiliar night sounds. *Was that a rat chewing?* The third day they finished the job, gathered up their supplies, and flew back to Yarinacocha. *Was that John snoring in accompaniment with the droning engine?*

So . . . the next time you cut your grass, you can enjoy what an easy job you have.

Pod Project Without Pod

On June 1, 1990, John added a new responsibility as acting Director of Aviation. Flights were fewer at that time, but some big maintenance projects were scheduled on Helio 1312: installing a cargo door, adding a cargo pod under the plane, putting in JAARS safety seats, a 1,000-hour inspection, new windshield, and repainting. It was a lot of work!

We were excited that good friends were coming in June from the JAARS Center to help. Wayne Huyett and John had trained together at LeTourneau, and we had enjoyed times together with Wayne's wife Cheryl and their daughter Becca at the JAARS Center. The Wyses also came.

But the pod was hung up in customs. Our man in Lima had said, "You'd better call off the project. It doesn't look hopeful to get the pod released." We prayed, and John took some different approaches. The men began to strip the plane.

At the end of June, the pod was finally released and trucked to Yarinacocha. The project continued on schedule and finished before Huyetts left mid-August. It was then easier to load the plane and to distribute the weight more safely. Passengers didn't need to be surrounded by baggage. We were grateful to friends from Brookfield Bible Church in Harrisburg, PA, who helped fund the pod.

The Fleet

Through the years the Aviation fleet had changed to meet the needs of the translation programs. The first teams in Peru had it tough, traveling by road as far as possible, then hiking through jungle, or possibly using river travel. After several weeks, they arrived exhausted at the village where they worked.

The first plane to initiate JAARS flight service for Peru in 1948 had been an unusual one. An old military surplus "Grumman Duck" lifted the translators over the rough terrain to their tribal allocations in only hours. That noisy, amphibious machine could deposit people on land or water. As the program in Peru had grown, so had the fleet. In the 60s and early 70s up to eight planes had busily carried tribal workers back and forth from the Jungle Center at Yarinacocha.

With 20 translations already completed in 1991, the flights were fewer. Five planes handled the load—four Helio Couriers and one Cessna 210. To our pilots and mechanics, each one had its own personality and were called by their serial number:

1. "Old 951" had been with us the longest—since 1971. It had been "rolled in a ball" twice, repaired, and was still their favorite workhorse.
2. 1000 was nicknamed "Millie" because the number thousand in Spanish is *mil*. She was a venerable old float plane with over 10,000 hours of service.
3. The Vietnam Vet, 1188, had come to JAARS headquarters as military surplus. It had been modified and relicensed in the U.S. for service in Peru. It also was on floats.
4. 1312, the "New Kid on the Block," was a favorite with passengers because it carried about 30 kilos more than the other Helios. It also now had a pod under its belly where cargo could be distributed for safety and comfort.

   Since these Helios had encountered different experiences, each had its unique little bumps and dents, just as people have warts and freckles. Yet the four were a look-alike team with identical two-toned blue and white paint jobs. Their instrument panels were equipped with the same buttons and dials in like configurations for easy pilot transition from one to the other. Each had JAARS safety seats installed. Made with energy absorbing foam and S-frames, these more crashworthy seats had been developed in a joint mission aviation research project.

   (While Helio Couriers were no longer in production, they still served us well because of the short takeoff and landing "STOL" capabilities needed for the short grass strips in places with no room for long runways. The strong tubular steel structure provided protection for passengers and pilot in the event of an accident.)

5. Lastly, there was the "Queen of the Fleet"—1291. The Cessna 210, equipped with a Robertson STOL, given to us by the Bolivia Branch when they completed their work there, added to the fleet in 1984. She was fitted with a turbo charger, with which she could develop sea-level horsepower up to nearly 20,000 feet and thus fly higher and faster. Also radar equipped, she could avoid severe weather and know exactly where mountain ranges were in relation to the flight path. She was the one used for flights over the Andes to mountain locations, or for emergency trips to Lima. Sometimes the Queen worked in partnership with a Helio; she carried a load quickly to a location and the Helio shuttled it to a smaller strip.

It had taken hours of paperwork and maintenance to get each plane to Yarinacocha and make it useful for our program. Challenges were constant, but providing wings for translators was an essential service the aviation team was happy to provide.

Our aviation team also interacted with SAMAIR (South America Mission Air Service) located not far away to help each other when needed.

Completions

After a two-year effort and various complications, our contract renewal was finally signed by the President on July 19, 1990, just before the change of government! Thankfully it was for ten years and renewable.

The last months, our Peru Branch Director's major effort had involved personally seeing many officials. We felt that the Lord had raised up special Peruvian friends to help us and had given us favor in the eyes of leaders at various levels, any number of whom could have closed the door. Linguistic analysis, anthropological studies, community development, and literacy training which our personnel did, were of great benefit to Peru, as well as an integral part of the translation process, and of ministering to the whole person. We appreciated the privilege to be in Peru and hoped we didn't take lightly the responsibilities involved.

Another completion was celebrated by a crowd gathered to greet a plane arriving at our airstrip with translator Hattie Kneeland and her companions, Noyda and Sylvia, from their stay in a Matsés village. We held an impromptu praise time thanking God for their completion in rough draft of the Matsés New Testament while in the village. Another milestone!

The Matsés previously had been called Mayorunas. I remember reading a story about the Mayoruna contact years ago in a Sunday School paper. It was an exciting event . . .

> The new language group had been discovered during a survey in the early 60s. Harriet Fields felt called to work on this project. In 1965, Joe, who after living for several years with the Mayorunas (Matsés), had escaped. He was picked up and taken to a military post. Our Jungle Center was contacted, and Harriet had the opportunity she needed—someone who spoke the language. Joe spent over a year working with Harriet. However, he became lonesome, and planned to return to the Matsés, even though it could mean death. He was flown near the Matsés location and went off into the jungle. Harriet told him she would be at the river waiting in three months' time in case he could bring some people to meet her. That was August 1966. But it wasn't until 1969, after various efforts, that a peaceful contact was made at a campfire at the end of a freshly cut trail, and Harriet was able to converse with four Matsés men in their own language!

Harriet and her partner Hattie subsequently worked for years on the Matsés translation. Hattie had recently shared at a Sunday evening meeting that her last stay with the Matsés had included considerable difficulty. "I hate medical work," she told us, yet there had been four medical emergencies, including one death even as she was finishing Revelation. "I hate spiders," she said emphatically, "and I've never seen so many spiders out there." This indicated to her that the final New Testament revision process would likely receive strong satanic opposition. She felt the need for faithful intercessory prayer.

Ephesians 6 tells us to put on, with prayer, the full armor of God. The sword of the Spirit—the Word of God—is our strong weapon. With words from Scripture, we can send the enemy running. No wonder Satan wouldn't want the Matsés to have it—or us to use it. Thankfully, during the translation process many Matsés had already committed great quantities of God's Word to memory. The Lord was blessing in their lives and had blessed the work. We celebrated His goodness!

Conditions Deteriorate

That year about 540 students from communities all over the jungle attended the bilingual teacher training courses on various levels. Linda Potter, who helped in the training said that, of a group of 10 bilingual teachers who had met in her home the previous year for church services, two had already been killed by subversives. As those key people went back to their communities, they were targets because of their leadership roles. Many schools would not be functioning because communities had fled to the jungles for safety. In another case, a community church service had been disrupted by subversives, the pastor killed, and Bibles burned. Despite the danger, a Chayahuita teacher, Mamerto, who had committed his life to the Lord during his time at the training, was so excited that he eagerly shared about his newfound joy upon returning to his village. When he asked how many wanted to follow the Lord, half the village responded!

Peru continued in its most serious economic crisis in history, with reserves depleted, new monies being printed to meet payrolls, and spiraling inflation. Postal rates shot up 100%, with inadequate supplies of stamps available. Strikes of various entities paralyzed progress in many areas including medical facilities, transportation (even airlines), and government agencies. Electric company workers were on strike, then health workers. Some bridges on the road between Lima and Pucallpa were destroyed by terrorists, limiting produce, gasoline, and other supplies from reaching the jungle area.

Our flight department, after great effort, chartered a Hercules air shipment for aviation fuel. In Lima electricity was limited due to ten power pylons downed by terrorists. Seven policemen and an electric company driver returning from guarding power pylons were killed when their van drove over booby-trapped bombs. Two car bombs exploded in Lima during a blackout. The former Social Security president was killed. Terrorists destroyed buildings and vehicles at an agricultural station. Terrorists shot the district mayor of a town. Terrorists attacked the $3 million U.S. built anti-drug base.

Most of our translation teams were unable to work in their allocations because of danger to them or to the community by their presence. Community leaders and pastors were often targets of subversives. Fifty men, women and children were shot dead in a town in the high jungle as a column of heavily armed subversives arrived at the village in early evening. They called the people to the square and searched out those who hid in their houses. Without warning, the attackers opened fire, then set offices on fire before leaving. Marine infantry reported eight terrorist suspects killed by crossfire inside a military base when a Sendero Luminoso column attacked the barracks trying to release some prisoners. Travel advisories sent out by the U.S. Embassy indicated areas to avoid.

We prayed for peaceful elections and for wisdom for the new president and congressmen. During the hotly contested race, two congressional candidates were killed, one in Huánuco (along with several of his bodyguards) and one in Lima. You had to be brave to run, or to hold office. The results required a run-off election for the two highest presidential candidates. Then surprisingly, the candidate who came into the running in the last couple months gained a substantial margin to win. Reports indicated that election procedures went smoothly and safely. Alberto Fujimori took office on July 28, Peru's Independence Day. He faced enormous challenges.

By December of 1990 there were times when it seemed uncanny that so many things could go wrong, and we felt like saying, "Lord, that's enough, please!"

In our Print Shop our best Peruvian employee was caught stealing supplies. He with two other workers had stolen large quantities for several years. As other employees were aware of this, we had to ask for the immediate resignation of the three involved. This left us with only two inexperienced Peruvian workers to carry a print shop load that used to be handled by five. The unskilled workers were slow and made costly mistakes.

At the same time there were mechanical failures with two presses. There was a large quantity of paper received of substandard quality that wrinkled going through the presses. There were problems with ink being too sticky. The electrostatic plate maker with which we burned our paper plates would not function well. Rain leaked through the roof dripping on equipment in our office, and shorting electricity. Project funds were depleted for printing literacy materials.

For several months our new Print Shop Manager, Rich Reid, was seriously ill with Undulant Fever. When he was able to start back to work, he learned that his mother in the States had experienced a heart attack, and he felt he should make a trip home. The result was turtle pace production—a heartbreaking situation when so many of the translators' books-in-progress should have been printed and distributed long ago. There were two urgent projects for the press: The book of Luke in Huaylas Quechua, the first printed book of Scriptures for that group, which had been held up because of orthography (alphabet) issues, and now was wanted ASAP. A hymn book for the Campa Ashanincas, many of whom were scattered from home due to serious confrontations with subversive groups. Music was important to them, and this hymn book could be a great encouragement. When the pressman began working on the hymn book, the press motor burned out.

But. Somebody must have been praying so that we had strength to keep going even when we didn't feel like it. One of our Branch goals for that year was spiritual vitality for our members, and we requested prayer for that. We sensed a spiritual battle and trusted for God's power to be strong against the spiritual forces of evil—especially as there were now six New Testaments in final revision processes. Translator, Nancy Black, had recently finished the North Junin Quechua New Testament in rough draft.

Cholera and Calamities

In addition, Peru made the international news with an epidemic of cholera. It spread quickly because of unsafe water supplies. Fish and seafood along the coast were contaminated. The major contributor to the widespread outbreak was a popular dish called *cebiche*, which is fish marinated with lemon juice which changes its texture, though it is not really cooked. Combined with sliced onions and special spices, it's very tasty. But, with the resulting severe diarrhea and vomiting, people became quickly dehydrated.

The very poor people who lived in shantytowns with poor sanitation and no clean water supply were most susceptible. By March of 1991, about 300 had died, and up to 50,000 people had contracted it. Measures had been taken to curtail the movement of fresh vegetables from the problem areas. Fishermen, farmers, and vendors had their meager livelihood seriously threatened.

Various countries donated tons of medicines, mainly a powdered concentrate with potassium, salt, and sugar, to be mixed with water (hopefully boiled) to be drunk as a rehydration fluid or given intravenously. We were pleased to receive some 1,000 doses free for our Clinic distribution. Later cholera did spread to nearby Pucallpa, but with a minimum of cases. During that time, we did not eat out in any restaurants.

The epidemic continued to move through Peru and seemed to "wax and wane" in various areas. One report later indicated 285,400 cases in Peru with 2,340 deaths. We expected that many cases in remote areas were undiagnosed and uncounted. Some linguists adapted a cholera pamphlet produced by the Ministry of Health and translated it into various languages, which the people appreciated immensely.

For ourselves we were concerned about increased subversive activity on facilities identified with U.S. and other allied countries because of the Persian Gulf War. In Lima two Kentucky Fried Chicken restaurants and a Pizza Hut were bombed, along with the U.S. Embassy, the Italian Embassy, and 20 banks. Local authorities indicated that our jungle facility could be a target as well. We asked prayer for the Lord's protection and for wisdom on the part of our people—what we did and where we went.

Through one calamity after another, we still saw smiles on the faces of our Peruvian friends. We wondered how they could be smiling. In fact, I found myself becoming numb to tragic news. Maybe we just got used to trauma, or perhaps it was a survival instinct the Lord gave us for coping with difficulties.

In the Print Shop office, our key desk-top-publishing person, Kathy Bergman, was called home to care for her parents after her dad had a bad fall. She had told her aging parents that if the time came when they needed her, they should let her know. And they did. So, she would be faithful to keep her promise to them. Before she left, she gave a crash course on Scripture preparation using the Ventura Publisher program to Judy Reid and me. It was a complicated process, and I took thorough notes.

It was exciting for me to be working again on Scripture preparation, as I had done in Bolivia. By this time, we used equipment and methods hugely advanced from those days. It was stimulating and very challenging, and I loved it. But, for me it was not to last for long.

(*Later Kathy got set up with equipment to continue Peru projects from her parent's home, which was a very unusual, special arrangement in those* days. *She continued doing that for many years, preparing New Testaments and Scripture books for press.)*

Journal of a Tribal Trip

In August of 1991 a plan came together. After several cancelled trips, I would join Carolyn Fowler for a short trip to the Nahuas. Come along with us!

It was finally happening. I was flying in our Helio Courier to visit the Nahua village of Putaiya with Carolyn Fowler. She wanted to make a medical check on the village since Kim's chronic fatigue still sapped half of his strength. Bill and Pat Pinch also accompanied us—the couple who had come from Phoenix to help keep our Print Shop going. This gave them an opportunity to visit tribal people. Also, their fares and mine contributed to the cost of the expensive flight, lessening the Fowler's financial burden. Pete Lawry was our pilot and would stay overnight with us to allow a two-day visit. We headed south from our Yarinacocha Jungle Center with one stop at Miaria (Mee-ah-REE-ah) two hours out to pick up fuel, then 20 minutes more to Putaiya.

In the right front seat, I looked down at thousands of trees with a ribbon of brown river twisting through them. We were flying low under a cloud layer, so details of the terrain were visible—the green-yellow slime on closed water channels, beaches exposed during low water of dry season, and squares of green indicating garden plots. I saw tiny white specks that flickered and moved over the terrain near the rivers (they had to be birds) and a few isolated jungle houses along the river edges. Pete tilted the plane and pointed. "That's Galilea over there," he mouthed. We wore earplugs to protect against the roar of the engine, so conversation was limited.

After an hour of smooth flying, the clouds increased. As the sun shone on clouds just below us, their brilliant whiteness was almost blinding. We flew around and between them, like a bird among giant white cotton candies. Then we had to fly *through* some. Too bad I hadn't found my Dramamine to take before the flight, but I tried an anti-acid tablet Carolyn gave me. Then, I decided more fresh air would feel good and turned the little knob to open the tiny window vent beside me. Pete recognized the signs and made sure I had a sick sack handy. I tried to wish away those familiar feelings, but using the sack was inevitable. Descending and banking to land at Miaria didn't help my nausea, but as soon as the wheels touched, I felt better.

We taxied down the grass strip with rows of jungle houses and several hundred people on either side. It had rained there and was damp, so Pete decided to pick up fuel later, but delivered some letters for people there. We climbed out to stretch our legs and greet the people. This was a Piro community, but some spoke Spanish. Two young Peruvian ladies from the Alliance Church in Lima were working there as missionaries and told us they were having a week of special services at the Piro church. They asked us to pray for the people. *(The Piro New Testament translation was one of the first completed in Peru about 30 years previously.)* The friendly people waved us off as we taxied away. Children knew to get off the strip, thankfully, and soon we were airborne.

And just as soon, my nausea returned, and I sought another sack. I missed seeing the Sarejal where some Nahuas were building a new village on a river bend. I was glad when, through the clouds, Pete pointed out a tiny airstrip next to the river among all those trees that was our destination.

It had rained there also, and the three-to-five-inch grass glistened on the airstrip as we touched down. Only one small simple jungle house adorned this strip. It was elevated several feet on poles, with bark walls and thatched roof, no windows, one door, and about 50 Indians waving excitedly

from and around its open porch. Pete taxied near to it and cut the engine. Then the children were at the doors of the plane to greet us.

As Pete was scheduled to pick up and deliver some other people to Miaria, he needed to unload the plane and be on his way. He asked if I could guard the supplies on the porch while he unloaded. With my camera and drawstring bag over my shoulder, I carried the first box and lost my balance going up the unusual steps to the porch. Grabbing a pole to keep from falling off, I managed to avoid injury even if I did lose my dignity. I determined to observe the correct procedure to mount the inclined hunk of trunk with high and low horizontal chunks nailed to it. Best to take advantage of an adjacent stump to serve as the middle step.

Cute little boys helped carry the supplies inside. Because of the weight allowance, we didn't have much, but I could tell it looked like a lot to them—a couple boxes with medicines and trade goods; one with food and a kettle; another held the remains of our lunch (I hadn't eaten); one with cookie treats for them; a citrus sapling bagged in soil ready for planting; a duffel and some large plastic bags that held our sleeping gear, a change of clothes and a few personal items.

Everyone was greeting Carolyn, and she "introduced" us. Part of the greeting seemed to be pats on arms and shoulders. Some were telling Carolyn in high whiny voices that they didn't feel well. Others came to join the group, and the porch seemed to bounce with the weight. We all watched as Pete took off. He would return later that day if the weather held.

We visited with the people. The old Chief was happy to see us and wanted some medicine. He prayed with Carolyn; it was touching, though I didn't understand the words. A lady carried us a bucketful of water from the creek across the airstrip. Some men brought firewood, and Bill got a fire started. He had to use some newspapers we had brought, as the wood was damp. Later Carolyn showed Bill where to get water, and as it began to sprinkle rain, he brought back another bucketful. She also showed us where the latrine was, about 100 feet behind the house and into the trees a little—a hole in the ground with wood slats over it.

Some of the babies had colds and fevers, so Carolyn began some medical treatment. One child couldn't hold down the cough medicine and vomited.

Peru (1988-1992)   191

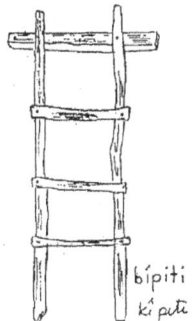

I got out my sketch book and began to sketch objects around us—a ladder to the loft and a banana palm. Little boys gathered round to watch and tell me the names of the things: *bípiti (or kípiti)* and *prátano (or máñina)*.

Some held the notebook sideways to look at the funny lines. I drew a very tall tree that branched at the top like an umbrella. That they called *pona*, or *ëbë*, or *pida*. Then moving to the other side of the porch, sitting with our feet dangling, I sketched a "bush" of long narrow pointed leaves which I thought was lemon grass. I spotted a papaya tree and drew that (with the pretty blossoms I knew indicated the "male" tree which would not produce fruit but help pollinate others). That they told me was *popayu*, or *burso*, or *bursho*.

As it grew darker and cooler, people began leaving until there was only one family left, and then it rained. It was only 2:00 p.m. but felt like 6:00. Carolyn shared some cookies with the family, and we took a break inside to have some tea and cookies. I ate the chicken sandwich which I hadn't eaten earlier on the plane.

Later the rain stopped, and people came again. Their homes were stretched out mostly across the river. At one point the people got excited and said, "Papa José!" Some visitors were approaching. José came to the house with a couple Nahuas. Apparently, they had just arrived from the

Manu (Mah-NEW) Park, an area of National Preserve, where fauna and the primitive people who lived there were protected. He knew some Spanish and said there was a very sick man in a canoe, which he had left upriver some distance. He said the man was about to die, so he had brought him for medical help. He also told of Mestizos putting so much poison in the river (to stun and catch fish) that the whole fish crop was devastated, and people had gotten sick from eating the fish. He wanted us to report it to authorities. He stayed a while, and Carolyn continued medical work with the ones there. Then he left with his group.

Carolyn also played cassettes on the tape player from time to time. They enjoyed hearing choruses that Yaminahua Christians had recorded. New to them were songs of Yaminahua Scripture put to music of their style by Mary Ann Lord (linguist waiting for Moronahua contact). Some listened carefully and repeated the song a phrase behind, as if trying to memorize it. They also heard a recorded testimony of Gustavo, the Sharanahua pastor, who had visited them before.

It rained off and on during the afternoon. We didn't know if Pete would make it back, but in the late afternoon the sky brightened. The people heard the plane two or three minutes before we could. Pete landed and parked the plane close to the house. I was happy to see that the people here also knew to get back off the airstrip when a plane was moving.

Pete set up his mosquito net and sleeping bag in a corner of the house, and we started to set ours up also before it would be too dark to see what we were doing. Five could just fit nicely along one side and filled half the house. Jungle living makes close fellowship!

The people on the porch got excited again. They saw a large canoe arriving on the river below. They said it was more people arriving from the Manu. Quite a few of the people ran down to the river, then all left as darkness fell.

We lit candles and set out supper—the rest of the sandwiches, cut in half and crumbly by now, liver pate spread on large crackers, carrot sticks, cookies, tea, and coffee—on the high bench which served as a table. Oh yes, also turtle eggs we had been given—a new experience for me. They were about half the size of chicken eggs, with a wrinkled and tough shell. Though they had been cooked in boiling water 15 minutes, the "white" was slimy and seemed undone. I scraped that off on my plate and left it. I cut the yolk and shared it with Pat. It tasted similar to the yolk flavor I knew, but stronger and with a grainier texture. While this might be a delicacy served at a gourmet restaurant, I decided I wouldn't seek it again. The candlelight seemed to draw us into a special camaraderie, and our conversation lingered as we sipped our tea.

As the weather front was from the south bringing rain and cold winds, it seemed unlikely that we would be able to fly out the next day. Carolyn wondered if it would be possible for her to stay longer, maybe a week, to follow up some medical needs. She was also concerned about the newcomers, and if there was enough food for all of them considering the fish problem. I was willing to stay on with her, although Pete thought the flight schedule was already too full to squeeze in another flight. He would check in the morning.

We cleared up supper, brushed our teeth and prepared for the night. As the candles burned lower, we crawled under the mosquito nets and into the sleeping bags—except for Carolyn, who organized her medicine supply and planned what she needed to do the next day.

At first it felt great to stretch out nice and flat, but as the hours passed, I seemed to feel the floor slats through the inch of foam under my sleeping bag. I turned and shifted one way and another trying to find a comfortable

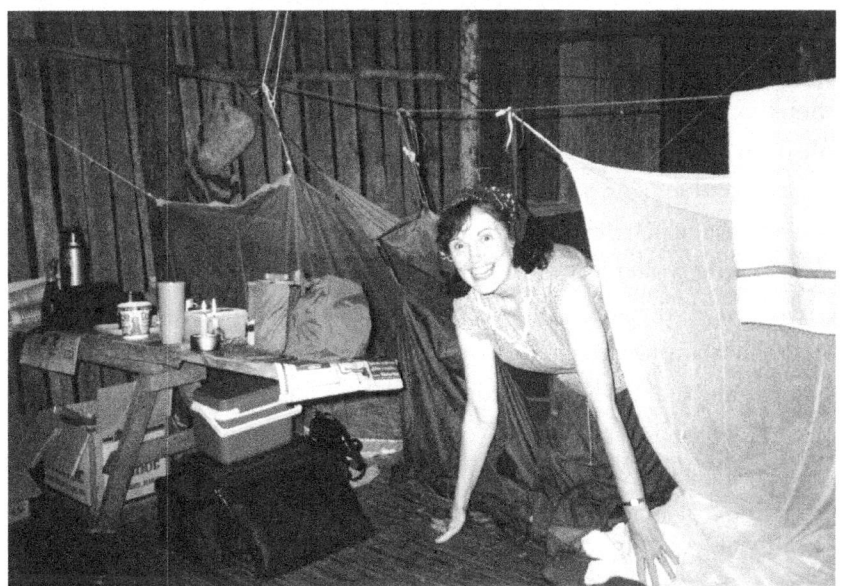

position. It grew cooler through the night, and the breezes blew through the slats of the walls (normally a blessing in hot weather). It seemed I didn't sleep much, but perhaps I slept more than I realized, for soon Pete was dropping his ropes and rolling up his sleeping gear with practiced precision. Just then I found the comfortable position I had been seeking all night, so lingered longer in the warmth of the sleeping bag. Pete went out to the plane to check things and called our Center on the radio. Sure enough, the flight schedule was full for several weeks. As we had only enough food for a couple days, the option of staying on was pretty much limited.

I helped set up breakfast, and before we could eat it, Nahuas were arriving to visit. Carolyn knew she needed to eat before beginning her day's activities, for she might not have much time later. I gobbled some granola and coffee quickly and went out on the porch to entertain the early comers with my notebook and pen in hand—also my small New Testament in hopes of having some devotions. I sat on the bench nearest the wall to avoid the cold breeze. The Nahuas were shivering with cold, yet wore few clothes, and a couple children were naked as the day before. I felt guilty in my three layers: white blouse over blue printed blouse over cotton knit pullover, and blue jeans under my jeans skirt. They checked over my layers with envy, pointing out their ragged shirts and blouses.

I endeavored to read some Scripture for myself as most of them warmed by the fire, but soon curious children were checking out my colorful bookmark, beautifully handwoven threads in a nice pattern by nimble Shipibo fingers. They tried it on their wrists, but the part was missing through which the end strings could be pulled to make a bracelet.

Abandoning my devotions, I took out my notebook and began sketching a bench in the middle of the porch—a log cut in half with four (by now) oddly angled leg posts. They told me that was called a *cita duro*, or *dulo*. How do linguists ever decide what is the correct word or pronunciation for something when they give so many variations! Then he wanted me to draw the *avion* (airplane) which was a bit more of a challenge.

Later we noticed a row of young girls sitting along the edge of the porch each picking lice from the hair of the one in front. When they found one, they would gleefully display it on the tip of their index finger, then eat it. Bill and Pat thought this very amusing. I had seen it before and decided that to be social I might join them. I sat down in the front position, and the first girl delightedly sifted through my hair. Another even joined her to check out this unusual gringa crop. They dutifully showed me on their fingertips a couple treasures from my scalp! I thanked them graciously but didn't offer to eat them.

As more Nahuas arrived, Carolyn played some tapes, reviewed reading vocabulary words on flashcards, gave vitamins, and treated babies with colds and fevers. One of the new men who had come from the Manu sat straddling a log facing the fire. Bill wanted to move the spoke-like arrangement of logs toward the center to get more flame and to set the kettle on them to boil water, but the man couldn't seem to get the hint to move. He wore only a shirt and a "G string" with a fluff of bark over his private parts. As Bill fanned the fire, the ends of the bark fluff were singed, and the man quickly jumped up to snuff out the red glow. Bill apologized profusely, put the pot on, then went inside the house to hide his laughter at what he had done to the poor man.

Later Pete and Bill went with a Nahua man to chop down some trees at the end of the runway. As the man had admired Bill's sweatshirt, he offered to give it to him for his machete work. (Bill told us later that Pete could chop a four-inch-thick tree with 10 machete strokes—a balsa tree that is!)

Carolyn had planned to go looking for the "deathly ill" man José had told us about, to see if she could help. But to her surprise, he came walking to see us with José and some others. He looked appropriately grave but seemed to only have an inflamed boil on his hip. Carolyn prepared a shot of long-acting penicillin. On her first puncture of his thick skin, she drew blood with the syringe and had to jab again in another spot. I could see that Carolyn's couple years of nurses training were a great help to their ministry. (Many linguists are called upon to meet medical needs for which they have very limited medical background.)

Later in the day the man looked greatly improved to me, and I even caught him laughing once when he forgot how sick he was. The people seemed to crave the attention they got if they were ill, and so magnified their slightest pain. Carolyn needed the Lord's wisdom to separate the true needs from the imagined ones.

Pete came to call the Center on the plane radio again and check to see what weather reports had been called in from other stations. It looked good for departing that day, and he suggested we plan for the first shuttle with Pat and Bill at 1:30 p.m., and 2:30 for Carolyn and me. (The limited length of the grass strip restricted weight allowance on takeoff.) As Bill was still cutting trees, I helped Pat take down their mosquito nets and roll up the sleeping bags, which seemed to roll up larger than before. We set out some lunch, and each helped ourselves as we were able. Carolyn was scrambling to get done as much as possible in the time left. Then the wind began picking up again, and Pete decided it was too gusty for takeoff. We would stay another day. Carolyn was delighted to have the extra time, but she felt badly that Pat and I had worked so hard to pack up the bedding.

Later in the afternoon Carolyn took Bill, Pat, and me to visit some Nahua homes. She determined that the steep slippery bank at the river crossing would be too much for Pat to negotiate (having had a sprained ankle in the recent past), so opted for a trail across the creek which had not been used for a while. Bill went in the lead with a machete to chop the way clear, however it was so overgrown we got off track at one point. It went down to a place where three wobbly logs spanned the creek which flowed 10 to 12 feet below. We took turns crossing the 15-foot span like cautious tight rope walkers.

Then as Bill chopped and slashed, we wound our way up and around toward the main trail. Considering Bill had chronic asthma and had already had his heart replumbed in a triple bypass, I could hardly believe his energetic activity and named him "Don Guillermo of the Jungle." The thick vegetation held lovely, unusual flowers which we admired. Pat prayed we wouldn't see any snakes. We climbed over huge fallen trees and negotiated steep inclines. We considered turning back, but Pat said she could handle it. The last 25 feet or so, a Nahua man came from the other end and opened the trail for us.

With a new freshness, we proceeded on the smooth trail which wound through areas of tall banana palms the Nahuas had planted, yuca growing well, pineapple and squash. Their jungle houses were scattered through this area, with extended family groups living together under simple pole and thatch-roof dwellings. They had no floors or walls or furniture, but hammocks hanging here and there with fires built right beside them on the ground for warmth. "Is this where they live? This is their house?" asked Pat when we approached the first one. It looked more like a picnic pavilion to cover a couple picnic tables. Yet, there was a certain cozy atmosphere as children played, dogs lounged (or ran to bark at us), chicks pecked, and big pots of yuca boiled over the fires. It seemed we had arrived at supper time.

We didn't stay long, but proceeded down the trail, and at each place yuca was cooking, also some meat, bananas, or corn soup. Carolyn was thankful to see they were eating well. We even saw some enjoying cooked fish, which they had gotten downstream. At one place I tried playing some soccer with a couple of little boys who had befriended me earlier. I couldn't make a goal against their quick, nimble feet. Carolyn spotted her latrine seat at one place, which had been carried off from their house, and they gladly returned it to her.

Suddenly we realized it was later than we thought, so we began a hasty return, lest the sun leave us before we had negotiated the obstacle course back across the creek. There would be no moonlight to guide us with the overcast sky. From this direction we had to climb up a steep incline with little foothold and a huge log in the middle. Teamwork helped us get each other over. We could barely see when we arrived back at the airstrip. Thankfully Pete had gotten water and even cooked bananas and turtle eggs for us.

We enjoyed another leisurely supper over candlelight. Carolyn enjoyed the wonderful flavor of the "fresh" turtle eggs, breaking just the end of the shell and sucking the juicy part to eat along with the yolk. I guess that was the proper way to do it, but I declined to try again. I enjoyed a corned beef and cheese sandwich, banana, and hot orange Tang.

Soon we crawled into the warmth of sleeping bags again. It was colder than the night before. I expected to sleep much better this time, but again spent most of the night searching for that comfortable position which I found just at sunrise. We had planned to shuttle out at 8:00 a.m. and 9:00, so Pete was up and rolling up his gear early. As I made no indication of moving soon, the guys started untying my ropes, dropping the mosquito net down over me. Such wonderful help!

We quickly ate and got the gear packed in the Helio for the first shuttle. Nahuas began arriving to visit and say goodbye. After Pete took off, Carolyn played the tape explaining the dangers of cholera and how to avoid it and treat it. Mary Ann Lord had carefully researched how to say this and had recorded her information. Carolyn hoped the people would listen well, which a group of them did. She played it again so they could catch it better. They laughed at the part where Mary Ann told of the value of digging holes for latrines. Carolyn chose the lady who had listened most closely and left rehydration packets with her.

Then José had the men line up who had said they wanted to work cutting the airstrip. They stood like soldiers with machetes, tip upward in their left arms. Carolyn wrote their names in her notebook, so she would know who to bring items for on the next flight to pay for their work. I saw a little girl had sneaked into the house and I went to check on things. She saw me enter and quickly passed something through the slats to a lady outside. It was obvious I had seen, so soon a package of cookies surfaced and was returned. I told Carolyn and she decided it was time to pass another round of cookies to the guests. She got the remaining packages, and we passed three cookies to each, the best we could as eager hands reached from all directions.

Then Carolyn walked to the end of the airstrip to make sure the "crew" knew what was needed. I waited with the people till she returned, then we began packing up the remaining meds and supplies. Pete returned within the hour and with a warning that the winds were beginning to pick up again. We quickly finished final details and carried boxes to the edge of the porch so Pete could load them on the plane. I quickly found my Dramamine and swallowed it without water. There was just time for a few final photos, a prayer for us by the Chief, and goodbyes to the people. We climbed into the plane and were off.

In 20 minutes we landed at Miaria, where Pat and Bill waited. They had enjoyed attending one of the special meetings at the church during the interval. Pete reshuffled the load while people surrounded the plane and watched from all sides.

Then we were off. As the Dramamine took effect and made me sleepy, I felt secure that I wouldn't get sick. We flew under the cloud layer, and between dozes I watched the endless trees below and the river ribbons which we followed.

Just after noon I recognized the now-huge-to-me city of Pucallpa below and then we were over Yarinacocha. As we circled to land against the wind, I spotted John by the hangar waving a welcome up to us. The wind gusts required Pete's close attention as he skillfully set the plane down on its home pasture of short, well-kept grass.

I thanked the Lord for my experience, for safety, and for those involved in the effort to bring God's Word to all language groups—even the small, humble group of near-primitive Nahuas living in the remote Amazon Jungle.

Several months later Kim and Carolyn returned there for a six-week stay. That time they took some trial copies of the first reading book adapted from Yaminahua to Nahua, which I helped prepare. We had cut in word replacements and made 20 books using the copy machine, then added a nice, printed cover.

Pressing Forward

Though our work was curtailed in many areas, translation projects continued. The Pastaza Quechua team finished translation of their New Testament in July and moved to the final checking stages. That made *seven* New Testaments in final revision! Revision committees worked diligently on final corrections and checks. That included consistency in spelling, key terms like "believe", ensuring the inclusion of all chapters and verses, appropriate footnotes, illustrations, etc.

Kim and Carolyn finally had a long stretch of six months at Putaiya, progressing in language learning despite recurring chronic fatigue symptoms. Carolyn taught reading with a small but enthusiastic group, who sometimes woke them in the morning asking when it was time for their class. Younger ones learned quickly, while the older folks had more difficulty. Fowlers realized that the Nahua people preferred to be called Yoras, so the official name designation was changed. But I had a hard time changing. I felt that they would always be Nahuas to me.

New Direction

John was encouraged to attend a Townsend Institute seminar held in June of 1991 in Waxhaw, NC. This program presented leadership and counseling skills to "equip participants to optimize their competencies." He appreciated the opportunity to attend these valuable sessions. While in Waxhaw he was approached by several people asking him to consider job slots there, as they had several needs. One that caught his interest was helping direct the new Africa Transportation Service program which was exploring ways to best meet needed land vehicle transportation over rough and muddy terrain. While John was not eager to leave Aviation, he was open to change, and desired to help where needs were greatest. Though it would be hard to leave Peru after 14 years of involvement, he was willing to consider something new. It seemed like good timing for him personally as the Peru flight program would be reducing with the completion of many translation programs. We requested prayer from our partners back home for our decision.

In October John traveled again to the JAARS Headquarters at Waxhaw, NC, for the annual Aviation Technical Conference. While there, plans were firmed up for John to help this new venture with Africa Transportation Service, which aimed to help provide transportation for our personnel serving in the 23 sub-Saharan countries in Africa. In his new assignment, scheduled to begin the first of July 1992, we would be based at the JAARS Center in Waxhaw. With those plans in place, we slowly began preparations for closing out our work and our house in the next months before heading home. Our departure was set for February 27.

Finishing

In November, prior to our 1991 Annual Branch Conference, the highland and jungle teams each met together to plan strategy for the coming year. One key decision was setting a date for closing out the Yarinacocha Jungle Center—1996 was proposed. That would not be the end of the translation work in Peru but a shift in emphasis to mountain programs as there would only be a few jungle teams still working on translations by that time. It's always hard to process closing something which had taken great effort over the years to build up, maintain and improve. It would be an emotional concern to those for whom the Center had been home for most of their lives. We had been through similar decisions in the Bolivia Branch. Our mission's policies were to concentrate our efforts on Bible translation and not to become entrenched in other projects. They did not want our personnel to hang on forever, but to turn over the work to the people. There were also other missions who specialized in other areas of service, like running Bible schools and medical work.

We had been prayer partners with Kim and Carolyn Fowler since 1984, so we would surely carry their prayer concerns with us. They were just beginning to make good progress. They worked on adapting Books 2, 3 and 4 from the Yaminahua reading series. I prepared camera ready copy for Book 2 which we ran on the copy machine, and printed its cover on the press. It made an attractive trial edition. I wished I could help prepare the others.

(Sadly, Kim Fowler passed away suddenly in 2017 in the Pucallpa hospital. At this writing, Merilee Goins and Mary Ann Lord continue with Carolyn Fowler to finish as much translation as possible and help with the medical needs of the people.)

Packing for a trip is one thing. Packing for our move was another. Each item in the house demanded a decision: to sell or give away, ship ahead or carry with. "Be ruthless," said John as I sat one day sorting through file folders. What he meant was, throw away as much as possible.

John was a wise husband, knowing my weaknesses too well. He wanted me to begin the process to avoid a last-minute panic. We sold some household items in the Christmas boutique. In January as our walls began to echo against the bareness, he said, "I'm pleased with the good progress we're making."

Then I came to the shelves and drawers in my special work area with computer books and Things-to-Do files. I opened the notebook which held copies of newsletters from our whole time in Peru. And I began to reminisce as I looked through them. I reread about when 10,000 new copies of New Testaments (five different languages) had to be rebound by hand because they came unglued in the jungle humidity . . . and when the water flooded the hangar . . . and when the currency changed from soles to intis.

"I'm getting nowhere with the packing and the decisions," I thought. "I need to put this in the pile for shipping." But the next letter caught my eye, and the next. I kept reading, feeling guilty that I was wasting time. Finally, I realized that I needed this review of our history to help with the parting process. A time of remembering and reflection was necessary to say goodbye to this segment of our lives and be free to look forward to the new.

So, released from the guilt, I began systematically with the earliest letters, reviewing our history. I was reminded of hard times. I was refreshed by the joys of published Scriptures, of new believers among the jungle groups. I reviewed special projects John had been involved with through the years. I remembered when the Lord answered prayers to bring us through impossible situations. And as I read, I could see where God had led and provided. Then the absolute deadline arrived when the notebook had to be packed.

Much we leave behind, I thought, *but much will also go with us. Yes, they were good years. But now we move on. Thank you, Lord, for the memories.*

We anticipated our new assignment. But first there was furlough March through June.

---------৯৫৯৫---------

(It took longer than anticipated for the Peru Branch to finish up the remaining jungle translation projects. The Jungle Center closure date was moved several times. Finally, the Center was turned over to the Ministry of Education around 2004 to be used as a college for indigenous peoples, which had been Wycliffe's founder Cameron Townsend's original dream. The linguists working on the remaining jungle projects, which had begun later than the others, found housing in nearby Pucallpa—not nearly as convenient or secure as our Center, and without the previous support services, but workable. Flight services were provided by SAMAIR with South America Mission.)

Chapter 9
Africa Transportation Service
Those Barely Passable Roads

———————————————✈

Back Home

In and out the door went boxes and suitcases. Ours went in, and our renters' belongings went out. They moved just a few blocks away to their newly constructed house. That was good timing! It was June 30th, 1992. Our furlough, with a big trip out west, was over, and we had arrived at the JAARS Center in Waxhaw—this time to begin new assignments.

What a blessing to have a home to come back to! I considered it a "miracle house" remembering how the Lord had stretched and multiplied our limited resources back in 1976 when we built it. We had lived in the house less than a year when we had been asked to go to Peru for 18 months. Now 14 years later it was there for us. Meanwhile, it had served to house various JAARS missionaries. Our rental charge had been less than the local market price. Yet, God used the rent to pay off our house loan!

As we opened boxes that had been stored for years, we were so grateful for the Lord's provisions. But we would try not to hold those things too tightly. After all, we were just pilgrims passing through. Our real home was in heaven. *(Hebrews 13:14 KJV - "For here we have no continuing city, but we seek one to come.")*

New Program at JAARS

John enthusiastically began his new work with the Africa Transportation Service (ATS). Still in developmental stages, ATS had been started a couple years earlier in response to needs of translation and literacy personnel who needed to travel in very remote and inaccessible areas of the vast African continent. The goal was to provide surface transportation in three main ways:

1. To handle the purchase of vehicles at a reduced price through an arm of the United Nations, shipping them directly from the factory (usually in Japan) to the specified African port.
2. To help raise funds for extremely high transportation costs. For example, if $18,000 purchased a vehicle, the cost to import it into the country could be another $18,000.
3. To develop no-frills, durable 4-wheel-drive vehicles for use in Africa costing approximately $6,000, and to field test two prototypes in Congo by July 1993. Development was moving along with the recent completion of Prototype #5.

In addition to that, ATS had put together a maintenance facility in a container for Zaire and a boat project on Lake Victoria.

Our members served in 23 countries south of the Sahara Desert. The 450 million people in Sub Saharan Africa represented 10 percent of the world's population, the fastest growing population for its land size in the world. Possibly one million would die from AIDS in the 1990s. Severe famine was widespread. Language groups there totaled about 1,900, with four major language families overlaid with English, French, Portuguese, and wide use of Swahili. About one-third of the remaining world-wide Bible translation task was in Africa.

We learned that the role of our personnel in Africa increasingly involved being facilitators, trainers of often well-educated and well-motivated Africans in translation principles and methods, enabling them to translate and to develop national Bible translation organizations. In that way the efforts could be multiplied for the huge translation task. But the physical challenges for transportation of our personnel working in undeveloped areas was huge.

John initially ordered eight vehicles, arranging for banking and shipping. In September he made a quick trip to Sonora, California, to check progress and discuss possibilities with two volunteer engineers, Gino Bartomeleo and Mike Lundgren. They were working on Prototype #6 of the 4-wheel-drive vehicle, dubbed the Gazelle after the fleet-footed animal common in Africa. John was impressed with what they were doing.

In January John was named director of the ATS Program. He faced the decision of the practicality of continuing the development and production of the Gazelle. With added improvements to the prototype, the cost projection increased, which might make the result not worth the immense effort that would be involved.

John flew again to California to discuss the final version of the Prototype #6. He then drove that demo vehicle across the U.S. to Waxhaw for further evaluation.

On the way he stopped at LeTourneau University in Texas since they had requested its display at a mission's emphasis program. John thanked friends for praying that he stay awake during long hours of driving alone.

This latest Gazelle prototype made extensive use of existing commercially made parts, which seemed like a realistic approach, requiring many less man-hours to produce/assemble. This vehicle's foundation was a rugged four-wheel drive version of the Toyota Pick-up, modified to meet the unique requirements of third world transportation. The adapted cab and bed allowed removable rear seating. A camper shell protected passengers and cargo area, while a cargo rack doubled as an external tubular roll cage. A diesel engine replaced the gasoline engine. Keeping cost under $7,000 seemed a possibility. Also, importation costs on "used vehicles" were much lower than for new ones.

Each previous prototype had helped the team learn something, and now we hoped that translators on the field would soon reap these benefits. Gino and Mike then began work on two additional prototype #6 Gazelles for field testing in Africa.

In and Out of Africa

John's supervisor had made a recent trip to Africa and other countries where exciting opportunities were opening for JAARS to be of service to our translation teams. He recommended that John travel to Africa to begin working out some details. John made flight arrangements, got shots, requested visas, and communicated with those serving in Africa. He purchased a 30-day ticket to conserve costs.

On February 5 John departed the Charlotte Airport with Ray Berry, a JAARS Board member. From Nairobi, Kenya, they boarded our JAARS DC-3 for a cargo and supply flight nearly all the way across central Africa.

They arrived in Bunia, Zaire, to a situation with bombings and killings between two tribal groups. They learned of the tense situations that translators and literacy teams worked in. After delays with customs, the DC-3 departed for Isiro, Zaire, where they unloaded much of the cargo, saw the vehicle maintenance shop funded by ATS, and visited the translators' location.

Next stop was Zemio in the Central Africa Republic to visit an isolated Africa Inland Mission station. They visited other mission stations enroute to the capitol Bangui, where for three days they helped set up communication facilities. When the DC-3, along with Ray, started their reverse trip back, John instead flew to Brazzaville, Congo. There he discussed ground transportation needs with the director and made plans to send a Gazelle vehicle for testing. On Sunday he worshiped with the translation family in a local church and learned of their struggles to reach the Mbochi people with God's Word.

John then flew through Douala, Cameroon, to the capitol, Yaoundé. Paul Haken, a friend from pre-Wycliffe days in Harrisburg, PA, met him. For several days, John conferred with various Branch leaders about their transportation needs. He enjoyed a visit with my cousin and her husband, Heidi and Pat Rosendall, who were attending the Africa Orientation Program in preparation for doing Bible translation in Nigeria.

Flying back to Nairobi, Kenya, John conversed with translators there. Then in Addis Ababa, Ethiopia, he visited with the director. After that he went down-country in a four-wheel-drive vehicle with a newly assigned translator to an area where he would work in the future. They enjoyed checking the capabilities of the vehicle.

He finished up in Nairobi, meeting with our Africa Area Group leaders and those from Sudan Branch and East Africa Group. Finally, he headed back home.

John had observed many similarities between South America and Africa, but also profound differences in the way the people lived and functioned. A big challenge was ahead of him to help with transportation in such a vast, diverse area.

His observations burdened him more than ever for the needs of our colleagues in Africa: deteriorating infrastructure in several countries, some on the edge of anarchy, isolated teams, and barely passable roads. He had seen firsthand the necessity for dependable ground transportation.

The JAARS Team

Back at the JAARS Center, John enthusiastically set out to help meet the transportation needs of our colleagues serving in Africa.

Meanwhile, in May the JAARS Center hosted Wycliffe's Triennial Conference, with 390+ guests, delegates, and observers from all countries where Wycliffe worked and "sending countries" from which our members came. The JAARS staff each did their part to help make the event successful. John oversaw several committees covering transportation, housing, and registration. Much business was conducted informally over meals or in passing, as colleagues were able to talk face-to-face with co-workers they only saw on rare occasions. Two delegates from Congo arranged for a container shipment for the first Gazelle and calculated how many mattresses and other items they could also fit in the container.

During this time, I worked again in the JAARS Print Shop. At that time, the printing press was located in the end of the Maintenance Quonset building, while the printing office was housed in a mobile trailer down the road. There we worked on computer typesetting, artwork, selling stationery, receiving/delivering orders, and running copies on the duplex copier. I learned some new procedures and a new graphics program, Corel Draw. I also enjoyed using the Ventura Publisher program again. I prepared a flyer for John with information about the Gazelle vehicle program. Our shop saved about 50% on the JAARS printing costs.

The print shop staff, like many departments at the JAARS Center, was in constant transition as personnel came from and to field assignments. Our print shop manager and one of the pressmen left for Colombia. Our office manager returned to the Philippines. With responsibilities falling on me, it was a stressful time, working too many hours and worrying too much. I tried to give my anxieties to the Lord, and He helped me relax. John didn't want me to be so tied up with my work that I couldn't help him, or to be so tired when I came home. As others were able to handle more, we split up responsibilities, and I tried to keep regular hours. *(Months later we encouraged Steve Kaetterhenry, back from assignment in Australia, to manage the Print Shop.)*

The ATS Program

In July, John completed the financial paperwork at the bank to purchase a new Toyota Land Cruiser for a family in Cameroon. As the U.S. dollar had devalued against the yen, the cost was $30,000 to cover the vehicle and shipping! With fewer contributions, ATS didn't have enough on hand to cover this expense. John reluctantly charged $30,000 to the translator's account. With nine additional approved requests to order vehicles, of which ATS had agreed to pay 50% of total cost, John was concerned. We asked for prayer for God's provision through interested people, and wisdom for John to make the needs and opportunities known.

The first Gazelle model to be field tested was completed in California, so John flew out to drive it to Waxhaw. While in California, he spoke about the Gazelle Program in some churches to familiarize local people there about the project. He also helped with final details on the Gazelle before he began his trip across the U.S. He tested the vehicle's endurance by driving up to 16 hours a day. I was glad I wasn't along on that trip! But he safely arrived home, though exhausted.

The model needed a few more details done at JAARS to make sure it was in good shape. They even tested out the winch operation in a nearby pond. Then our shipping department packed it in a container, along with mattresses and other items, for sending it to Congo. This vehicle was free to those testing it. They were excited to have the vehicle and eager for its arrival.

The second Gazelle for field testing was not yet underway. John was eager to get the testing done. Field personnel were beginning to request Gazelles, even before the field testing was completed. John had lined up groups of men in several U.S. locations who were excited to be volunteer Gazelle assembly teams if the project got the go-ahead.

August found John in Ona, West Virginia, helping to prepare for a Wings 'N Wheels weekend promoted by local Christians there. The following weekend he helped at a Mini Air Show and banquet in Kidron, Ohio. Proceeds from both events went to support the work of JAARS, including ATS.

In September I accompanied John in the Gazelle demonstrator vehicle to display it at a MATA (Missions at the Airport) in Woodbury, PA, held at the private airstrip of our good friends, Ed and Lois Sell. A local team worked hard to make it a successful event. Proceeds were designated to purchase a vehicle for a translator in Ethiopia. John and I went a week ahead of time to help them get ready. We stayed in a pop-up camper borrowed from my sister and family. During that week we also visited and spoke in my home church in Bellwood, a supporting church in Tipton, and two other local churches.

Damp, cool weather lowered Saturday attendance at the MATA, but Sunday afternoon the crowds came. The JAARS Cessna, Helio Courier, and helicopter were busy giving rides. JAARS staff had displays showing computer work, construction and maintenance work, JAARS books, shirts, and more. People viewed Wycliffe videos, enjoyed concessions, a sausage/pancake breakfast, and a chicken barbeque supper. Many found bargains at a yard sale, while local music groups entertained the visitors. A local man set up a ham radio so people could talk to field missionaries. John displayed the Gazelle vehicle. (*This experience prepared us for something we would do some years later.*)

After the MATA we returned the camper and found my mother in the hospital. We delayed a few days to be with her, then drove back to Waxhaw. Mom's diagnosis was Hodgkin's lymphoma. John suggested I return to PA to help with Mom's care, and my Print Shop supervisor also gave me permission.

We felt it was God's timing for us to be in the U.S. now so we could be available to family. Mom had been living with my sister and family for ten years, a great blessing. As my sister and her husband both worked long hours and rotating shifts, I was glad to give them a break during a time when Mom needed extra attention, and while they went on a long-planned-for 25th anniversary trip. Also, I drove Mom to medical visits and chemotherapy treatments. Mom was one of those sweet people that nothing bad should ever happen to, but she faced a long treatment.

On December 12, John flew to California to help finish the next Gazelle. He worked long hours for a week with Gino, then started his trip on the 18th to drive it to JAARS. Our plan had been to travel to PA on the 22nd for Christmas. So, John drove long hours each day, staying overnight with friends along the way. He stopped for a demonstration visit with a translator interested in getting a Gazelle, and even for supper with his sister, Joette, in Alabama. He arrived home at noon the 22nd, more tired than he realized. A beautiful snowstorm that night didn't deter us from leaving the next morning for PA, just one day behind schedule.

We enjoyed Christmas with my mother, sister, and family. Mom was tolerating the treatment, for which we were thankful. After Christmas, John drove the demonstrator Gazelle on snowy roads to Corning, NY, to show it to a group of volunteer men who were eager to do Gazelle build-ups. Then he headed back to NC. Passing through Virginia, John decided to stop at an airport where a former JAARS man now worked, and where a JAARS board member had his business. It was a providential visit since that man had missed the last two board meetings and didn't know much about the Gazelle. He thought it was a good project.

On January 5, 1994, John made a presentation to JAARS administrators requesting that the Gazelle project move from research and development to production. They agreed unanimously, and a FAX was sent to the members of the JAARS Board for their approval. John was excited when their approval came on the 13th. In God's timing, our friends George and Kathy Ellison from Peru Branch, could help John during their year's furlough. George especially understood diesels and vehicles in general, so could help get the second Gazelle ready to send to Congo for field testing, then help with others to follow. Kathy, who handled group finances in Lima, set up ATS accounting procedures for the build-up program.

Delayed by Civil Unrest

The long FAX from Congo was business-like, yet carried a sense of foreboding. It told of increased civil unrest, of a missionary family crouched in a hallway during nearby gunfire, of plans to move some personnel out of harm's way. And it said, *"We feel it is unwise to try transporting the vehicle at this time, so have put it in storage. Please pray that it won't be stolen or damaged. . . . And please hold off on shipping the second one."*

John was concerned for our people there, and for the future of the Gazelle program. That first field-test Gazelle had been shipped to Congo in September '93. The shipping company placed it on a different ship than listed, so personnel in Congo couldn't find it at the dock. Finally, the other ship was located, and the Gazelle unloaded. It was to be sent by train to the Capitol city, Brazzaville, then shipped by barge up-country to the remote northwest corner of Congo to be used by the Phillips in their translation work there. Feedback from using that Gazelle (and the second one) was to be received before proceeding with the program. Would this unrest mean additional delays to meet urgent transportation needs of other personnel in Africa?

We wondered if the hard work, and time already spent would be in vain. Maybe God had other plans. Yet John had been burdened, assigned the task, and had seen the Lord work in so many ways to get to this stage. Funds to subsidize new vehicle purchases were coming in very slowly, so it seemed that a low-cost alternative would be better use of the Lord's money.

Praying for wisdom, John tried another route. He asked permission to prepare other requested Gazelles, reasoning that its design, after research on five previous prototypes, was basically a refurbished Toyota truck—already a proven vehicle commercially. He could incorporate feedback from the field as it became available. For several weeks, we awaited the decision of the JAARS administration and Board. We were encouraged when the go-ahead was unanimous.

John excitedly began the next steps: bidding on used Toyota 4x4 trucks, gathering the parts and supplies for modifications, matching lay work teams with the projects, transporting items to work locations, and finding a garage or work area in Waxhaw for final wring-out before shipping.

Then word came from Congo that unrest had lessened, and personnel were returning to their locations. With the first test Gazelle air freighted to Brazzaville, we had the go-ahead to ship the second one, which was ready and waiting at Waxhaw. All the labor was worthwhile. The Gazelle program moved forward. We trusted God for continued wisdom to help translators who sacrificed personal comfort to bring God's Word to people in their own language.

Moving into Production

In May John flew once again to California, and met co-worker George Ellison there (who flew in from Minnesota). Gino had purchased two good used Toyota 4x4s at an auto auction. John and George helped Gino get some camper tops, racks, bumpers, and other parts. They got the emission controls checked and passed a safety inspection. Then, George drove one vehicle and John the other, heading back across the country. They used two-meter radios to communicate along the way, which was helpful if they got sleepy. They dropped off one vehicle in Spartanburg, SC, at Robert Houghton's alignment shop for a volunteer crew to do the conversion according to directions. Following that, helpers at Waxhaw would overhaul the engine, and check the brakes and suspension. That Gazelle

At Robert Houghton's shop

would be shipped to Guyana, South America (not in the Africa plan, but needed and approved).

It became clear to John that a shop with storage space was needed to finalize details on the Gazelles at the JAARS Center. Vehicles in various stages were parked around our house, with parts and supplies accumulating in our garage.

George Ellison in the trucking shop

They had been able to use space in the maintenance shop of the trucking department as available, but a more stable situation was needed. John looked for space in other shops on the Center, but only found temporary options. He looked for garage-type buildings in the area, even the possibility of remodeling an old firehouse presently used for storage. However, to bring it up to new building codes would cost almost as much as a new building.

The answer came when a Christian businessman offered to donate a 40x40 foot steel structure and two other businessmen offered to contribute financially. The JAARS Committee for Center Development assigned a location, and the JAARS Board voted their approval at their May session. John just needed to come up with funds for the cement pad, electrical, plumbing, and shop supplies. John shared about the program needs, exhibiting the demo Gazelle during various JAARS events and other locations, at Missions Conferences, and every chance he got.

On the suggestion of his good friend, Wayne Huyett, John contacted Wayne's brother Martin Huyett, the Wycliffe Associates Director. Then WA kindly sent out a fund-raising letter to help bring in funds for subsidizing purchase of *new* vehicles. As a result, Wycliffe Associates contributed a large amount! With this and other funds from Missions-at-the-Airport programs, ATS was able to help purchase and ship three *new* Toyotas for workers in Ethiopia, Tanzania, and Cameroon.

In September, the donated steel shell for the shop arrived by JAARS truck all the way from Sun Steel in Washington State. JAARS Construction and Maintenance (CAM) personnel, along with volunteers, installed a cement slab and assembled the steel frame. Al Schoonover, from John's home area, organized a work crew to put on the roof, most of the siding, and insulation. My Uncle Ralph came to make worktables, and a rolling tool cabinet. (He brought along my mother for a visit as well, since she had finished chemotherapy and felt better.)

The shop was almost ready by Thanksgiving '94. The inspector required final details to meet strict county codes. With JAARS friends in Kidron, OH, donating equipment, and Haney Reels of NY donating electrical and air reels, the project moved to completion. On December 20 it was dedicated publicly with a ribbon cutting ceremony and tours including coffee and donuts. Then, on  December 30, the final inspection was granted. After the light company connected electricity a few days later, equipment was installed, and the much-needed facility became a beehive of kingdom activity.

Two semi-retired men worked regularly—Ernie Rich on engine overhaul and Bob Murphey on repairs and final preparations. Other semi-retired colleagues and volunteers helped as able. Friends Craig Waldo and John Ingalls from NY came to make a cargo rack.

In the corner office, John worked to fill Gazelle orders in various stages, communicated with people on the field via e-mail and FAX, ordered and delivered parts. He networked to share resources of the Christian community. He needed a secretary and wished I could help him, but I was committed at the Print Shop and overwhelmed there myself. I was able to prepare an ATS newsletter, create a new brochure describing the program, and make a Guest Book to record volunteers. I also sorted and put photos in a notebook to showcase the various projects. Sometimes I helped in the evenings with his correspondence. He dictated as I typed. When needed, John also worked on vehicles.

The Schoonover crew from the Corning, NY, area also took on a vehicle modification project, adapting a Toyota for use in Kenya. They worked in a designated space in the camping facility owned by Dennis Smith, to rebuild the front end, complete the rear brakes, modify the cab, and do other specified tasks.

After delays transferring titles, two co-workers volunteered to drive two more Toyotas to Waxhaw from California. Meanwhile, the Waxhaw shop crew worked on a vehicle for Uganda, making minor changes in the cargo rack and camper installation.

The next vehicle was then ready to be delivered to a lay work team in State Line, PA, where friends Dale Hostetter, Pat Byers, and crew were eager to prepare a Gazelle for Burkina Faso.

John had orders for two more Gazelles. The program was in full gear, even as his staff diminished with the Ellisons returning to Peru.

Pat Byers and Dale Hostetter with vehicle for State Line crew

Other JAARS Departments helped with publicity. The November-December 1994 issue of the JAARS *Beyond* publication featured the Africa Transportation Service with a colorful description of the work. The Media Department prepared a six-minute video. It graphically showed the need for durable land transportation for translators in Africa and how ATS was working to meet that need.

Reports came regarding the two test Gazelle vehicles in Congo. Each told how the Gazelle had responded well to transportation challenges they faced. They also gave helpful suggestions which were being incorporated in future vehicles.

Excerpts from translator Gary Dawson's report:

> We recently made several trips to and from Ngo, our village allocation. The trip is about 150 miles and takes around 5-1/2 hours. The road condition has recently deteriorated in places because of the rainy season. There was a fair amount of mud and, of course, the usual craters (not just potholes). There were numerous times when 4-wheel drive was essential to get us through those difficult places. There was only one time when we got totally bogged down in mud . . . another large truck arrived, and it pulled us out after we had attached our winch to the back of their truck (no trees on the savannah) . . . .
>
> We have had numerous opportunities to carry heavy loads in the back of the Gazelle. During the months of September and October we built a water cistern at our house in Ngo. This is a necessity for us since wells cannot be dug in this area (because the water table is too low). Once I transported 12 bags of cement (about 1200 pounds) from Brazzaville to Ngo. I've also carried numerous loads of sand about 30 miles. I would guess that the sand weighed over 1000 pounds. I should also mention that the roof rack has been great for transporting long planks and iron rods. In everything the Gazelle has had no problem handling the extra weight.

When the crew in NY finished their vehicle in January 1995, John combined a trip to PA and NY. Although there was ice and rain traveling north, he drove one Toyota to the work crew in PA and was picked up there by John Ingalls, a friend from Corning, who drove him to NY. There, John's home church, North Baptist, had a dedication for the Gazelle adapted by the Corning area crew, with a special meal which included a cake decorated with a design of a Gazelle. John then drove that finished vehicle back to the JAARS Center. And so, the activity continued with projects in various stages.

John was doing his best to address needs in Africa, where many families were just beginning their Bible translation projects and were allocating in areas only accessible in four-wheel drive vehicles. We had seen the Lord work in many ways to help us address this need, and we were trusting Him for the resources to accomplish the task as He directed.

Meanwhile

During that time, we were praying for our JAARS friend, Ray Rising, kidnapped in Colombia where he did radio/communications work. He spoke Spanish well and enjoyed interacting with the local town's people, about four miles from their Lomalinda Center. They found his motorcycle at the back entrance to the Center. Possibly he had been abducted by the leftist Revolutionary Armed Forces of Colombia who took two New Tribes missionaries in January. That group had made threats against American citizens there. We waited for possible word from the kidnappers.

(Over many months hundreds of people prayed for Ray. We heard rumors he was alive. We all rejoiced when we received official word that on June 17, 1996, he was free after a two-year captivity!)

Earlier we had learned of the death of Rómulo Sauñe, (Peruvian husband of a daughter of Wycliffe friends). He had been killed by Sendero Luminoso (Shining Path) terrorists in Peru, along with his brother, a nephew, a cousin, and ten others, on the road 12 miles outside Ayacucho, Peru. Their vehicle had been suddenly stopped at a roadblock by a band of some 100 subversive forces. Rómulo, an outstanding Christian leader in Peru, was co-translator of the entire Ayacucho Quechua Bible. His grandfather had been killed by the same group a couple years earlier. Rómulo knew his work was dangerous and had moved his wife and their three children to the U.S. The Lord had protected Rómulo in previous dangers but allowed him to be called home at that time. The 5,000 who observed the testimony and songs of 2,500 believers who marched in the funeral procession, had never seen anything like it.

Many Involved

During 1995, the Africa Transportation Services program grew and adapted. John worked hard to get Gazelle production running smoothly.

Skilled volunteer work crews in various locations were doing a big part of the checking and the reconditioning. They considered it a privilege that from their home areas they could help meet transportation needs for translators on the front lines, making God's Word available in remote parts of the world. They could serve God with their talents as they worked together once or more weekly. Some shared their testimonies with curious on-lookers about how God had worked in their lives.

Several volunteers ferried Toyota trucks from California—always an adventure, and sometimes with a little competition to see who could arrive in the shortest time. John had a good vehicle source in California, and with no salt damage, so the effort was worthwhile. They did, however, find a couple workable vehicles nearby.

Terry Bacon with Alabama crew

As each succeeding Gazelle was modified for field use, they found various components that needed special attention. Perhaps a compressor in one, the engine in another, or maybe the pistons. Then John realized that it would be best to check all the components on each of the vehicles to ensure reliable working order on the field. Additional options proved very helpful, such as a limited-slip differential, 3-inch suspension lift, special shock absorbers, etc. But these safety features increased time and cost. John's concern was how to speed up the process and still have a reliable vehicle.

Trevie Henry in Taccoa, GA, made and donated heavy duty bumpers.

The ATS shop bustled with activity with the increased preparation needed. Diesel engines were overhauled, luggage racks assembled, custom-made auxiliary fuel tanks installed, as well as air-conditioning, heavy duty bumpers, suspension lifts, winches, and other items as requested. With ten orders in progress at various stages, John tried to keep the work flowing well with available parts, some of which came from Japan.

Full-time staff for the shop was in short supply, so John was very thankful for the great help from semi-retired JAARS members as well as volunteer short term helpers who worked as available: George Woodward, David Dirks, Paul Bartholomew, Don Vander Ploeg, Paul Schwenker, Dave Immel, Roger Dodson, Bob Hyland, and others. At times the shop was full and overflowing and the guys wished it was larger. The challenge was the very transitional nature of the staff. Of course, every vehicle was needed ASAP, so the pressure was on.

Too Many Challenges?

By March of 1996 problems were mounting. "How is my vehicle coming?" was a question John dreaded to read in his email correspondence from Africa. Often they were behind in completing the work in the anticipated time. Delays came in surprising ways: like a worn cylinder block discovered while overhauling a diesel engine, requiring it to be bored out to install larger pistons and rings; a bad air conditioning circuit board giving intermittent signals defying diagnosis; or when one more diesel part needed to be ordered.

International shipping delays were beyond their control, like when cargo was transferred to a different ship in Brussels, and it took a while to find the other ship. Another time a fire on ship caused a delay for insurance claims. Often there was a wait to release a vehicle from customs. In one case, a waiting recipient walked six kilometers daily to his work location carrying what he needed with him. Another rented a vehicle for $1.00 a kilometer while awaiting his Gazelle.

Costs continued to increase. More workspace was needed to work on several vehicles at a time, and some key workers were no longer available. John wondered if he should not accept new requests for Gazelles until they could catch up. He realized that present resources offered little hope for change to meet deadlines.

Meanwhile, as part of an effort at the JAARS Center to evaluate use of their resources, they planned to do a study of each JAARS Department. John requested, because of his frustrations, that ATS be the first to receive this study, hoping to get some good advice. (That may not have been the best thing to do.) As a result, the JAARS Administration concluded that while the Gazelle program addressed a vital need, the costs were too high. They requested that the current Gazelle projects be completed, but not to take any more orders. This was not the conclusion we wished to hear; we had hoped they would have made an all-out effort to help with needed resources. However, we could understand their decision. We needed to trust God's sovereignty working through their conclusion. The JAARS Board concurred with the verdict at their next session.

Other aspects of the ATS program would continue, such as raising funds to help purchase new vehicles for priority projects, acting as purchase agent with the Japan source, technical advice, etc. We asked for the Lord's wisdom if John should continue with this, or if it could be handled by other JAARS Departments—such as Purchasing & Shipping, and Public Affairs for the fund raising. There were probably other aviation needs where John could serve. Ten Gazelles were basically completed, with four more in progress.

By early September the last Gazelle was completed. All but one had been shipped. That made a total of 14 Gazelle projects, which we trusted would increase the efficiency of all the recipients.

We were very grateful to all who had helped with prayers, gifts, and by volunteering. We appreciated the lay work crews who enthusiastically gave of their time and skills, and our gifted engineer in CA, Gino DiBartholomeo, whose vision and selfless service "in his spare time" made so much of the program possible. We loved the JAARS volunteers and staff who did excellent work in the shop.

Arrangements were made to pass along the purchase program for new vehicles, and someone to respond to Gazelle questions from the field. John had been asked to do a special aircraft refurbishment project in Zaire.

I was disappointed to see the program close after all that had been developed. In any case, many vehicles were provided during a time of special need. We sent a final report and thank-you to those involved, including a chart showing all the recipients of vehicles from the program.

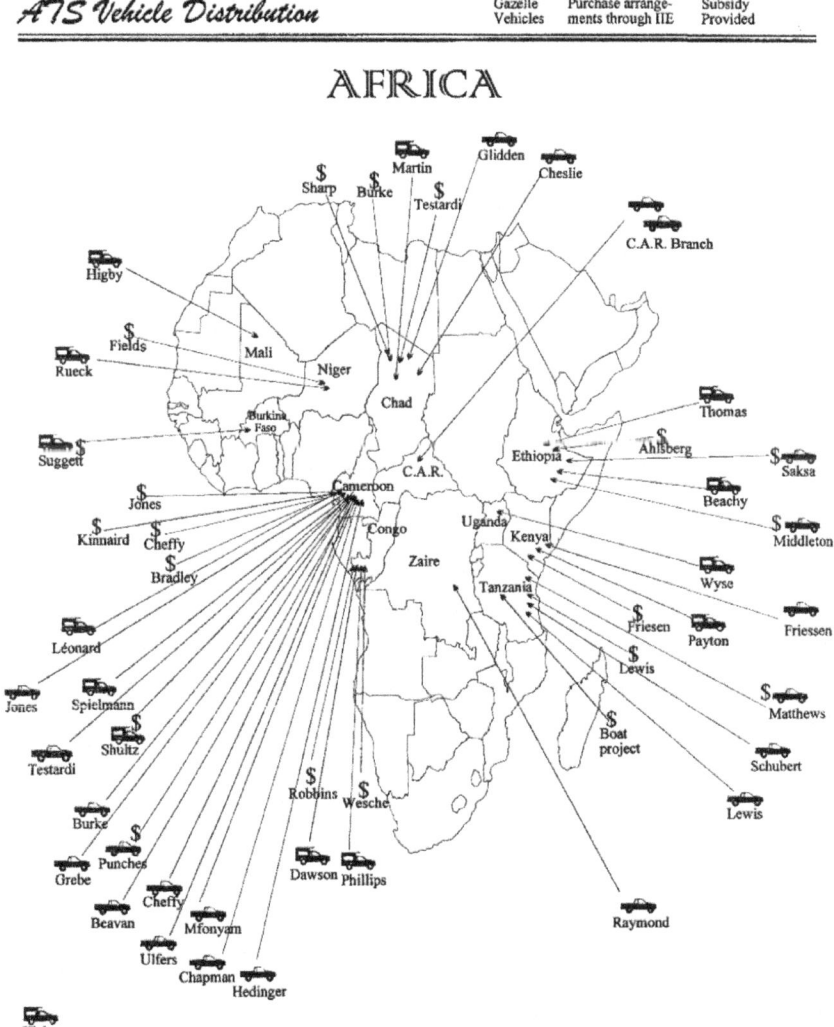

Chapter 10
Africa (1996-2000)
The Huge Continent

―――――――――――――――――――✈

Go Where?

"You go ahead to Africa on the aircraft rebuild project," I told John. "I'll be here when you get back."

Since the project was expected to take only a couple months, I didn't really want to go to Africa. I was now comfortably used to living in the United States again and working at the JAARS printshop. In the back of my mind, I hoped this wouldn't lead to future service in Africa.

"No, I want you to come with me," John said, promising that we'd take time for an African Safari.

On October 3, 1996, we flew from Charlotte, NC, straight to London, then on to Nairobi, Kenya. Our plan was to spend one week in Nairobi to obtain our Zairian visas, get acclimated, and meet the Eastern Zaire Group (EZG) staff working at the Nairobi EZG office. Then we would fly out to Nyankunde, Zaire, where there was a hospital and where MAF (Mission Aviation Fellowship) had a flight program that served their workers in Zaire. JAARS would be augmenting their program with a pilot (Steve Bevelhymer) and the Cessna 206 airplane which John would refurbish. That plane then would be designated the primary server of the SIL translation teams. It was the first aviation partnership without secondment for JAARS, and a creative way to face the challenges of mission work in Africa.

For our week in Nairobi, we stayed in the guest house at the BTL (Bible Translation and Literacy of East Africa) Center in the Upper Hill area of the busy city. The Center contained a walled-in group of buildings constructed with large, semi-rectangular stones. There were offices, apartments, meeting rooms, and a group dining room where we ate. Our simply furnished room had twin beds with mosquito netting, and the bathroom was down the hall.

Most of the people in Nairobi spoke English in addition to one or more of five major tribal languages. Kenyan English emphasized each syllable, with some unique expressions. We would learn a little Swahili which was common. Professional African workers tended to dress more formally; many men wore suits and ties. At the BTL offices, women wore dresses. My wardrobe was mostly "jungle-style" for hot, humid weather. With Nairobi at 5,889 feet above sea level and a mild climate, we were short on appropriate clothing, and John didn't have a necktie.

That one week in Nairobi changed to many weeks, as the situation in Zaire was changing drastically. Nyankunde currently had an influx of people (and aircraft) due to evacuations from areas of unrest. Rebels had taken over the cities of Bukavu and Goma along Zaire's eastern border where Rwandan refugees had fled. About a million refugees were caught without food and water. With troops moving through various areas of the country, translation programs were disrupted. In God's providence two EZG translation teams in that area were already on furlough, and another team was on a two-year break from translation to do administrative work in the town of Bunia.

With the current unrest in Zaire, it seemed best to start working on the plane in Nairobi. John was grateful to AIM-AIR (Africa Inland Mission air service) who offered John space to work in their hangar at Wilson Airport—even to use some of their tools and equipment.

For our housing, we remembered that our former Bolivia Branch colleagues, Willis and Becky Ott, had an empty house in Nairobi while they were on a short furlough. They currently served with our Sudan Branch, but lived in Nairobi because of unrest in Sudan. We rented their two-story stone house in the local neighborhood. It was surrounded by a high stone wall and a locked gate, as was common. A Kenyan house-help lady lived in a small house in their backyard. A night guard came at dusk each evening to keep watch from a guard house (which looked like an old telephone booth) by the front gate. When the night was cool, he built a small charcoal fire to keep warm. I prepared chai and bread for him each evening, and he left at daybreak.

The neighborhood was a conglomeration of cultures—people from East India (men with turbans, women with long-flowing gowns and veils); tribal Africans in a variety of colorful dress; Muslims in long white tunics; and other Kenyans in a mixture of western attire. Just a few blocks away, a Muslim Mosque gave a call to prayer via loudspeakers several times a day. (The five-a.m. call was not our favorite.) When walking through the streets we alternately saw piles of garbage and lovely flowers. Jacaranda trees were in bloom with bright lavender blossoms.

We also had use of Ott's vehicle, which made it workable to live there. In Kenya we could drive using our U.S. drivers' licenses. Learning to drive on the left side of the road was a challenge, especially in and out of the three-lane round-abouts (traffic circles). Ott's had requested that we use their security bracket on the steering wheel when we left their car unattended. They gave us the code which unlocked the mechanism by rolling six little wheels with numbers to a certain position. The first time we drove to the grocery store was an adventure. John accidentally locked the bracket in an upside-down position. When we returned to the car to drive home, John had to crawl on his back under the steering wheel to see the numbers and unlock the device.

As the unrest in Zaire escalated, John worked on the airplane in Nairobi. Zairian troops were moving through various areas, and we were concerned they might commandeer planes, vehicles, whatever.

Pilot Steve Bevelhymer also stayed in Nairobi to help with the plane rebuild. John hired a young Kenyan auto mechanic to help three days a week. He began stripping paint. They "opened up" the plane, removed both wings and the interior, and checked components that needed to be repaired or replaced. John installed a larger window, while Steve repaired the cargo pod. Next on the list were service bulletins and updates as well as an annual inspection and a 1000-hour inspection.

Our East Africa Group also worked out of Nairobi and had offices at BTL. They provided a Desktop Publishing Office where items for SIL entities were prepared for press. Suddenly all the personnel working there had to leave for health or family needs. Also, the well-trained Kenyan worker resigned. So, I was asked to step in to finish half-done projects and handle some new ones.

Without overlap, it was a challenge to figure out what programs and procedures had been used. There were people of whom I could ask questions, but basically I was on my own. I relied on the Scripture preparation crash course I'd had in Peru. I prepared alphabet charts with pictures for Kazinza of Tanzania and Budu of Zaire, and an eight page Christmas booklet with Scripture for Ngiti of Zaire. I also formatted a Budu primer and a translation of the Epistles for the Komo language of Zaire. In between there were prayer letters to get ready and other small jobs. Later I prepared a booklet, *Africa Area Annual Literacy Report for 1996*, describing literacy projects and items printed in the various languages by SIL in all of Africa. I also completed the Daasanach Gospel of Mark for Kenya and Ethiopia.

Each morning John and I left the house together in Ott's vehicle. At the place where John turned to head to the airport, I hopped out and walked to the BTL office. I had to cross a very busy street with hundreds of others who were also walking to work. When there was a pause in the traffic, people would swarm across the road, stopping oncoming vehicles until the crowd was all on the other side. Then I took a shortcut on a path through an area where there were train tracks to cross, and up a hill to the BTL compound. In the late afternoon, the procedure was reversed. I had to be back at the corner before John came by. He would pause briefly for me to jump in to ride together the remaining eight blocks to the house. (And we did this before there were cell phones to coordinate our time!)

A colorful aspect of Nairobi was the vehicle of choice for many who traveled around the city. The matatu (ma-TAH-too) got you there quickly, sometimes using the sidewalk or creating an extra traffic lane. Most were decorated with colorful graphics, and many offered loud music. These privately owned mini-buses seated 20 to 24 passengers, but would let many more squeeze in anywhere along the route. The more passengers, the more fares. Aggressive drivers competed with other drivers. Each matatu had its name painted on the side or back, giving the vehicle its own personality. John and I kept a list of names. You can imagine the personalities associated with the names in the box.

Early Bird	Shameless
Equalizer	Promise
Enigma	Gift of God
Galaxy	Lord Cares
Undertaker	Upon the Rock
Oops	One Love
Peace Worrier	Moon Raker
Ginuwine	In Style
Cyber Bus	Blue Chip
Millennium Bug	Sunrise
Internet	Cool Baby
Diana	Swoosh
Lewinsky	Thuggish
Monika	Wings
Daisy	The Nairobian
Bugs Bunny	Sun Splash
Too Frank	Electric Avenue
Delirious	Smasher
Be Happy	Stylish
New York Gangsters	Touch of Class
Rebirth of Sleek	Gas Explosion
Road Striker	Torpedo

The last week of October, EZG personnel gathered near Nairobi, Kenya for their annual conference. They invited us to join in the sessions. We hadn't planned to do that since the plane project was almost finished, and we would be going home. But we changed our minds and joined the group at a Baptist Conference Center, Brackenhurst, about an hour west of Nairobi and 1,000 feet higher. We appreciated learning more about the work in Zaire, and those who served there.

"Strategic Planning on the Entity Level" (SPEL) was a major agenda item. A SPEL document which stated the goals, rationale, strategies, core values and core tasks was arrived at by means of discussion groups reporting to the body, and by committees organizing and refining the information. It was quite an exercise in group dynamics, resulting in an unanimously approved plan. The mission statement of the document stated: *"In dependence on God, the mission of SIL-EZG is to partner with the Zairean church and others to provide all peoples of eastern Zaire with effective access to God's Word for their personal and corporate transformation."* There was a strong sense of the need to have Zairians take more responsibility in the programs to multiply their efforts. We were impressed with our colleagues there who were talented, dedicated people, with mature Christian faith.

Do What?

Representatives from Wycliffe Associates (WA) also attended the Conference—Martin and Sharon Huyett and another couple. They explained that the Lord was burdening WA leadership to connect a specific field entity with a geographical segment of WA constituents to "come alongside" with detailed prayer, generous support, and volunteers for work projects. A pilot partnership with Eastern Zaire Group would offer close involvement over a period of time to see Bible translation move forward.

A liaison person was needed to facilitate the projects and communicate closely with WA. Surprise! John was asked to consider that position after completing the Cessna project. It would mean being stationed in Nairobi, organizing work groups, and traveling into Zaire and to the U.S. as needed. I knew it! It seemed inevitable that we would end up in Africa. But we would pray about it and check with appropriate people about accepting that assignment. We had appreciated the involvement of Wycliffe Associates projects in Bolivia and Peru and knew many of the WA staff, so it did seem like a natural fit.

Unfortunately, during that Conference time, unrest escalated in Zaire. At the end of the conference, it was deemed unsafe for EZG translators and literacy staff to return to their places of work in Zaire. Some had come in with only suitcases for a couple weeks' stay. What to do now!?! Places to live and work in Nairobi had to be found.

We also needed to find new housing. When the Otts returned from their furlough, the hostess from SIL Sudan Branch found a small flat for us, very near the EZG office and the BTL office where I was working. She also loaned us basic necessities.

The Cessna project was moving forward well. John had added a more experienced Kenyan man to the work team, Daniel Kangethe. He had an A&P (Aircraft and Power Plant) license and helped the other man move along more energetically. After the interior was reinstalled and the cargo pod reattached, it was time to paint. To spray the wings, they strung them on ropes between two shipping containers with a tarp overhead to protect from the weather.

They gave the plane a shiny new coat of white paint with red trim to match the MAF fleet. The Cessna was completed in February. At a dedication ceremony in March, EZG members gathered to commit the plane's service to the Lord's honor. Although the unrest in Zaire prohibited its use there at that time, it was ready for service.

By that time John had agreed to take the liaison responsibility with Wycliffe Associates. We would be assigned to the Eastern Zaire Group, but seconded to WA. For the EZG responsibilities, John would do Resource Development. That included coordination of funding to support the language projects, recruitment to address the huge translation needs, the aviation program, and helping to establish supply and communication lines for people as they returned to a country where the infrastructure had been devastated by war.

We needed to head home first and arrange for a longer stay in Kenya. But we were asked to delay our departure for an additional month in Nairobi to help a WA work crew renovate a new office space on the fourth floor of an Africa Airlines building on the city's outskirts. Our Sudan Branch staff had offices on the first floor. Currently the EZG offices used one half of a duplex house, lacking adequate space to serve the now greatly expanded staff in Nairobi.

In February we heard that my mother had complications after radiation therapy for recurrence of Hodgkin's Disease at the same time as my sister was scheduled for surgery. I felt the need to help. John found someone traveling in two days from Nairobi to Charlotte, NC, the same route as our tickets. With room on that flight, John changed my ticket date, and on the 13th I was on my way with a traveling companion.

After I left, John prepared to host a five-man well-qualified WA work crew for the office renovation. WA provided John with a van for transportation, and John moved to a two-bedroom flat on the 4th floor of an apartment complex to house them. He bought a used stove and beds, borrowed a refrigerator and some other furniture and linens, set up a water filter and welcomed the men. Various EZG people invited them for breakfast or supper, and John arranged for lunches at the project site. During this time, unfortunately, the electricity was off in part of the city from about 1:00 to 5:00 p.m. daily, due to drought in Kenya affecting hydroelectric power. Then a broken water pipe near their flat meant no water on the 4th floor! They had to be invited out for showers and carry in water for drinking and laundry. Even so, they had a great time and did an excellent and efficient job preparing the offices for use.

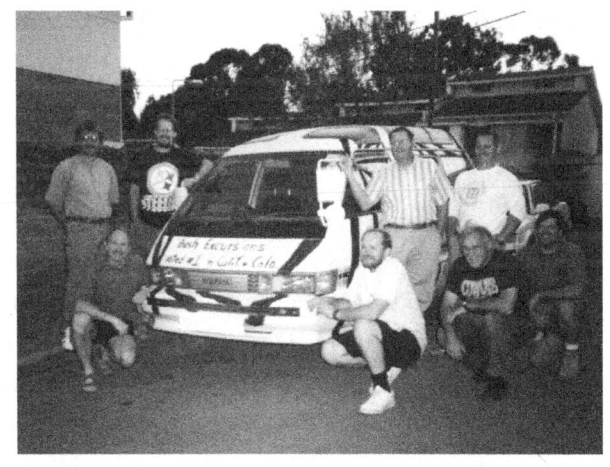

Near the end of their time John took them to the Nairobi Game Park on the edge of the city where they saw some of the African wildlife. Later, as a joke, they distracted John while they painted zebra stripes (washable) on the van to look like a tourist safari vehicle.

The completed office space had a passageway down the center, with offices along either side and work cubicles on the hall side of the offices—room for everybody. There was a reception area and mail room near the entrance and a meeting room with large tables. From windows on the south side, you could see the Nairobi Game Park in the far distance.

The staff was pleased to move into the new offices, as it appeared that they would be in Nairobi for quite a while. Rebels held all the areas where our people worked in Zaire. The military threatened a counter-offensive to recover the entire occupied zone—about one-third of the country. Retreating Zairian soldiers looted and destroyed some areas through which they passed. Foreign mercenaries arrived to assist the military.

The boarding school run by AIM at Rethy, where missionary kids studied, was ransacked and damaged. News came regarding damages to places where our people had been working. The MAF Center at Nyankunde had been evacuated in December. If our plane had been there as planned, we would have had to leave it in pieces, which may have been damaged when the Center was looted.

— The EZG team tried to assess how God was working in the situation and how they could help. They needed new ways to continue translations. Their desire to involve local people more directly was now a necessity. Except that some of the teams had fled to the bush for safety.

With the office renovation completed, John left Nairobi a month after I had gone. He flew to Charlotte, where he got some See-America tickets to travel to various places, including planning meetings in Dallas and the WA offices in Orange, CA, to work out details for his liaison job. I stayed on to help my mother.

In April we had another new experience. We traveled with a Wycliffe Associates banquet team on a tour of seven large cities in Kansas and Missouri. This area was selected to partner with the Eastern Zaire Group. These mega-banquets each had around 500 in attendance. We enjoyed working with the WA Area Directors, Rock and Ardis Leier. Doug and Beth Wright were flown in from Kenya to share heart-stirring stories about their translation project in war-torn Zaire. As John and I helped prepare for each banquet, we learned of all that was involved in set-up and tear-down, placing information on tables, name tags, talking with concerned people, etc. Through those meetings 900 new prayer partners were added, 128 signed up for volunteer trips, and many pledged ongoing financial support for translation projects in Zaire.

Meanwhile back in Africa, over the weekend of May 17-18, Zaire's capital Kinshasa was taken with little bloodshed by Laurent Kabila's ADFL troops (Alliance of Democratic Forces for the Liberation of Congo-Zaire). Mobutu Sese Seko stepped aside as president and departed the country.

Mr. Kabila declared himself the new head of state, changed the country's name back to the "Democratic Republic of the Congo" (DRC), set up a transitional government, and promised to form a constituent assembly in 60 days with a mandate to draft a provisional constitution for a period preceding the elections. The civil war had lasted about seven months. We hoped that Kabila's victory meant a great change for the better for the country. Thus far, our colleagues there had seen no indication that a Kabila-led government would be against the kind of translation and language development work SIL had been involved in since 1980. The Eastern Zaire group was now called the Eastern Congo Group (ECG).

Near the end of the war, several ECG staff had traveled to Arua, Uganda, meeting with Zairian co-workers who safely traveled there. Amazingly, these co-translators had been continuing to work on translation through their time of displacement from their homes, even while surviving in the bush. What dedication! The consultants found their translation work to be of very good quality. Also, church leadership was encouraging two-to-four-week trips into the project locations. The reworked Cessna 206 was currently leased short-term to MAF for air support to Medical Emergency Relief International. It was being used for relief flights from Goma, DRC, to help refugees.

Flexibility

Our airline tickets to return to Nairobi were dated July 8th. We worked through our to-do list in preparation. We had renters lined up to occupy our house in Waxhaw. We renewed my passport, and sent paperwork to Kenya to apply for work papers which we needed to have before our departure. We also needed to increase our monthly income to cover the higher cost of living in Nairobi. My mother, thankfully, had steadily gained strength, and even spent a month with us helping pack our things away.

Then, we received word from colleagues in Kenya that our work papers would probably not arrive until mid-August. We needed to revamp our schedule. The next date British Airways could schedule us was August 31. Our renters were scheduled to come, so what should we do? We remembered that the ECG administration had suggested I officially train for Scripture preparation, but we hadn't worked it into our schedule. We contacted the International Publications Department at our Linguistic

Center in Dallas asking if they could possibly train me during our limited time frame. Their regular training course took three months. Since I already knew the Ventura Publisher program they used, they kindly offered me to join another gal who was updating her training during that time—a special course just for the two of us.

Darlene Weidman was scheduled to start her training on July 7 before returning to do Scripture preparation in Ghana. We planned to head to Dallas July 5. God provided housing through three former Peru Branch colleagues living there. Just as those plans were in place, we received an email from ECG, "Yippee, your work papers have been granted."

But ECG said we should stay with the August 31 return date. The training for me went well, even though I had a hard time keeping up with Darlene. I learned how to use many tools for processing Scripture for printing, including complicated procedures for special characters, performing checks on the text, and preparing a big consistent changes table to format the text. If I didn't remember it all, I had good resource materials and knew who to e-mail for help.

During that time John took a self-study program in management training. He used a study cubicle in their air-conditioned library. (Dallas temperatures reached 100+ degrees for 15 consecutive days.) John was also able to pull together funding to purchase desktop publishing equipment for our Eastern Congo Group. That included a computer, monitor, printer/scanner, and software, received in time for us to take it all with us.

Enroute to Africa, in the London airport, there was an eerie silence. Everyone seemed to be in a state of shock and grief, having heard the news that Princess Diana had died.

Back in Nairobi, we needed to find housing with guest rooms for work crews. On a whim, returning from church, we stopped at a newly built apartment complex. It looked like they were showing some people around. They showed us an available flat on the third floor (fourth level), 63 steps, no elevator. The first level housed offices, laundry, and parking. A security wall surrounded the buildings, with a guard to open the gate when we honked. The flat was very nice, and we received an introductory offer for being among the first residents. They also partially exempted us from paying three months' rent in advance with a three-month deposit, which we learned was standard procedure. We had the honor to be the first people to move into the Nina Apartments. WA helped with some setup expenses and as funds were available, we furnished it.

After we moved in, the other apartments filled up. When John greeted the couple in the apartment across the stairwell from us, the lady asked, "Are you Christians?" Anita and Didier had met in the U.S., although she was from Tanzania and he from France. She worked to secure funds for a wildlife foundation, while he was a French chef who worked for an embassy. We became good friends. Didier blessed us with delicious baked treats for special occasions. *(We celebrated the birth of their first baby and kept in touch after they moved to another apartment. Later, they visited us in the U.S. with their two boys.)*

New ECG colleagues, Chuck and Diane DeVries, moved into the flat above us. They also became good friends. For my first six months in Nairobi, I did not venture to drive. John had to take me for groceries. One day Diane said, "Elsie, I don't think God brought us to Nairobi to live fearful of going out to do things." So, she and I took turns driving, praying for safety before leaving to do shopping or whatever. We braved many close calls, but God protected us.

From the window of our flat, during dry season we observed an unusual event. As we heard "Clinkity clink" in the distance, then more clinks coming closer, we looked out to see that the sound came from cow bells belonging to a herd of Massai cattle. They were ambling up the street below, looking slightly undernourished, some brown, some black, urged onward by a Massai herdsman. They stopped to nibble anything green along the way, and occasionally gobbled a bright pink bougainvillea blossom. Automobile horns joined the music as they edged their way through the herd, vying for their piece of the pavement, and more eager to reach their destination than

the animals. The Massai people, whose ancestors once enjoyed wider pastures to nourish these symbols of their wealth, still claimed this area as their own. And so, a begrudged welcome was given to them when the pasture lands outside the city dried up. Tall, thin Massai herdsmen usually wore red wrap skirts. I was warned that they often carried knives under their skirts. These herdsmen could walk huge distances, and even sleep standing up while guarding cattle. Their famous dance included jumping straight up to surprising heights.

Building Back Up

As safety increased in DRC, a few of the translator families took exploratory trips to their locations. Most discovered that repairs and cleanup were needed to return to their houses. Congolese teams were overjoyed to see them and shared moving testimonies of God's mercy and protection through the war.

In mid-October John took folks to the airport to fly on our JAARS DC-3 to Ibambi, DRC. This was the first complete team returning for a longer work stay. They reported settling back in despite challenges of high immigration fees, visa renewal problems, termites in rafters, dead computer batteries, a cistern needing repair, and mice-eaten wires in vehicles. They prepared for translation training and drafted five literacy booklets. They resurrected a laser printer and printed 200 copies of Luke 2 for church leaders before Christmas.

Five hundred attended their Christmas service in Ibambi, the first time their entire service was conducted in Kibudu, the language of the Budu people. As chapter two of Luke was read in their language, the people were amazed. Now they clearly understood it, rather than staring into space while children played around the benches. As the preacher said, "Amen," students attending from the preparatory Bible school burst out in African style spontaneous singing. Twenty-five women from the church's nearby maternity clinic went forward to receive Christ as Savior! What confirmation of the importance of having God's Word in their own heart language!

John was happy for a signed contract between our group and MAF for cooperative flight service based in Nyankunde, DRC. Our refurbished Cessna was finally flown out to join their fleet. Several MAF families were back there and resuming flight service to some areas. John also completed proposals for funding projects to reestablish in Congo. WA partners agreed to fund two large projects, one for "Congo Advance" and one for "Administrative Costs." JAARS also sent generous funds from the Missions at the Airport events. Plans were in process with WA partners to come for a "Vision Trip" to DRC.

I was happily set up with the new equipment, doing desktop publishing work on a Mangbetu pre-primer and a small primer which were run on risograph, stapled, and boxed to be sent to the Mangbetu people who were carrying on their literacy project in an area yet unsafe for our folks to return.

In January 1998, an MAF pilot flew John and the MAF Aviation Director to DRC in our Cessna 206, also carrying cargo for missionaries there. They had a stop at Entebbe, Uganda, on the way. John admired their nice modern airport. They also stopped at Bunia, DRC, then over to the MAF flight center in Nyankunde (where we had originally been scheduled to go). John found Nyankunde very similar to Peru's Yarinacocha Jungle Center. They made plans to change the registration on our plane to DRC and hoped the paperwork could be completed before February 4th when the annual inspection

ran out. This should avoid prohibitive fees to fly in the Bunia area. Two houses were being built there for our pilot and mechanic who would fly and maintain our plane. John saw construction progressing so well that volunteer work crews were unnecessary there.

During the annual ECG Group Conference in February, we enjoyed hosting a family in our flat. We sensed God's wisdom in the business sessions. We greenlighted ideas to multiply efforts. Most language teams had made progress despite the war. Luke's Gospel was nearing completion in several languages. Translator Jon Hampshire, currently unable to work in their unstable location, was elected director. He would assume leadership after a short furlough. We were surprised when John was elected to be the new Executive Committee Chairman. Since most of the ECG staff were young families, I think they appreciated John's experience. John prepared quickly for the first session a week later. In the coming months, more of our teams cautiously returned to their locations.

Then another challenge! The DRC government announced closure of all private airstrips in the country, only to be used with special authorization from the Minister of State for the Interior. This was difficult for our teams since air travel was basically the only way to reach much of the country. It seemed, however, that various regions interpreted the document differently. Fortunately, we were still able to fly where our people worked. For some places they required a policeman to accompany the crew, limiting the space and weight allowance, and paying him $160 a day.

I worked on desktop publishing projects, also helping with some books for our Sudan Branch since they no longer had a desktop publishing person and we conveniently worked in the same building. I helped train a Sudanese man who caught on quickly.

John gathered information for a work crew project to construct a building for the Budu translation project in Ibambi.

News came from home that my mother was now hospitalized with cancer that had spread, and she was unable to eat or drink. John had a planned trip to the U.S., so we moved his flight up and I accompanied him. While he traveled for appointments, I stayed with family. We were blessed to see Mom once again bounce back after surgery. I stayed another month, then returned to Nairobi alone—with all kinds of complications. It seemed that travel went much more smoothly when I was with John!

Work in DRC was gearing up after the war. Translation personnel were out working in four locations. We looked forward to three families returning from extended furloughs along with four new families. Momentum was building.

Here We Go Again

However, in early August we heard of new insurgent activity in DRC, an apparent attempt to overthrow the *new* president. Fighting was first reported in the capital city of Kinshasa, where a curfew was imposed and two of Kabila's ministers fled. The shooting followed the president's decision to expel from the country Rwandan Tutsi-dominated troops who had helped bring him to power. Fighting broke out in the east, with some borders and airports closed. Initially the activity was to the south of our personnel, but it was moving quickly into other areas. It was difficult to get clear information, as some areas were taken by rebels, then retaken by government forces.

Our administration activated the Field Crisis Management Committee to decide on possible evacuations of our families. In the absence of this committee's chairman, John served for several days in his place. Pressure mounted to develop an evacuation plan. The committee communicated with AIM and MAF personnel, pooling information to coordinate important decisions. Our administration asked two families who could drive out to leave their locations. We were concerned about our remaining workers as hostilities spread, with decreasing options for getting them out. Before we could react, all airstrips were closed.

As John and I worked in our shared office on August 7, 1998, a loud boom shook the building. I thought it was an earthquake; John said it sounded like an explosion. From our office building roof viewing area, we saw smoke rising from the area of the U.S. embassy about five kilometers away. Radio reports verified that a blast had targeted the U.S. Embassy, and buildings next to the embassy were destroyed.

Hospitals became overloaded with people needing emergency care. Two of our colleagues who were nurses went to help. Some gave blood. The number of fatalities increased to nearly 200 as rubble was removed. Around 5,000 were injured. Two of our Kenyan staff had lost cousins. Joyce, our Kenyan receptionist, learned that her husband was cut severely from falling glass. As an accountant for a security guard company, he had just left the building where he was trying to collect payment for guard services. Those to whom he spoke minutes before were killed. He had been taken to one hospital which was full, then to another, so it was hard for Joyce to locate him. She thanked God he was alive. We were all shocked by the incident, thankful for our own safety while grieving for those suffering.

At that same time ECG administrators, including John, were planning to visit our embassy to clarify the situation concerning our people in DRC, and maybe get help to evacuate them. Our men could easily have been at the embassy when the bombing occurred! Was this God's special protection? The embassy staff quickly set up in another building temporarily, and our men were permitted to go there. Embassy personnel encouraged our team to go ahead with an evacuation; they would flight-follow via radio.

Several missions planned together, but problems beyond their control developed on August 12. They felt they only had a brief window before the area would be overrun. Foreigners would not be treated kindly if that occurred. The men worked long hours praying and planning. On Sunday morning the 16th they launched two planes, with our men flight-following from the hangar. The planes flew in quickly while most of the people were in church. Evacuees, including nine WEC International missionaries, needed to be ready for a brief stop by the planes on the village airstrip. From the moment the first plane touched down until the second one lifted off was just eight minutes. All 18 adults and four children entered Uganda airspace at 2:20 that afternoon. We rejoiced with great relief and a loud "Praise the Lord."

After debriefing, the evacuees needed to remake plans for the coming months. Most again needed to find housing, furniture, and household goods in Nairobi. This was emotionally difficult for those who loved the Congolese people and wanted to be with them in their danger. Folks in Nairobi shared clothing, toys, and basic needs with the evacuees who brought very little with them. We were happy to host a family for two weeks while they made plans and found a flat to rent. We prayed for God's protection on the Congolese colleagues who remained in DRC, and for the church leaders. We also prayed for protection on household and work supplies in our linguists' homes so recently re-equipped. We prayed for wisdom to benefit from another "waiting period." How could work proceed on a displaced basis?

John's planned trip to DRC was canceled. He had hoped to move the vehicle repair garage as its use had not developed in the Isiro area as planned. He wanted to check the site at Ibambi for a WA classroom construction project. A WA Vision Trip to DRC in August had been postponed. We saw God's leading in that, as the visitors could have been surrounded by fighting. Violence continued to spread in DRC, complicated by ethnic hostilities crossing borders into other countries who helped on both sides of the conflict. It appeared that unrest would be ongoing.

Thankfully, some of the project teams had received translation and literacy training, and were continuing to translate as able—in their homes or having fled to the bush. The Logoti Gospel of Luke was consultant-checked in October. I began preparing the manuscript for printing. We prayed for ways to complete Luke in Budu, Mayogo, Ndruna and Komo. I prepared a Logoti Folk Tale book with cute drawings. It included animal stories with a moral—to build reading skills. Then 5,000 copies were printed, with 50 copies sent with someone traveling to Congo. By combining desktop publishing services with our Sudan Branch, I had plenty of jobs to do. I worked on several literacy books for them, some of which I printed on my office printer and stapled together.

We were greatly relieved when we heard from several of our village teams in November and December, that they had kept working while keeping a low profile. But from other teams we had no news.

New Strategies

In February of '99, an Africa Area administrator led the ECG staff through group discussions. The clarified conclusion was that instability in DRC would continue indefinitely. We expected pockets of calm and pockets of fighting for years to come. Although our ECG folks would not be able to live and work in DRC, we anticipated short trips in and out. It seemed God was forcing us to make new strategies and to involve more Congolese church organizations. We needed to move the 13 existing projects forward, and somehow reach out to the possibly 140 groups in DRC needing translation. We would trust the God of the impossible. By being forced to regroup and rethink, ECG might be building a stronger foundation for the long-term work in Congo.

John prepared a "forward-looking" Project Funding Request to help Bible translation and literacy on a displaced basis, anticipating needs. That involved a lot of paperwork and approvals, with the challenge to predict when project funds would be needed, and to document the need. This included funding items like trips to Uganda or DRC, publishing Scriptures and literacy materials, communications, vehicles, workshops, and training of key Congolese personnel.

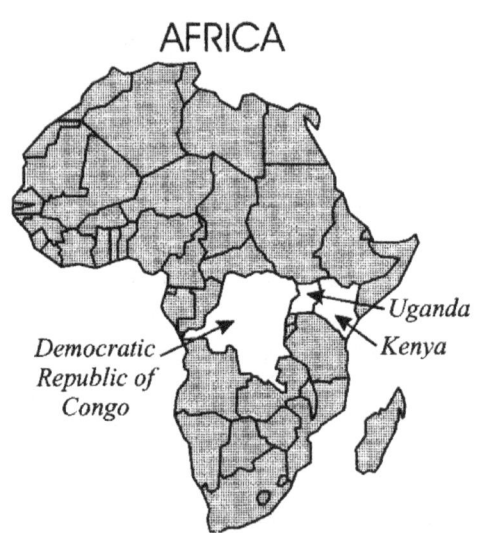

In June several linguists met in Arua, Uganda, for an Orthography Workshop with Congolese colleagues from several language groups, to finalize how to write their alphabets. Some Congolese traveled through DRC on bicycles to attend. Others passed through a partially blocked area due to a hemorrhagic fever epidemic. Some experienced culture shock, leaving their country for the first time. At the workshop each language had its challenges: like changing from a phonetic alphabet, how to write tone, or whether to add a new consonant.

Concurrent with the workshop, a consultant checked Budu and Mayogo Scriptures of beginning translations in Genesis and Acts, giving training along with the process. We were all encouraged by this progress.

Holding workshops in Arua, Uganda, became an encouraging means to continue the work. In September most of our language personnel participated in a big, exciting workshop with 11 staff and 22 Congolese from six language groups. Logo, Tembo, and Ndruna men worked with consultants on translation checking of Acts and John. Sessions in Bible translation principles, computer training, and manuscript preparation were held using new computers.

Another linguist trained two new literacy personnel. Two Komo men were there, with whom we had lacked contact for several years—a huge opportunity for their team to get re-motivated to continue translation. We thanked God for His protection from malaria, prevalent in that area, and for good health for all.

Holding a workshop like this was not easy, but it was a way forward. Travel to Arua was problematic for some participants who had to pass through areas of ethnic violence, where they saw people pulled from vehicles and beaten, and saw dead bodies along the way. Some narrowly escaped serious injury when their truck rolled. Staff tried to fly those people back home, but at that time flights were delayed because airstrip grass awaited official orders to be cut.

Meanwhile, I finished preparing Logoti Luke for press. We adjusted the font settings for good letter spacing which was affected when diacritics on vowels bumped into hooks and seraphs on adjacent letters, also adjusting letter combinations which appeared to be too far apart to read smoothly. I added illustrations with captions and footnotes, then the introductory text, glossary, and map.

Providential Banquet Tour

John was scheduled to speak on behalf of our Eastern Congo Group at six Wycliffe Associates banquets in North and South Dakota and Minnesota. These cities were being added to the special partners of ECG. Then, WA suggested that I come along to help. That turned out to be a miracle of God's incredible timing.

John planned to first attend the JAARS Aviation Technical Conference in Waxhaw, NC, while I visited Mom and family. We also looked forward to overnighting with Uncle Ralph, who picked us up at the Dulles Airport in VA. But there he had news for us. My mother was in serious condition in the hospital after falling and hitting her head. They recommended that we go directly to see her. So, Uncle Ralph drove us that evening to the hospital. Mom was having seizures from a brain hemorrhage. Between seizures we talked, and she was glad to see us. The next day she couldn't really talk. Seizures increased, and the nurse said she had only days to live.

John had to go on to the JAARS Center, and I was so thankful I could stay there, as we took turns sitting with Mom, day and night. Mom fought

for her life, surprising the medical staff. We tried to tell her we would let her go to heaven. And she did!

We made funeral arrangements, and John arrived back for that. I felt sad that we had spent so many years away from her, since family was her most important thing. I was so thankful for Carol and Mike and their children who had made a home for her with them. And I was thankful to be with them for her last days and the funeral.

Then, we were scheduled to do the speaking tour, so off we went. While attendance was lower than normal at the six banquets, the response of those who came was very good, and we were glad they sensed the needs in way off DRC.

We delayed our return to Nairobi by a week to help with decisions related to Mom's homegoing. We accompanied Uncle Ralph, the designated Executor of the Will, to the bank to handle some details. Mom had left some money for Carol and me. While in the bank office, suddenly the grief hit me. The tears came as I thought of how Mom was always so frugal for her own needs, but she delighted to buy gifts for the family and to help in time of need. We really missed Mom but were thankful for how she had blessed us through her life.

Stuck in Entebbe

In December, back in Kenya, John learned that literacy specialist Bettina Gottschlich had headed out to DRC, very excited to be with her Budu friends for their big Christmas celebration. She planned to train new literacy workers, prepare to train teachers for a big literacy program, do some literature production work, and "Scripture Use" training. But she was stuck in Entebbe, Uganda, because of plane problems. The ECG Cessna 206 needed an engine changed! Our Cessna was currently leased to AirServe (commercial organization related to MAF) out of Entebbe, and ECG pilot Shawn Brandt was contracted with them for that year. Since an engine from the U.S. would take months, John quickly put together a plan to help.

Miraculously, AIM AIR had a recently refurbished engine which they didn't need, so John was able to buy it at their cost. John offered to drive the engine to Entebbe and asked Daniel Kangethe to go along. (He had refurbished the plane with John in '96.) Translator Roger VanOtterloo asked if his son Nathan could go along. Nathan, a high school senior, was interested in aviation and was on his Christmas break. I was glad John had company, and they could help change the engine. It would be an adventure for them, but not without danger on the roads.

On December 17, they spent the morning getting papers in order. John got export papers for the engine and propeller; got the propeller disassembled at a shop so it would fit in the truck; received a fax from our pilot in Uganda requesting they bring a new Ugandan importation agreement for duty exemption. I picked up a letter for John from our director explaining the reason for transporting the engine, and arranged for John to pick up a copy of the legal agreement stating that SIL was a registered

NGO (non-governmental organization) in Uganda. Daniel got his papers to leave Kenya. All that so that they could hopefully cross the border! They were off at 2:00 p.m. Then they showed up again at the office at 4:00! They didn't have necessary papers with them for the truck they were driving! They left again, planning to get about three hours down the road and overnight at a hotel. It was a 12-18-hour drive, depending on what they encountered.

With only minimal problems at the border, they were able to drive on. They quickly installed the engine and tested it. Amazingly, although Bettina was delayed several days, she did get to Congo for Christmas! The men got back from Entebbe, driving straight through, thankful that their goal was met.

After the trip, John was overdue submitting a funding report listing money spent in various categories for the "Congo Forward Thrust" projects. He was ready for a rest when the office closed between Christmas and New Year's Day. We wondered if Y2K would affect our delicate communication connections as we moved into 2000, but alas there was a lot of worry over nothing.

Two Celebrations

Many had prayed that God would enable two important Scripture dedications to take place in DRC, even in a time of war. January was a time of great celebration.

The Gospel of Luke in Logoti was eagerly anticipated by the Logo people. To travel to Todro, DRC, translators Doug and Beth Wright drove the ECG Group Hilux truck all the way from Nairobi. They carried boxes containing 5,000 copies of Luke and 3,500 new Logoti hymn books. Others flew via Entebbe to Arua, Uganda, and joined up with the Wrights there. The road from there was

mostly dry, although in poor condition after the rainy season. They traveled without getting stuck, with no mechanical problems, and no accidents, despite three close calls. And they had easy border crossings.

After their three-day road trip, they arrived Saturday afternoon to decorations of flowers and palm fronds, and with singing by a choir. After greetings, they formed a human chain to  unload and pass the boxes of precious books from the truck to the office. Doug tried to clean the dusty boxes before passing them to the pastors dressed in their nice suits. But they said not to worry. They were just delighted to be receiving the printed Scripture.

A Sunday morning service was held at the church, and then the four-hour dedication service took place in the hot afternoon on the lawn between Wrights' house and the translation office. Nearly all the pastors of the region and top church leaders attended, having been there that week for a pastors'

training seminar for graduates of the Bible Institute. The dedication service focused on the Lord's faithfulness through many trials. Pastor Etsea cut a symbolic ribbon on the door to the translation office and distributed pieces of it to key people. He gave thanks to God for all those in SIL and their supporters who made the work of Bible translation possible. The Chief said, "Now that we have the gospel I fear, because we are without excuse. We can no longer say, 'I don't understand.'"

At that time, you would hardly know the country was at war, except for very few vehicles on the roads, very limited commerce, and an acute shortage of medicines and food. Many came to the Wrights with serious, legitimate needs.

Because the oldest pastor was not well enough to attend the service, Doug and our director visited his home to take him a copy of Luke. Over 90, Pastor Madrangi was suffering painfully from a dislocated hip, but he shuffled out to visit with them under the thatch of his verandah. When Doug handed him his copy, he was very quiet, just staring at it with eyes sparkling for a long time. Then he smiled, still not saying anything. Finally, he spoke, almost laughing, "It's really true. God has given us His Word before I die!" He had prayed for that since he was a young boy, and he had faithfully encouraged the Logo translators. He had often come by the translation office and said, "I just came to pray." Many times during the painstaking details, Doug had been inspired to keep pushing forward because of Madrangi's desire to have the Word in his language. The pastor's quiet ministry of encouragement had been a great blessing for many.

The Wrights were greatly encouraged as they saw the Logos reading Luke and singing from their songbooks in the light of the evening fires. Already 600 copies of Luke and over 1,000 songbooks had been sold, with more dispersed by bicycle. The team was gearing up to start more literacy classes. It was very encouraging for all involved.

The second celebration in January was for the Kifuliiru (Key-foo-LEE-rru) New Testament. That translation project had continued through incredible challenges. Let me back up and share that story.

Only a few miles from the border with Rwanda and Burundi in 1980 Roger and Karen Van Otterloo had begun working among the Bafuliiru people whose language was called Kifuliiru. After 15 years of translation work, Roger and Karen expected to finish the translation in two or three years. However, when they heard that funds had run out to pay their local co-translators' salaries, they needed to complete it in just one year. Roger worked from 7:00 in the morning with the co-translators, then he did revisions until 9:00 at night, covering himself and the computer with mosquito net to protect from gnats.

Translating Kifuliiru was especially challenging with more than 25 tense/mood possibilities, and 30 distinctions for each—totaling 750 possible variations for each verb! By God's grace and their tireless persistence, they reached their goal just in time. Joyfully, and with a sense of relief, they handed two computer diskettes to the senior checking consultant before leaving for home in summer 1996.

Then they found out why the Lord had allowed such pressure to finish the New Testament. Full-scale war had broken out, with one of the first major battles in their village of Kiliba and surrounding areas. Rebels swept down the mountains into Kiliba and simply began killing people. They looted Roger and Karen's house of everything: furniture, dishes, keepsakes, tools. They stripped lights, toilets, doors, and even ceiling.

But the Kifuliiru New Testament was safely in the hands of the United Bible Societies of Kenya, being prepared for publication and printing in Korea. God had given a window of opportunity to do the translation. Would He also give a window to dedicate His Word in Kiliba?

Returning to Nairobi in August of 1999, Roger had carefully traveled to Burundi and DRC to visit Bafuliiru colleagues and friends for the first time since two wars. He found most project workers still there, but having suffered much. But they were eager to continue the work where they had left off three years earlier. They planned for an early December dedication of the New Testament.

But, because of delays in transporting the 10,000 New Testaments, the dedication was postponed to January 23. Then security deteriorated in the area as a two-front offensive was launched by government forces. Roger received letters from the project workers that, despite difficulties, they had finished a back-translation project. They had worked on hymns, but when their small tape recorders were taken, they tried to remember the tunes. They asked for prayer "night and day." One said, "Hunger is attacking us, and there is much poverty." Another wrote (after back-translating in Corinthians) that they saw themselves as "sacrifices about to be offered." It broke Roger's and Karen's hearts to hear of such dedication.

Even so, in a time of war, God gave a window of opportunity for a special dedication service at Kiliba. Roger traveled first. Then a charter flight, organized by a Wycliffe Associates video specialist, transported the Van Otterloo children with their mom and a video crew to document the event.

Despite war conditions, an additional 500 people showed up to join the 2,000 who normally attended the Sunday morning church service in Kiliba. They crowded inside the large, stucco cement-block church building, sitting on nice wooden benches with backs. Dignitaries, guests, and choirs sat in the front seats, with aisles packed with people sitting on chairs brought from home. Others stood in doorways or sat on school benches outside under the trees. All were able to hear, thanks to a good PA system. Everyone was dressed in their best clothes. Roger said, "The Bafuliiru know how to dress, how to cook and how to sing."

Five choirs impressed guests with incredibly beautiful choral music accompanied by unique instruments. A favorite was a large hollowed-out gourd with goat skin stretched over it. A stick inside was rubbed to vibrate making a tuba-like sound. Many songs used traditional tunes with words from Scripture. (Since they had a collection of 300 Kifuliiru Scripture songs and hymns, many had already memorized Scripture.)

It was truly a celebration—not worshiping a book but giving recognition to the importance of the book and worshiping God. The regional Vice Governor talked about the power of forgiveness. ECG Director, Jon Hampshire, encouraged the people to really read their New Testaments and not just leave them on a shelf. Roger explained their usability and durability, with the pages sewn in the binding, so they wouldn't lose "Timothy" as he experienced with one of his English Bibles!

Unfortunately, the truck with 10,000 copies of the New Testament didn't arrive in time for the celebration. At least Roger had brought 165 advance copies. There was some "holy jealousy" of the few who received books. They made plans for when the container did arrive, that it would be stored in a secure place and sales would be handled by the Kifuliiru Literacy Project leader.

This translation provided significant benefit for hundreds of other languages. It could be used as a base translation for about 500 related Bantu languages spoken in nearly 20 countries of southern Africa. Since the grammar in the Kifuliiru New Testament had already been "Bantu-ized," translation teams didn't need to "re-invent the wheel" for each new Bantu language. Their time to produce a translation could be significantly shortened, and overall quality improved.

Mission Leaders Lost

We were just beginning to get to know new neighbors in the flat across from us. Our Africa Area Director and wife, Bob and Ruth Chapman, had previously served with our Cameroon Branch. The WA video team had interviewed them as they described how vital it was for people to have Scripture in their own language, especially in a time of need, as it had spoken to them when they lost their two boys to cerebral malaria. *(That recorded interview became part of a touching WA video presentation.)*

We heard the news broadcast that a plane had crashed off the Ivory Coast. We knew that Bob and Ruth had traveled to visit our workers there. Then it was confirmed that they were aboard the Kenya Airways flight from there to Nairobi on Sunday January 30th, which crashed just after takeoff in the Atlantic Ocean. We hoped they would be among the few survivors, but that was not the case. A week later, their bodies were found, identified, and repatriated to Canada. A memorial service was held at Nairobi Evangelical Graduate School of Theology (NEGST) jointly with the United Bible Societies who also lost two people in that crash.

The Chapman's daughter, in college at the time, was now the only one left in her immediate family. She came to Nairobi for a week with an aunt, uncle, and family friend, so she could see where her parents had lived and worked, go through their possessions, settle their bank account, and handle paperwork. Her friend stayed in our flat. It was a very hard time, but good to give closure. The Chapman's testimony remained, illustrated by the plaque on the door of their flat: "God is good in all His ways." It was hard to reconcile that truth with the tragic loss, but we trusted God to bring good from it.

On the Road Again

Having had a good experience in November of '99 speaking at six Wycliffe Associates banquets on behalf of the Eastern Congo Group, we embarked on another tour. It was one of the four regular WA spring banquet tours, this time in 25 cities in Pennsylvania and Ohio.

Tour Cities:
3/27 Erie, PA
28 Pittsburgh
30 Bloomsburg
31 Lansdale
4/01 Lancaster #1
03 Altoona
04 Lancaster #2
06 Philadelphia
07 Reading
08 Allentown
10 York
11 Chambersburg
13 Middlefield, OH
14 Youngstown
15 Akron
17 Hartville
18 Sandusky
(Easter Break)
24 Fulton County
25 Mansfield
26 Marion
28 Wayne County
29 Tuscarawas County
5/01 Cleveland
02 Holmes county
04 Lima

We trained with speakers of three other tours in Chicago, March 23-25. Then we traveled again with WA Area Directors, Ralph and Mary Wheeler. They worked hard between each meeting, checking with local coordinators for reservation counts, confirming meal counts with facilities (sometimes an educated guess), getting good prices on hotel rooms, having supplies sent when we ran short, coordinating the banquet timetable with head servers so the program wasn't delayed, calculating the results of each banquet, even working ahead on plans for the fall banquets.

We spoke each evening except Sundays and Wednesdays (prayer meeting night for most churches). On Wednesdays we washed clothes and caught up. Ralph joked that some people called this a chicken tour, as many of the meals were chicken dishes, but we enjoyed them all. Each location had a different dynamic, depending on the staff, room arrangement, and attendees. After the meal, Ralph described Bible translation, explained the faith promises, and showed video segments. Then John spoke and I shared some stories. We talked without notes, so had to remember our material

Africa (1996-2000) 251

well. We had to keep it within a time limit, always aiming to finish the program by 9:00 p.m.

After the banquets each evening, the Wheelers opened the response envelopes and prepared to forward gift notices and cash to their headquarters. The following morning, after a relaxed breakfast, we headed to the next location in their van. Fortunately, there were not long driving distances between each banquet. It took us an hour or more each time to set up video equipment, sound system, table information, welcome table, and table displays. We sometimes changed into our good clothes in a restroom.

At one banquet, the large crowd maxed out the venue. After the meal, we moved to an adjacent section for the program, where chairs were set up in rows. Ralph brought in his small platform so people could see the speaker. Ralph had encouraged John to keep forward on the stage to better interact with the people because John tended to back up. In that crowded room I sat in a chair right in front of the platform. As John talked, he stepped backward and lost his balance on the edge of the wooden box, flailing his arms in circles to avoid falling. He joked about it and kept on. But it struck me as hilarious. I started giggling and could hardly stop as John continued.

One night was especially memorable. I wanted to be helpful by starting video segments, as Ralph had been stepping down from the platform and then up again to do this. Three video segments showed work in Kenya and DRC, including the Kifuliiru New Testament dedication. The last segment was the Chapman's interview recorded just weeks before they had lost their lives. It was an emotional close to the program following John's stories of the challenges faced by the Eastern Congo Group.

The banquet was at Good & Plenty Restaurant in Lancaster, a place we were familiar with. Several of our local friends were among the 300 who attended. As John finished his talk, I took the cap off the lens and pushed the start button on the remote control to show the last segment. Nothing happened! Had I aimed wrong? I tried again. Nothing. This was about the worst thing that could happen! What had I done wrong? Had the bulb burned out? Some tried to resolve the problem. I made a comment to the crowd, "This is just like on the field when the electricity goes off!" John attached an extension cord to a different plug, and voilà, there was power. We showed the last touching segment. But the momentum was lost. We later learned that an employee had turned off various circuits unaware that we were using one. So, it wasn't my fault, but such was the excitement and challenge of a banquet tour.

Completing the tour, we took some time to decompress and help my sister go through Mom's possessions. Then we headed back to Nairobi.

Pushing Forward

In Nairobi we continued with our responsibilities. I had taken on a project to key from dictation an English back translation of teacher's manuals for a Kifuliiru Bible curriculum. Schools in many African countries required religion classes. Students could choose from three main religions. This English translation would be used by other language groups to translate the Bible curriculum into their language. It had great potential for wide use. *(This was the beginning stage of a project that would mushroom and years later be used as Bible curriculum in schools across several countries.)*

At the same time, I kept other projects going as well. I worked on corrections to the text of the Budu Gospel of Luke in the Neta dialect, preparing it for press. Next was Ndruna Matthew, Mayogo Luke, and a Lika alphabet chart. Each month I compiled a prayer guide, the PFOA (Praying for One Another), with requests from our ECG members for each day, then sent it out to a lot of people who prayed faithfully for us.

Kenya was experiencing a major drought with many people suffering from lack of food and water. In Nairobi, there were increasingly wider problems with water and electricity distribution, dependent on hydroelectric power. In early June electricity rationing increased, triggering protests about unequal distribution. Our office building had power Monday, Wednesday, and Friday mornings, then Tuesday, Thursday, and Saturday afternoons, and alternate Sundays. Where we lived was the opposite. A new generator was installed for the office building. After initial problems, it kicked in when power was cut off, so that we could continue working. Our Thursday evening ECG prayer meetings, currently held at our flat, were lit by candlelight and flashlight.

Roger Van Otterloo was looking for someone to key from dictation the English back-translation of the entire Kifuliiru New Testament. We needed someone not already assigned to other jobs to undertake this huge project. Louise Anderson remembered Janet Yost, guest helper at the JAARS Center in Waxhaw, N.C. I also knew Janet from a supporting church. An excellent typist, we asked her if she could come to Nairobi to take on that project. We invited her to stay with us in our flat. The project ended up being a little more complex than anticipated, but she plugged away at it, and had the experience of her life. *(Some years later, I accepted her Power of Attorney, and became responsible for her care until her death.)*

In DRC measles, chicken pox, meningitis, and convulsive malaria broke out in many areas, with medications hardly available. Flour was scarce. Fighting involving Rwandan and Ugandan troops resulted in about 500 deaths. Unrest escalated, and by August of 2000, half of the population was affected by war, with thousands displaced. Military movement increased in the area of our Bunia, DRC office, complicated by ethnic clashes.

Reports indicated around 760 people killed in the Kisangani area. A bomb fell on a pastor's home there, injuring his seven children. They were taken to a hospital which then was also bombed, but they didn't suffer further injury. His wife had been at the bomb site minutes before it hit. About 10,000 Congolese had reportedly fled to Uganda, around 6,000 to Central African Republic, and some 60,000 to the Republic of Congo. Although a few ECG personnel made short trips into safer areas, it was apparent that John would be unable to take WA volunteer work crews into DRC. WA funding projects had greatly helped, but hands-on trips could no longer happen.

Re-evaluating

John and I discussed our personal long-range planning. We were scheduled for furlough in the fall of 2001. After that, we could continue in Africa or in the U.S., maybe again at JAARS. As we green-lighted, John asked me to consider other options. He had visited the Wycliffe Northeast office near Lancaster, PA, while we were on tour, encouraging their help to recruit translation personnel for Eastern Congo Group. He had also learned of the need for a director at that office and had been asked to consider that. When we mentioned that possibility to our family, they loved the idea.

As John communicated with the Northeast office, they indicated that the need was immediate, and asked us if we could move up our departure time from Kenya by a year and take up that new role by the first of January 2001. Wycliffe Personnel released us from our ECG assignment a year early. It all happened so quickly. We would complete projects, pack, and move in mid-October, with a shortened furlough before the new assignment.

John completed reports on project funding, clarified accounts, and passed on information. Fortunately, someone returning from furlough could take over his responsibilities. I finished three books for printing, each being the first Scripture book for those languages: Ndruna Matthew and Budu Luke in two different dialects. I had also helped the Sudan Branch with work on the Ndogo New Testament. Mayogo Luke was at the printers. I hoped that book would be ready for Jill Brace to take when she traveled to DRC mid-October to prepare for a dedication celebration.

(The Mayogo Luke dedication was held November 4 in DRC with 3,000 attending, despite the wartime situation!)

It was a blessing that a Wycliffe Associates short term volunteer, Kari Allen, was just arriving in Nairobi, to help where needed. She would take over our flat purchasing most of our furniture and household items.

It was sad to leave the Eastern Congo Group, but we had spent a lot of time on the field. It would be a special blessing to be close to family and still be serving with Wycliffe.

Side Benefits

We would have many special memories of our time in Kenya—with the small group of dedicated ECG personnel with a huge task to do, figuring out ways to continue Bible translation. We were glad we had been able to help for a few years.

Other memories included a promised genuine safari experience. Our opportunity had come when Jim and Louise Anderson organized a group trip to the Maasai Mara Game Reserve, a popular Kenya safari destination stretched along the Tanzanian border adjacent to the Serengeti. Annual wildebeest migration passed through it. In addition to many species of birds, the "big five" of African animals were all there: the African elephant, lion, leopard, cape buffalo, and rhinoceros. Other animals included cheetah, hyena, hippos, crocodiles, baboons, warthogs, topi, eland, gazelle, impala, waterbuck, zebra, and others.

Every six weeks or so, tired of city life, we visited the Nairobi Game Park. We packed a lunch and invited any new helpers, visitors, or friends to go with us. The park on the city's edge was only a ten-minute drive from our flat. With resident passes we entered at a discounted cost. We were permitted to drive around ourselves, and John discovered the best places to find animals. We stayed in our vehicles, except for designated areas.

We had never had the joy to personally attend a Scripture dedication, but when John was away for meetings, the Andersons invited me to attend a Duruma New Testament dedication near Mombasa, Kenya. This was not a language of Congo, but of Kenya, where we lived, and it was an *accessible* location. I flew with the Andersons a day early to enjoy the beach at a coastal hotel. Our bus crossed on a ferry with other vehicles to get to our destination.

Louise asked me if I'd like to ride a camel. On the beach area she negotiated well with a Kenyan man in Swahili for a reasonable price. The lift-off surprised me. I could easily have been dumped headfirst over the camel's neck. The view from high atop the hump was mesmerizing as our  guide led the camels down the beach. I balanced carefully when the camel kneeled for me to get off.

The following day we joined a group for a two-hour chartered bus ride to the village. As honored guests we sat along one side of an outdoor quadrangle set up with chairs, platform, and sound equipment. We had no difficulty hearing. I videoed much of the six-hour ceremony—some in Kiswahili, some English, and mostly Duruma. Speeches were interspersed with choirs from 12 different churches, accompanied by African rhythm and motions. The highlight of the program was the procession to carry in the boxes of New Testaments. We heard singing in the distance, and excitement mounted as the box-bearers with the New Testaments came closer, stepping forward, backward, and sideways, waving branches with leaves. The crowd cheered as they entered the quadrangle. They opened the boxed treasures on a table and displayed the precious books for the first time. Church leaders gave dedication prayers. The crowd listened attentively as three people read selected portions of Scripture in their language. They presented New Testaments to certain people who had been involved in the translation process.

Afterwards New Testament copies were sold at a subsidized price. That day the Duruma people joyfully received God's Word. I was privileged to witness it!

Just a couple weeks before we headed home, we took a grand finale safari trip. Friends, Chuck and Diane DeVries, invited us to go with them to the Ngorongoro (En-GOR-oh-en-GOR-oh) Crater. We went together in their vehicle, driving all the way.

We stayed at the crater's edge in a safari lodge constructed of local stone that blended into the natural elements, practically invisible from the crater below. We enjoyed a day-long tour in a park vehicle with a guide.

The unique ecosystem formed by a giant volcano that had exploded and collapsed, created rich grazing land for many animals in the 100-square-mile area. Local Maasi herdsmen also grazed their livestock in the crater.

Those special trips were like a reward for serving in Africa. Although I hadn't wanted to go there, I was so glad for the years of working with the Eastern Congo Group and learning about the challenges of serving in Africa. We would continue to pray for the work in DRC the rest of our lives.

Chapter 11
Northeast Regional Office
Mobilizing and Caring for Workers

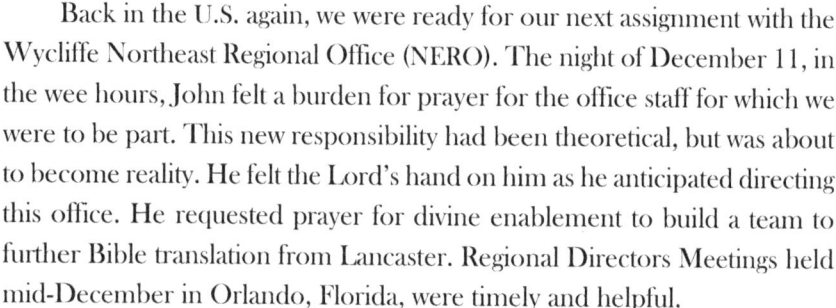

Back in the U.S. again, we were ready for our next assignment with the Wycliffe Northeast Regional Office (NERO). The night of December 11, in the wee hours, John felt a burden for prayer for the office staff for which we were to be part. This new responsibility had been theoretical, but was about to become reality. He felt the Lord's hand on him as he anticipated directing this office. He requested prayer for divine enablement to build a team to further Bible translation from Lancaster. Regional Directors Meetings held mid-December in Orlando, Florida, were timely and helpful.

Wycliffe USA had taken up a challenge to move ahead in new ways. A new commitment adopted at the 1999 International Conference was called Vision 2025: *To begin work in every language group that does not have God's Word in their language by the year 2025.* Given the rate of Bible translation starts at that time, we would need more than 100 years to complete the task. Meanwhile people were dying without ever hearing God's message of salvation. We were challenged to envision how we could fulfill Vision 2025. It wouldn't happen just by working harder, but by adding and multiplying our efforts. Considering that, Wycliffe USA was working to "beef up" the six regional offices. We needed an effective plan for our region to raise awareness of the challenge. NERO needed to grow, adding full-time workers in strategic locations, and building a network to challenge and resource churches to join in the task.

From the 14 states in our northeast area, over 800 active Wycliffe members served around the world. It was important to encourage, strengthen, and help those colleagues. NERO was staffed by Wycliffe members who were assigned to work in the U.S., or who were on furlough,

or on retired status, as well as long-term volunteers from the local area. Some worked part time and others full time. The staff at NERO served in four key areas:
1. Member services—Career guidance, housing for furloughing members and/or staff, personnel services including training in partnership development, a free clothing "boutique", and a donated vehicle program.
2. Mobilization—Recruiting new members, conducting "Windows on Wycliffe" events in various areas for those interested in applying to Wycliffe, and tracking contacts.
3. Media Services—Providing Wycliffe videos, films, slide sets, displays, literature and books.
4. Church Relations—Interacting with churches to provide information about the need for Bible translation, coordinating missionary speakers, and providing resources to aid church programs.

Supporting these programs, an efficient staff served in the mail room, finance office, maintenance, computer services, prayer ministry and receptionist. The director's secretary kept track of many aspects and was a big help to John.

Our Regional Office had evolved over the years. In the 1950s and 60s, representatives were located in MA, PA, Washington DC, and GA. After that the east coast representation served from Waxhaw, NC, then moved again in 1974 to downtown Washington DC. In 1980 it relocated to Falls Church, VA.

Late 1983 the active Wycliffe Associates Chapter of Lancaster, PA, urged the northeast office to move to Lancaster, PA, because of good interest there and opportunity to include housing for staff. Local businessman, Marlin Thomas, offered to sell Wycliffe land in the Willow Valley Retirement Complex below cost and to provide site development (road, water, sewer, utilities). Also, Wycliffe could rent office facilities in the Willow Valley shopping mall, with exposure to tourist traffic. With funds raised from local churches and others, Wycliffe Associates volunteers completed the first six-unit apartment building by 1987 and the second by 1989. Over the years, a series of directors moved the work forward: Clay Johnston, Tom Hopkins, Ron Yaddaw, Dan May, Ray Huber, and as interim directors: Tom Hopkins again and Carl Campbell.

John started serving there in January of 2001. His most urgent project was to rework a proposal to the Wycliffe Board on a building project—a new office for NERO. The current office space at Willow Valley Square had served well, but was expensive to rent, using about half of the budget. It had lost a main entrance when Darrenkamp's Grocery store expanded. The difficult-to-find entrance was now around the side of a building and up a back stairway.

Also, we needed a larger space with room to grow. Land for the new building and utility permissions had already been acquired. Architect, Steve Fry, scaled down the earlier multi-mission proposal pro bono. Then John traveled to our Orlando headquarters to present the adjusted proposal to the Board. As he met with them and with the Board Financial Committee, he realized that he knew most of the men personally from previous contacts during our time with Wycliffe. What a blessing that was, as it made it easier for John to interact with them. They voted unanimously to give us a green light on the project.

Another priority was preparing the program for an upcoming NERO retreat scheduled for January 23-25. John put me to work on that. Being too late to find a special speaker, we chose to present some material which the Lord had recently placed into our hands. John did sessions on adapting to change, using materials from a motivational book, *Who Moved My Cheese*. I did sessions on team building. While we were personally stretched to prepare and present those, it was a good opportunity for us to get more acquainted with the team.

My new work responsibilities included several areas. The first was to prepare a monthly newsletter to encourage the 800 members from our northeast region. I also prepared flyers and pamphlets for our various events. I became the temporary housing hostess for our Wycliffe apartments, coordinating reservations and preparing the apartments for new residents. Short-term and long-term guest apartments were rented to NERO staff or furloughing families.

(Then, when new volunteers arrived, Marge Olsen became the housing hostess, and her husband Fred worked with the donor car program.)

Meanwhile we had been living in a Wycliffe apartment while trying to sell our house in Waxhaw to buy a house near the Wycliffe office in PA. After lots of looking, one in Strasburg seemed just right for us, four miles from the office. We reserved a week in March to go to Waxhaw to clear out our house there and get furniture ready for moving. On our last day there, we signed a contract for the sale of our house. On April 30th we moved into our new home, even having guests right away. What a blessing of the Lord's care in our lives after a lot of temporary living!

In between speaking trips, participation in mission conferences and visiting Wycliffe Associates chapters, John dealt with getting the new office building project going. A zoning hearing was planned since questions had come up regarding expiration of a previous permit. Also, some stipulations previously given on use of the property were very limiting, depending upon interpretation. It could be an opportunity to have the agreement clearly defined. So, we were thankful to receive a good ruling. Now we could begin a funding drive and "vertical construction."

By July the "capital campaign" was off and running. Two special gifts gave us a good start: $20,000 from Wycliffe Associates and $40,000 from our Wycliffe Orlando headquarters, added to the $20,000 on hand. John needed to raise $500,000, and another $500,000 was being borrowed from Wycliffe. John invited Earl and Audrey Bowers of Wycliffe Associates from Waxhaw to be the project supervisor and volunteer coordinator. We knew them from projects they had led previously in Peru—neat people who did a professional job. They invited many past-project friends, who kindly helped once again. Some came and stayed for several months. Sherm Guyer (a Wycliffe member who just returned from serving in Papua New Guinea) became the head contact person to work with Earl Bowers. Sherm was from

Lancaster and had been a contractor in the area previously. He already had a good start on preparations, including relating to the zoning board and getting a work permit.

I prepared a flyer explaining the project and our need for it. We sent out a mailing and asked God to burden people to help us move forward by contributing financially, volunteering labor skills, and upholding the project in prayer.

The name of our Northeast Regional Office was changed from NERO to WNE for "Wycliffe Northeast." This accomplished consistency with the other five regional office names. We were grateful when four couples and two single Wycliffe members arrived to help WNE gear up. In addition to regular responsibilities, the team pulled together to carry out events.

Around 3,000 people attended the second annual Wycliffe Family Weekend at Smoketown Airport near Lancaster on August 25 and 26.

About 30 JAARS staff from Waxhaw joined us, bringing displays, three airplanes, and a helicopter. Rides were given to 995 people. Local parachutists topped off a Helio Courier demonstration on both days. Volunteers helped our staff to man food tables and exhibits. Translators made presentations, a panel answered questions, and musicians demonstrated ethnic percussion music from around the world in a "Heartbeat for Missions" program. Some attendees seriously considered getting involved in Bible translation in some way. Some signed up for volunteer construction work

on our new building. Many people were made aware that there was a Wycliffe office in Lancaster and that Bible translation was a worthwhile and challenging task.

In the fall, 60 golfers played in the first annual "Wide-World-of-Wycliffe Golf Tournament" at Tanglewood Golf Course, organized by Carl Sands. This event raised funds for effective local Wycliffe radio spots not included in our budget. Golfers experienced nine holes of regular golf and nine holes with unique missions' object lessons—golf like they'd never played before, but they were good sports! Several of our friends played, including a Corning, NY group.

While Al Schoonover golfed, his wife Jeanette and I were asked to watch for a hole-in-one shot, for which there was a very special award. We were to drive a golf cart to that location and monitor the shots. Neither she nor I had ever driven a cart. We imagined jerking forward, or crashing in full view of the lined-up players. Fortunately, the cart eased along slowly and safely, so we did not make a fool of ourselves. However, nobody made a hole in one.

John and I attended the Regional Directors' meetings in Orlando, FL, September 5-13. Once a year, wives could accompany their husbands, who met quarterly at our headquarters. I met other regional directors and their wives at a two-day prayer summit. Then while John was in mobilization meetings, I planned to read and catch up on correspondence in the hotel room. And so it was that on the 11th, I happened to be watching TV as news broke of the Trade Tower incident. I watched in horror as the first and then the second tower was hit. Everyone knew this was not an accident as the tragedy went from bad to worse. For two days I watched scenes and reports as our country was in turmoil. John anticipated that our return flight to PA on the 13th would be canceled. He quickly reserved a rental car to drive home, along with another member from our office.

By November the hole for the office building foundation was dug, with grading completed for the parking lot and water drainage areas. Footers were about to go in for the foundation.

The Bowers set up a construction office in a nearby house. Volunteers met there with Earl for devotions each morning before beginning their work.

And they enjoyed meals there, which Audrey prepared with help from volunteer wives. These ladies also did sewing projects for the Water  Street Mission in Lancaster. They even sometimes helped with construction! Audrey also kept the financial books for the construction.

I worked to prepare and send another big mailing as there was still a significant amount of funds to be raised. John applied for additional borrowed funds from Wycliffe to enable cash flow to purchase building materials. Don Toland (our Stewardship Ministry Director) hosted a businessmen's breakfast and invited the Wycliffe USA President as a speaker to inspire our guests with the importance  of Bible translation and to encourage donations for the project.

➤ Many construction volunteers for the building continued to come at a steady pace and as needed, staying weeks or even months. Specialists came for specific tasks, like drywall taping or mudding, painting, and window trim

installation. It was a special joy for us to have workers come from our own home areas of Bellwood, PA, and Corning, NY. One volunteer from Michigan suffered a heart problem, needing a triple bypass, extending his stay in the area to recuperate. Sherm Guyer, our Wycliffe coordinator, slid off a slippery snow-covered roof, breaking his wrist. Fortunately, he recuperated quickly and was soon back on the job.

Work progressed on the siding of the building. Kitchen cabinets and floor coverings were installed. Our IT staff, Jim Baptista and Rob Roberge, ran miles of cable and phone lines throughout the building and installed the latest software. Two staff ladies and I chose carpeting, tiles for bathroom and kitchen, and office chairs to match the cubicles—all provided at a special price for us. Betty Baptista decorated our four guest rooms, each with a different theme.

Meanwhile, along with other duties, our WNE team hosted our second annual fundraising golf tournament and the third Wycliffe Family Weekend.

On August 12, 2002, we hosted 230 guests in the Palm Court of the Willow Valley Conference Center to celebrate the office completion. Our program included a video prepared by one of our office volunteers which showed scenes from the building process. Our guest speaker brought into perspective the reasons for our building and the challenge of Bible translation. We thanked the Lord for the 317 Wycliffe Associates volunteers from CA, NJ, OH, IN, IL, MD, MI, NC, DE, NY, NH, FL, VA and PA, who contributed 10,297 hours to complete the building in less than a year. These servant-hearted volunteers gave of their time and talents. Earl and Audrey Bowers had given us a year of their lives to coordinate the project. Sherm Guyer was now in charge of maintaining our new facility and grounds.

John presents a plaque to the Bowers.

They all had done excellent quality work! The banquet offering of about $15,000 helped defray building costs.

We could now host events in our own Wycliffe Northeast facility, starting with a Partnership Development Workshop in September led by our Member Services team. In November our Mobilization team hosted a WOW program (Window on Wycliffe) for 32 people considering joining Wycliffe. After the day-long session, the team said, "It is so nice and convenient to hold it here in our new office, with no hauling of supplies to another venue." *(This program had been developed by Jim Baptista who had served in various administrative positions in Wycliffe/JAARS and now was our IT specialist.)*

The large basement served several purposes: 1) a mail room with shelves for storing books and supplies; 2) an area with a large, donated scale to weigh packed items for shipping overseas; 3) a "boutique" with donated used clothing and miscellaneous items (manned by volunteers). Items were free to Wycliffe members. Furloughing missionaries appreciated finding seasonal clothing there (like warm winter items when coming back from a tropical climate).

On November 1 we held an Open House with a dedication service for our new building. Over 375 friends joined us for tours, videos, and fellowship with snacks. I had decorated the walls with cultural artifacts and wall hangings, and created a tour script with Wycliffe Bible Translators' goals, including Vision 2025.

The garage, which sat behind the building was also open to view, having been completed just in time for the Open House. For that, 32 volunteers had contributed over a thousand hours of labor. Three bays, one with a lift, enabled safe repairs to donated cars. Our donor car program had provided 80 cars for furloughing missionaries the past year, working in a small garage. With 20 more currently ready to be checked, the process would be much more efficient in the new facility.

Meanwhile, at home we did some home renovations. First, we added a guest bathroom with my Uncle Ralph's help. Then we turned our basement recreation room into an apartment suite for John's sister, Karen, to come live with us. With her boys now on their own, Karen wanted to sell the mobile home she was living in to pay off her debt. Her counseling job, which she loved, did not pay well, so that was a challenge. She brought some of her furniture and used a little of ours. It was nice to have her with us.

John continued to travel for speaking engagements. In September I traveled with him to Orlando for the dedication of the new Wycliffe U.S. headquarters there. In meetings with the other regional directors, they discussed ways to align more closely with the Orlando office. In October John traveled for a week in Ohio with Don Toland (Stewardship Ministries) to visit churches and friends of Wycliffe. In November, he traveled with Aaron Hoffman (our Church Relations Coordinator) to visit churches and friends in New York. Other trips followed to various churches, Wycliffe Associates chapter meetings, and Orlando headquarters.

John was open to being aware of opportunities to gain knowledge that would be helpful in his job. He heard about a mission course that was being held at Calvary Church—*Perspectives on the World Christian Movement*, a unique 15-week study experience created by the U.S. Center for World Mission. He had been encouraged to take it, which he did, and enjoyed it immensely. It was to have a huge influence on him. "I wish I had known these things before our service on the field," John said when he finished the course. Although we had experienced a lot of great training when becoming members of Wycliffe, this course dealt with a lot more. John was so enthusiastic about his experience that the leader, Ray Lucas, encouraged him to take the coordinator training, with the idea for John to co-direct an upcoming course. We had the perfect facility to hold the classes, so John checked with his leaders, and they agreed to this.

We hosted our first Perspectives course starting in January of 2003 with 45 students meeting each Tuesday evening for 15 weeks. They learned how God has been at work through the ages among different cultures, what was happening currently, and the remaining task of giving all peoples the opportunity to know the true God. The course encompassed four areas: the biblical, historical, cultural, and strategic aspects of God's heart for the nations. Each week a different guest lecturer shared his/her knowledge and experience on the lesson topic. The course could be taken for undergraduate or graduate credit, or for a certificate. We wanted the participants to contemplate how they could serve God with their gifts, whether on the field, in their church, or other ways. And we hoped that some would be inspired to serve with Wycliffe.

⁓ *(Each year following, John continued as Coordinator of the Lancaster Spring Perspectives Course, while Calvary Church held a course in the Fall. Sometimes he traveled to other classes to teach one of the history lessons.)*

In May of 2003, 19 young adults studied in our first five-day "TOTAL-It-Up" program. This "Taste of Translation and Linguistics" course included introductory classes in phonetics and phonology, grammar, language and culture, translation, and semantics. Students discovered whether or not they were gifted for further translation training. Staff members taught classes, prepared meals (including delicious ethnic dinners), shared testimonies, gave field reports, and interacted informally with the students. Our office kitchen served well for preparing meals. John, Janet Morris, and I prepared a Peruvian meal of *lomo saltado*, tropical fruits, and flan for the dessert.

The all-purpose dining area had plenty of space for tables in various configurations. The students stayed in our guest rooms and in our apartments. Eleven students showed interest in career service with Wycliffe in Bible translation or other related areas, such as literacy or Scripture use. Five were interested in service with Wycliffe in a support area.

A Partnership Development Workshop, hosted by our Personnel team gave practical training to help members share effectively with churches and friends. With available resources and ideas, they could prepare meaningful presentations to interact well with their prayer and financial teams, enabling them to have their needs met while serving the Lord full time.

As plans were made for the fourth annual Wycliffe Family Weekend scheduled for August of 2003, we received news that JAARS would not be able to give airplane or helicopter rides. There was special concern as insurance rates had increased so much since the 9/11 incident. We struggled to plan a meaningful program without the rides. So, we were excited when we received word that the JAARS Board had reinstated the flying, with the stipulation that those taking rides sign a form. Other attractions for that year included a concert by the Jacobs Brothers and three different dramas by Maranatha Productions. In a tent, special "Kingdom Kids Corner" programs encouraged children to consider Bible translation work in their future.

In response to the Vision 2025 initiative, efforts by Wycliffe and our SIL's field personnel were bearing fruit. New translation programs increased from about 25 yearly to an average of 54 in the past three years (66 including all mission organizations). At that time there were 1,410 translations in progress worldwide (1,260 by Wycliffe/SIL).

During 2003 as John met with other Regional Directors at Wycliffe headquarters, a major discussion topic was realignment. Headquarters desired the six regional offices to align more closely with their Orlando office. As a result, each office was reorganized into five departments (or silos), each of which would report directly to Orlando headquarters. That included: Mobilization, Personnel, Stewardship Ministries, Information Technology, and Administration. Since this eliminated Regional Directors, John became Director of Mobilization for the Northeast.

Our office continued to hold the various events each year. In August 2004 we added a Youth Concert on Friday night to the Wycliffe Family Weekend. We tried running programs simultaneously in the hangar and in a large tent throughout the day. Carol Orwig and I created a Treasure Hunt game for children to search for information from various displays and presentations. John coordinated the event, with great help from volunteers, sponsors, and WNE staff.

In 2005, the Wycliffe USA Mobilization team was reorganized. John was asked to take a new role as Director of Specialty Mobilization, overseeing several recruitment departments and reporting to the new Mobilization Vice President of Wycliffe. Brad Steele from our office replaced John as Northeast Mobilization Director. John and I were asked to move to our Orlando headquarters. But, after just investing in our home in PA, I didn't like that idea. I was very thankful that they permitted John to work out of our PA office. He would communicate by email and teleconferences, with frequent trips. That also enabled John to continue coordinating the Perspectives Course and the Wycliffe Family Weekend. It would also allow me to continue my work there.

It was an exciting time for Bible translation progress as we began to see the possibility of the task being completed in the next generation. New translation projects were being started every four days on average! Wycliffe was proceeding with new urgency, motivated by Vision 2025. Mobilization's goal was to double Wycliffe USA's personnel by 2014.

Because many local people showed interest in short term trips, Don Toland organized a "Bible Translation Catch-the-Vision Bus Trip" in May. Don and his wife Norma, along with their daughter Laurel Lynn, and John and I, co-hosted a group of 46. We toured JAARS headquarters in NC, Wycliffe USA headquarters and Word Spring Museum in Orlando, plus Campus Crusade, and the Holy Land Experience. During long travel days on the bus, we shared our stories from the field, Wycliffe videos, singing and games, with different themes each day. We all gained renewed vision for Bible translation. John and I had never been on a bus tour before, so we learned a lot about how bus tours worked.

Meanwhile at home, our star boarder, Karen, enjoyed visits from a former friend. She had dated and been engaged to Jim Hastings as a young lady. But they had broken up due to some miscommunication and each had married someone else. A couple years after Jim's wife died, he contacted Karen. A platonic relationship became serious, and they married in September. Karen had been with us almost two and a half years, and we missed having her around, but were very happy for them both.

One of John's trips was to Puerto Rico to meet with a group of volunteers who recruited there for Wycliffe in their spare time. They had formed "Wycliffe Puerto Rico." This congenial group was eager to help, but lacked necessary resources, like Wycliffe literature in Spanish, office equipment, and training to do TOTAL-It-Up programs. They were grateful for John's visit and help, and we looked forward to more Wycliffe members from there.

When the Northeast Mobilization Director left to pastor a church, John now had two roles. Fortunately, he enjoyed the challenges and opportunities. As he wrote for one of our prayer letters:

> It's really rewarding to see people moving forward in following the Lord's leading into involvement in building the Lord's work. Not long ago I attended a commissioning service for a new missionary. Afterwards she told me that it was my closing statement at the end of our Perspectives course that the Lord used to get her to take the step forward and get started in missions service. Just last week I talked with the father of a young family that has moved to northern Asia to start a business and be "tentmakers" to have opportunities to share Christ. He and his family had also been part of our Perspectives course. It's wonderful to see them moving along in what the Lord has for them.

I organized office tours to share about Bible translation. To visually illustrate our talking points, I worked with a committee and a graphics specialist from our Northwest Wycliffe Office to create large descriptive wall panels. We adapted some graphics files from other Wycliffe offices. I hung the panels in our foyer, hallway, and in various rooms. This was made possible by a generous financial gift from our friend, Roger Hannay. At the same time, our resident artist, Michael Harrah, painted a three-panel mural for us in the foyer.

In 2007 a new recruiting tool called "Explore Wycliffe" was created—a one-day event for interested participants to receive insight into the process of Bible translation. A mono-lingual demonstration showed how linguists elicited words in a new language. Attendees heard of opportunities in translation, literacy, language survey, and support services. Held at our office and other northeast locations, each of these events yielded several participants indicating their intentions to join Wycliffe.

Requests came from all over the world for teachers to fill critical vacant positions. If the educational needs of missionary kids were not being met, families left the field and translation work was delayed. At that time 300 teaching positions were vacant. A special information session for teachers called "World Class Encounter" was scheduled at our office.

John recruited four new recruiters for our office, and they attended a training session in Dallas. Now we had six recruiters working out of our office, each responsible for a certain geographical area. We also had recruiters located in southern Maine; the Philadelphia, PA, area; Cincinnati, Ohio; and the greater New York City area. We were thankful for the good team.

For the past year John had been covering two job responsibilities. It had been a challenge for him to handle all the aspects of both jobs. So, they reallocated some of the specialty recruitment responsibilities to regions and shifted the reporting structure to give John a more manageable load.

At the same time, I did some serious evaluation of my situation. While I had always been heavily involved in my own areas of service with Wycliffe, I felt at times that I had neglected family and home responsibilities. It seemed I could never catch up with my list of undone tasks. I thought it would be good to take a year's "sabbatical" to be more organized at home, cook better meals for John, catch up on correspondence, file the piles of accumulated papers, spend more time in the Word, and generally slow down and reduce the stress level, while being available to help John when needed.

I also made an eye-opening discovery. While talking with a friend about her daughter's ADD challenges, I suddenly realized that I had many of the same symptoms. Through the years I had struggled to keep focused, to complete projects rather than jump to another project or get sidetracked on less-important tasks; my mind often wandered when I tried to concentrate. Sometimes I started to do something and then forgot what I wanted to do. So, now I had identified a cause for my frustrations. (Some would say an excuse.) In one sense I felt relief; but also discouragement, because it was too hard to change the way I was. Medicines didn't work for me. I had to rely on making lists, but it took enormous energy to keep to the listed tasks. I realized that whatever I accomplished was through great effort, and with the Lord's help.

Since I amazingly had reached retirement age, I decided to go on Wycliffe retirement status (remaining a member of Wycliffe). After a year, I planned to serve as a retired volunteer. John, being younger and without "retirement" in his vocabulary could keep serving for many years. I tried not to feel guilty about my decision. I told myself that many missionary wives primarily took care of the home situation. Someone had said that with us, it was "two for the price of one."

(As I was to discover, my sabbatical never materialized, since I continued to help John from home and went to the office sometimes to follow through on some work. I kept busy for years to come.)

Our Personnel team held "Wycliffe Connection" programs regularly for members coming on furlough to give them updates, advice, and helpful resources for their time in the U.S. In July 2007 there were 25 adults and 13 children attending. Of special interest was a panel of local pastors who discussed such questions as "What is the current climate of the Evangelical Church in America?" and "How can missionaries best connect with the body of Christ in America?" John talked to them about how they could be great recruiters while on furlough. There were also programs for the children. We hosted one family in our home.

That year's Wycliffe Family Weekend gave 680 helicopter and plane rides. Special attractions included: Steve Saint with his plane used to make the film *End of the Spear*, a Drama of Tyndale, Ventriloquist, presentations by translators, toy train rides, and more. Our Adult Bible Fellowship from Calvary Church planned and prepared the pancake and sausage/bacon breakfast, taking that responsibility off John's hands. Donations went toward a new Kodiak airplane. I helped prepare some advertising

materials, displays, and a Wycliffe Puzzle, and worked at the Welcome Table.

In September our Information Technology team hosted a new workshop called "Check IT Out." About 20 people with good computer skills attended, with three probably moving on to serve with Wycliffe.

In the fall I accompanied John on a trip to headquarters, using his frequent flier miles. While there, I was requested to do a project—to put together a newsletter for the Recruitment Ministries team. They set me up with a computer and I started work on it. I then became responsible for their bi-monthly "Recruitment Ramblin's." I gathered information, wrote it, formatted it, and sent it out to over 100 members involved in recruitment. This helped inform the widely spread team, encouraging them in their work.

The year 2008 began with a continuation of events. But 2008 was to be a year of great change. There had already been a lot of changes with new strategies, but the biggest one yet was coming. We had heard that some regional offices would close, but we felt safe that ours would not since we were a very active office. Ours had the most efficient cost ratio because of so many good volunteers. (Many offices now had paid employees.) We were in a new building—only six years in use. When two representatives from Wycliffe leadership came to our office to make an announcement, we were apprehensive. They read a statement to our assembled group. Our office would close in November! We all sat there stunned.

It was felt that with changing times, more people saw us first through the worldwide web, not at an office building. The plan was to invest in new strategies and multiply resources.

From my perspective, the decision was hard to understand. John had worked hard to see the office building built, to grow the staff and grow our impact. Many of our local friends had volunteered to help construct the office and apartments and were greatly disappointed. I was proud of John who decided to hold all those things loosely. God was in control, and we would see how He would continue to lead.

We had a closing banquet to thank local friends for their involvement and to serve as closure for our team. Darlene Weidman and I prepared a power point of remembrances. I also prepared a booklet that chronicled the Northeast Office history with information gathered by Don Toland and Helen Miller. We met on November 6 at Grace Church at Willow Valley with the theme "Stones of Remembrance."

Then we cleared out our offices. Headquarters oversaw the sale of our building. The apartments went to the control of Willow Valley Retirement Communities. Our volunteers "retired." Our members were encouraged to work from home or find a new place. This proved difficult for some, so a small office space was rented for five of the staff, representing Personnel and Recruitment, which was able to function for five more years before being closed the end of 2008.

We began to set up an office in our basement for John. However, these events launched another new adventure for him.

Chapter 12
Missions Fest Lancaster
Let's Go Big

---✈

With the closing of the Wycliffe Northeast Office, John began setting up to work out of our basement. Meanwhile another solution was evolving—with two concepts coming together. Did God have a better plan?

John met for breakfast with some men who had helped with the discontinued, yet successful Wycliffe Family Weekend. They loved the event at Smoketown Airport which had motivated mission involvement by people unlikely to attend a more formal program. The men explored the idea of continuing that type of event, carried out by volunteers rather than Wycliffe staff, even expanding it to include other mission aviation programs.

John's Wycliffe supervisor agreed that the idea would serve well. The men met regularly as a team planning for an August Fair, inviting other mission organizations to participate. While most of the team had close aviation connections, they wondered if the event could expand to an even larger mission vision.

Meanwhile, John continued attending a monthly Lancaster Missionary Fellowship (LMF) Luncheon, held at the World Mission Associates (WMA) office, as a learning opportunity and to network with others. Lunch was followed by a presentation and discussion on current mission topics, with emphasis on good ways to "do missions." At one meeting, LMF Director, Glenn Schwartz, reported on his recent visit to a huge Missions Fest Conference in Vancouver, BC, Canada. That event had developed from one congregation inviting other congregations to organize a bigger and better missions conference than they could do on their own. The conference had grown incredibly with added churches and great attendance. Glenn wondered if such an event could be initiated in our area, asking anyone interested to contact him. John shared with Glenn how the Aviation Fair team was exploring similar possibilities.

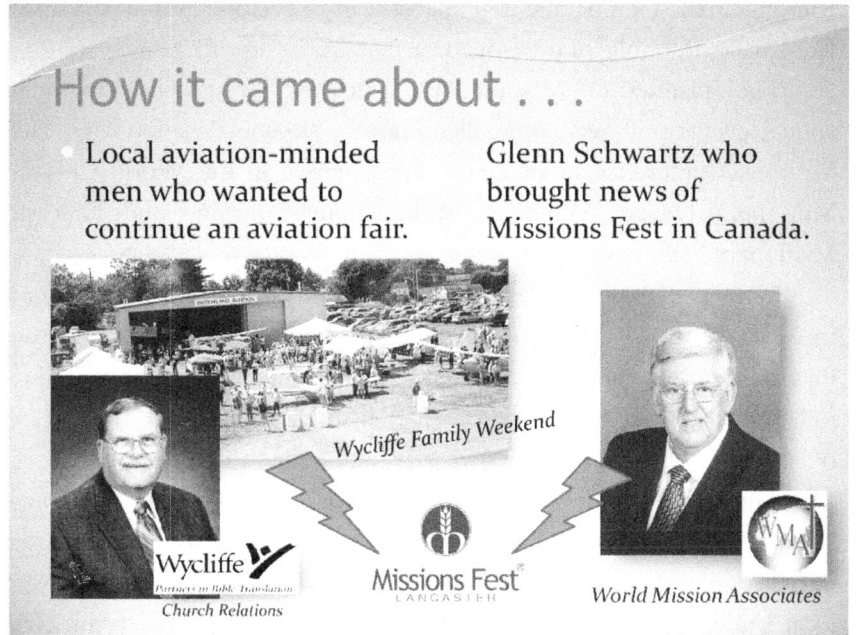

The team liked the idea of connecting with an existing organization to grow their event. In that way many of the legal aspects were already in place and organizational procedures validated. They researched possibilities and felt the Lord's leading towards Missions Fest International. The result was "Missions Fest Lancaster," a franchise-type organization under Missions Fest International. John was appointed Executive Director. It would be his job to get it up and running in the greater Lancaster area. With Wycliffe, John's responsibility fell under the Church Relations Department. The team, along with Glenn Schwartz, became the Advisory Board. Glenn offered John office space at the World Mission Resource Center, with use of a nice room for seminars, luncheons, and classes. WMA would handle our initial finances through their system.

The board was excited to join this international organization whose goals were to spread a vision for global missions; to help people find a place where their interests and abilities could best be used; to create an atmosphere in which congregations, individuals and mission agencies could cooperate in the overall task of the Great Commission; and to demonstrate

Christian unity. We joined other registered member cities of Vancouver, Canada; Seattle, Washington; Yaoundé, Cameroon; Lubumbashi and Kinshasa in the Democratic Republic of Congo; Pretoria, South Africa; and Brazzaville, Republic of the Congo.

They planned for Missions Fest Lancaster (MFL) to hold two main annual events and several smaller ones: a Mission Aviation Fair, large Missions Conference in February, Perspectives on the World Christian Movement course, Women's Spring Luncheon, and the Lancaster Missionary Fellowship Luncheons.

I was personally a little overwhelmed with this new venture. Board member, Marlin Horst, encouraged me, "Wycliffe Family Weekend closed for God to grow us into something bigger." Yes, when God allows something to happen, we need to wait to see what His purpose is. And, of course, we often never know. But God is sovereign, and we trust Him.

The official launch for MFL was a "Kick-Off Breakfast" on Friday, August 22, 2008, at the Eden Resort Hotel. Area pastors and church leaders were invited to learn about Missions Fest. About 250 attended with several local leaders participating in the program. A video showed activities of Missions Fest Vancouver. John introduced the board members and challenged churches to become involved. Steve Saint was the special speaker.

Our "Mission Aviation Fair" followed immediately on Saturday and Sunday afternoon. Board members took responsibilities for various areas of the Fair, with Randy Pearson as Fair Coordinator. A number of missions came as exhibitors. Steve Saint came with his airplane that he had flown in the movie, *End of the Spear*. It was a replica of the one his father Nate had flown in Ecuador when he was martyred in 1946. Steve demonstrated the spiral bucket drop, developed by his father, and used in preparation for that fateful contact with the Aucas (now known as the Waorani). A JAARS helicopter

and Cessna gave over 600 rides. Of high interest was the first Kodiak aircraft off the assembly line and its developer, Dave Voetmann, to tell his story. Over 100 rode in this plane especially designed for missions, and available commercially. With the addition of other mission exhibitors, our outreach had expanded.

The following months were a time of building up the organization. MFL would function with a small staff and lots of volunteers. They hired an Event Coordinator, Sara Costalas, to handle details for our events and serve as receptionist for the World Mission Resource Center. Later Mike McKeever, former Wycliffe Northeast colleague, became administrative assistant to John, working with finances. Funding for Missions Fest Lancaster would come from sponsoring churches, patron donors, individuals, exhibitor fees, advertisers, event offerings, and sales. One of the first steps was to get churches and individuals to sign up as sponsors and to be involved. A mailing was sent out to follow up with attendees of the Kick-Off Breakfast.

We began hosting the monthly LMF Luncheons and the 15-week Perspectives course. John contacted local churches. So far four were actively involved and five more were working through the process of their church's approval. I made a power point presentation explaining Missions Fest, which we showed in several churches.

To help prepare for our big missions conference, John attended the Seattle Missions Fest in October to see how they did it. He received valuable information and made helpful contacts.

In January 2009, Mike McKeever joined John to visit to the Vancouver Missions Fest. That festival drew 40,000 people in one weekend, the result of 26 years growing the event! There were 240 mission agency displays (including Wycliffe) in the exhibition hall and a huge selection of seminars. About 800 volunteers served. It became clear that we'd need many volunteers to successfully replicate such a local mission event.

We requested prayer as we moved forward in the planning. We wanted God to be glorified as we challenged regional congregations to work together to make Christ known globally. As someone said about Missions Fest, "You're a real answer to prayer. On our own, our church couldn't bring in well-known speakers or present so many opportunities. By working with other churches, we can do so much more."

In May a Missions Fest Lancaster Women's Luncheon was held in the private dining room at Lancaster Bible College. About 75 ladies heard Kate Ring share from her experiences as a Wycliffe translator about the importance of being courageous and trusting, whether here or "over there." John shared our dreams for Missions Fest Lancaster. The offering covered costs and a nice contribution to MFL. Many ladies volunteered to be involved, to pray, or encourage their churches to be involved.

In August 2009, prior to our Mission Aviation Fair, we held a Friday Missions Fest breakfast, sponsored by World Mission Associates and Hope International. The program included mission updates and a video of pastors in Canada speaking highly of the value of their churches' involvement in Missions Fest. Nard Pugyao, a JAARS pilot and Filipino by birth, was the keynote speaker. He shared how Scriptures translated into his Isnag language led him to follow Christ. He skillfully challenged attendees to realize the urgency and importance of listening and responding to God's mission call. He praised organizations like MFL, which educate and mobilize people for missions.

After the breakfast we headed to the Smoketown airport to set up for the following day: tents, tables, chairs, signage, machines for popcorn, slushies, soft ice cream, and more. That year we moved activities to the other side of the airstrip, with more space and the use of several hangars. Displays were set up by 14 aviation and 12 non-aviation agencies.

ITEC's Maverick flying car!

Special aircraft were placed in static display. A large rainstorm threatened us, but we thankfully saw it part and pass by on both sides.

Early Saturday morning we made final preparations as a light rain fell. Friends from our Adult Bible Fellowship class arrived and began cooking pancakes and sausages for breakfast. At 7:30 the rain stopped as people began arriving to enjoy the delicious food. Served on a donation basis, about $1,000 was raised for the ministry of MFL, most of the food having been donated by local businesses. Around noon the sky cleared sufficiently for missionary plane and helicopter rides. When we were closing for the day, the rain began again. Sunday afternoon the weather was great.

In all, almost 3,000 people from 137 different churches attended. JAARS gave about 450 rides. Special speakers included Steve Saint, Nard Pugyao and Jim Leamer with his IT presentation. We were blessed to see the good interaction as people visited the exhibits of various missions and interacted with the mission staff. Many had contacts to follow up for future mission service, or to help in some way. We appreciated the many volunteers who helped make the event possible.

After a summer pause, the monthly Lancaster Missionary Fellowship Luncheons began again. The facilities at the World Mission Resource Center served well for events. In October we held a dessert coffee for pastors and missions committee members informing them about MFL and their opportunity to be involved as sponsoring churches. In November we hosted a pastor/leader's luncheon. Beginning in January John again held the Perspectives Lancaster Spring Course.

Plans accelerated for our first big Missions Fest Lancaster Conference on February 19-21, 2010, at Lancaster Bible College. It was located just "around the corner" from the Missions Fest office. Their beautiful chapel would be the site of our plenary sessions, with seminars in classrooms of adjacent buildings. There were now eight sponsoring churches, and volunteers from various other churches, who helped prepare for the conference, along with six corporate sponsors providing monthly support for office operations.

What's in Your Hand?

↫ The theme was "The Changing Face of World Missions." Exhibitor applications came in from various Mission agencies. Committees were organized to handle hundreds of details. Four great plenary speakers were scheduled:

- Steve Saint, I-Tec founder, author of *End of the Spear* and son of missionary martyr, Nate Saint
- Jo Shetler, Wycliffe Bible translator in the Philippines with the Balangao People, a great communicator
- Glenn Mason, Executive Director of Carver International Missions
- Morgan Jackson, International Development Director of Faith Comes by Hearing.

I prepared a 32-page conference program magazine, including centerfold advertisements, learning the InDesign program to do it. The magazine included info about daily schedules; plenary speaker information; youth program, children's program; musicians; exhibitors; bookstore; prayer chapel; seminar schedule with descriptions, location, and presenter bios. We developed a key code to identify 18 seminar "tracks" (such as Church Missions Committees, Disaster Relief, Bible Translation, Technology in Missions, Medical Missions). E.J. Rittersbach helped by keying the extensive seminar information. And Sara Costalas gave editorial assistance and information about all she was organizing as Event Coordinator. DavCo Advertising gave me helpful preparation advice and a discount on the printing. The prepared copy deadline was prior to Christmas, so that the printed magazine could be available several weeks ahead of the conference. Because it was such a huge project, I didn't do much personal preparation for Christmas. We ordered 6,000 copies—perhaps a bit ambitious.

John arranged with the food service company at Lancaster Bible College to have meals available for conference attendees. He had to make a commitment for a certain number of meals for an unknown quantity of people, as we did not require registration to attend the event.

A flurry of final preparations, with threatened snowstorms, didn't stop the enthusiasm. There were 72 exhibit tables side by side in the first and second floor lobbies of the Good Shepherd Chapel. People circulated well to visit them. Sixty different seminars were offered in different time slots. Plenary speakers gave excellent presentations.

Music played a big part also. Four musicians from Indonesia, Kenya and America kicked off their "Beyond Idols Worship Tour" with a Saturday evening concert, after being finalists in American-Idol-type competitions. They were devout followers of Christ, traveling to various states with Global Disciples to present programs. The Lancaster Evangelical Free Church Praise Band led worship sessions. Lancaster Bible College Chamber Singers, Mennonite Children's Choir of Lancaster, and McCaskey High School Gospel Choir sang at various sessions.

About 225 students came to a Children's Program on Friday afternoon coordinated by Brad and Maxine Waldman (of the Caribbean Children's Ministry Network). It was set up as a "Field Trip" from home schools and Christian schools. They held a Children's Rally and a session of revolving workshops, followed

by speaker Kurt Jarvis with Chronological Bible Storying for Kids. The children learned about missionary work and had a good time together. We hoped that some would become missionaries someday.

Our attendance for the conference was lower than expected—about 2,000 for the weekend. A busload of folks came from Florida and a Missions Committee group from Michigan. A special joy for me was that my niece Wendy brought four girls from their youth group in Maryland. We felt that those who came would encourage lots of others to come next year, and that this "new thing" for our area would really catch on.

Meanwhile, back in October John and I had been advised that our name had arrived at the top of a list for cottages available at Calvary Fellowship Homes in Lancaster. My uncle, Tim James, who lived there, had encouraged us to put our name on the waiting list. We thought that it would take several years before that opportunity arose. They were offering a 15% entry fee discount and had three cottages available. Would we like to check them out? "I always like to look!" I told John. One seemed perfect with an additional discount if we liked the existing carpet. We felt this was God's provision for the best financial opportunity to move there. We put our house up for sale. Viewings were slow. Our realtor said that it would be a miracle if we sold by our February 1 deadline. Missing that date, we would need to pay the monthly fee to hold the Calvary cottage for us. We trusted the Lord for His best timing and provision.

All through this time we were waiting for our house in Strasburg to sell. We had expected that it would sell quickly. Finally in March we had a contract, with closing on April 30, 2010. By then I was so tired of getting the house in order for showings and open houses, vacating each time with our dog Frodo.

Actually, the timing served us well, following the very busy preparations for the February conference. Our house sold right at the end of the extended period in which Calvary Homes would hold the cottage for us. Our dear Uncle Ralph came to our rescue and paid for our three months of fees. We downsized with a yard sale, donated some items, and moved in early May.

Our new location was close to John's relocated office, our church, and grocery stores. John was happy to no longer cut grass. With his shop tools set up along the side of our garage, John built several pieces of furniture to fit perfectly in special spots in our new home. We felt very blessed to be at Calvary Fellowship Homes.

The Mission Aviation Fair continued to grow. About 3,000 came in August for a wonderful time of learning what God was doing in various parts of the world. We started off Friday morning with Russ Stendal speaking at an Eden Resort breakfast. Friday evening, we showed the film *End of the Spear* in Hangar Z with an explanatory introduction by Steve Saint himself. As a bonus, Steve also personalized it by stopping part way through to point out those in the film who were the actual people involved in the real-life story!

On Saturday and Sunday, attendees enjoyed a pancake breakfast, 30 exhibits, parachute jumpers, plane and helicopter rides, flight demonstrations, a selection of yummy food, and much more.

At speaker sessions, Russ Stendal shared how God opened incredible doors for ministry in Colombia after his capture there in the 80s. Jim Leamer told how various technologies facilitated ministries around the world. Paul Dye shared his nail-biting account of escape from Colombian kidnappers, along with lessons God taught him through that time. Steve Saint shared how the Lord was using his continued ministry and I-Tec organization.

A special Children's Kingdom Kids program was again directed by Brad and Maxine Waldman who brought with them a youth group of helpers from Allentown, including one who accepted the Lord as Savior during that time. With explorer passes, children attended activity areas earning "cash" for the "store" and learning the Great Commission verse:

"Therefore go and make disciples of all nations, baptizing them in the name of the Father and of the Son and of the Holy Spirit," -Matthew 28:19 (NIV).

Many shared how they were blessed. Over 100 volunteers participated. One person even connected with a job offer! Contributions and food sales covered the cost of the event!

Julie Iddings was now our Event Coordinator, organizing details of our various events. It was a big responsibility, and she enjoyed doing it. Her friend Alyssa Soule worked as administrative assistant for MFL and World Mission Associates, while also handling the reception desk. For a time, Alec Millen served part-time as Promotional Coordinator contacting churches.

The Missions Fest Lancaster Board of Advisors wanted to go big for the 2011 conference in February. "Let's go for it and hold it at the new Lancaster County Convention Center," said one. They agreed. John and I accompanied Julie to the Convention Center, meeting with their events person to make arrangements and determine the spaces we would need. Exhibits and plenary sessions would be on Level 1 in Freedom Hall A and Freedom Hall B with concession stands in the adjacent passageway. Seminars would be held on level 2, as well as a special area focusing on "Business as Mission." Lower-level space was designated for children's programs. Special MFL hotel room rates were available for those who would stay-over. A parking garage connected to the center. Other municipal parking lots were nearby. Shuttle buses were planned to transport people from satellite parking locations.

Using the Convention Center was going to be expensive. We needed to add more sponsoring churches and corporate sponsors. Exhibitors' fees would help. Admission would be free to be accessible to any who wished to attend.

I began preparing the Conference Program magazine, gathering advertisers to help cover the printing cost. I also prepared newsletters for our growing list of constituents. For our Fall 2010 newsletter, John wrote an article:

> The growth in technology stuns us as we try to keep up and use it effectively. Some think the missionary task must be nearly complete, considering all the resources available today. Yet, the most challenging areas of the world await the Good News of salvation. How can we best reach those areas? Is time running out for the unreached people

groups? How can our churches best be involved in the Great Commission task? Do those who already enjoy God's blessings still really care about the others? Are we willing to sacrifice a bit of personal comfort? Do those who are concerned know how to plug in with the resources and talents with which God has blessed them? Are there different means and methods we should use to gain access to restricted areas? To address these issues, our February Missions Fest Lancaster Conference . . . .

The Conference kicked off on Friday, February 18th with an RSVP luncheon at the Convention Center. Gracia Burnham spoke and gave us a taste of what she would present at the conference plenary session. (Gracia and her husband Martin had served for 17 years with New Tribes Mission in the Philippines where he was a jungle pilot. In 2001 they were kidnapped by a militant group and held for 376 days. Martin was killed in a firefight; Gracia was wounded but was freed. Since then, Gracia had authored two books, *In the Presence of My Enemies* and *To Fly Again*, and had spoken widely of the lessons she had learned through her experiences.) The room was so full, I almost couldn't find a seat.

A Friday afternoon Children's program, "The Commission Kid's Adventure," was again led by Brad and Maxine Waldman. Also, during all Plenary Sessions, children could attend hands-on, interactive programs.

A Friday evening Youth Rally featured speaker Shelby Abbott from Campus Crusade for Christ, who with humor and candor challenged students to consider their mission in life.

During Saturday and on Sunday afternoon, it was a thrill to see over 90 exhibitors in Freedom Hall presenting the ministry of their various missions. Five of our supporting churches displayed, as well as several Christian schools and camps. God was using each in a special way. As attendees interacted at the various exhibitors, some conversations of eternal value took place.

We were delighted and blessed with incredibly devoted plenary speakers:

Gracia Burnham told of the Lord's sustaining power when she and her husband were held by a militant group and of opportunities for continued ministry to that group.

Paul Borthwick, with Development Associates International, shared God's unchanging message in a changing world and practical ways people can live as "Great Commission Christians." Their ministry worked to identify and resource emerging leaders through ministries like the Lausanne Committee for World Evangelization and International Fellowship of Evangelical Students. Paul sought to influence the next generation towards world missions at Gordon College and as an Associate for the Urbana Student Missions Convention.

Chuck Bentley, CEO of Crown Financial Ministries, and host of MoneyLife radio broadcast, told of their widening ministry which included producing short Bible story films in various languages, which illustrated

God's principles. Their main ministry focused on biblical principles of managing money so that God's purposes for one's life could be fulfilled.

Dr. Ron Blue, coordinator of the Spanish Doctor of Ministry Program at Dallas Theological Seminary, and former missionary and president of CAM International, enthusiastically challenged us to consider "The Bottom Line, Sending." His exciting stories illustrated his points.

Board member, Charlie Kreider, made DVDs of all sessions, which were available afterwards. Bill Snyder handled the Book Sales. Many others took responsibilities, including Jean Hassel, who came on board as Volunteer Coordinator for over 100 volunteers.

There are always pros and cons for choosing a venue. The Lancaster County Convention Center was a great facility for such an event. The exhibition hall was perfect for placing many exhibitors. The auditorium area was more than ample; seminar rooms were nicely appointed. However, some attendees were confused about going to different levels. Downtown parking challenged those unaccustomed to city traffic.

Our biggest concern was the cost, which rose to double what we had planned because of various additional unanticipated charges. Although we received funds after the conference, we struggled financially. To help pay our debt, a board member kindly set up a $15,000 matching fund for donations. For future conferences we would need more sponsoring churches. According to Missions Fest International protocol, each sponsoring church would appoint one or two representatives to participate in planning events, encourage involvement from his/her church, and to make a yearly contribution (recommended $2.00 per church attendee) to help enable the events. Currently, 12 churches were partnering with Missions Fest Lancaster. One very active church participated with 30 volunteers at our conference! To financially cover large events, we set a goal to add 12 more churches by September.

Meanwhile the current Perspectives course was in full swing. At one session John asked the class, "How many of you at this point are considering full-time missions?" Half of the 24 participants raised their hands. After students finished each section of lessons, they completed a "Personal Response Form" where they described what was most important to them. Reading those was an incredible blessing. For example, one student wrote:

This course is challenging, but in the same sense, so rewarding. I've felt a call to missions for a long time, but I'd never been really willing to accept the call to go. Through the reading, the speakers, and the stories, I know this is truly what God has for me. My heart has been touched and challenged, but beyond anything, I've just gotten excited about the mission that God has called us to! We are chosen to spread his word, and missionaries aren't an elitist group. We all are missionaries, we all are called, whether to send or go. I feel such a strong tug in my heart to go, and I know if God would ever take that burden from me, I would still feel the need to send out missionaries to help fulfill his goals. . . .

Our Event Coordinator, Julie Giddings, kept busy planning details of each event, one after the other. She and other helpers prepared the lunch each month for the Lancaster Missionary Fellowship. She organized the Women's Spring Luncheon in May, held at the Gathering Place in Mount Joy with Cheryl Pfautz as speaker. Cheryl's husband was Director of Finances for Global Disciples. Her presentation burdened us for those still waiting to hear the Gospel.

The 2011 Mission Aviation Fair began with a Friday film night. Again, our Adult Bible Fellowship prepared the popular Saturday morning pancake breakfast, which motivated people to come early for the day's events. The airplane and helicopter rides attracted a lot of riders. Among the volunteers, John's sister and her new husband blew up  and tied balloons for the children. Attendees registered for door prizes provided by various organizations. This gave us valuable church and individual contact information for follow-up, as well as learning how they heard about the event to evaluate advertising choices, and if they would be interested in volunteering for a future event.

A silent auction helped raise funds for event costs. The Children's area with creation stations reported that several children had dedicated their lives to the Lord as a result of the mission activities tailored to them. Despite rain on Sunday, about 2,500 attendees learned about mission aviation.

In January 2012 John started another Perspectives course at the World Missions Associates office with 24 participants.

Our third Missions Fest Lancaster Conference was held at the lovely campus of Lancaster Mennonite High School on February 17-19. Their facility included ample parking space, a sizable gym for 72 exhibits, concession area, dining hall, and a gathering room on a lower level for the children's activities. Classrooms at the Academic Center provided space for 25 seminars, during five seminar sessions. Millcreek Bible Church was the site of the Children's Field Trip on Friday afternoon.

Friday evening a Youth Rally featured Mike Yankoski who shared about his life on the streets. He and a friend purposely became "homeless" for five months, living in six different cities to observe how Christians would interact with them. He had authored a unique book, *Under the Overpass*, telling of his experiences. Brett Rush, a popular local musician, performed a concert for the youth, as well as leading plenary session worship. Simultaneously on Friday evening, two movies were shown in the dining hall.

Dr. Ronald Cline, Ambassador for HCJB Global Radio, spoke at a Saturday evening banquet. For some years Ron had a radio program "Beyond the Call" on Christian radio stations. Both Ron and Mike spoke in plenary sessions.

I helped by again preparing the program magazine, posters, signs and the MFL display. Lots had been put in place to offer information, challenges, and opportunities for people to see how they could be involved in missions.

It was our desire to grow Missions Fest Lancaster to serve the U.S. east coast. We wished more people had come out to benefit from the conference and get excited about missions. But we struggled to meet operating expenses. While the third conference came close to breaking even financially, we were at a critical stage. To continue, we needed more financial input—especially from additional sponsoring churches and patron donors. While the hugely successful Vancouver festival was a grass-roots movement by churches, ours was in a sense top down. We had to convince the churches of its value.

We were thankful that Doris Dagen joined our team part-time as Church Relations Coordinator. And Alex Turoczi also helped part time with Church Relations. We hoped they could help bring in more churches. It was interesting that some of the large churches, with their own well-developed programs, did not seem to be interested in helping for the sake of the smaller churches.

Our annual Women's Spring Luncheon in May met at the Four Seasons Banquet Facility in Landisville, PA. Our featured speaker was Nancy Sebastian Meyer, an international speaker, musician, and author with her ministry called "Hope 4 Hearts." With an obvious passion to help women, she shared her own incredible story about how to love even when it is difficult.

For the 2012 Mission Aviation Fair we looked forward to having Steve Saint with us again to fly his Maverick flying car. We were sad to hear that he had suffered a serious accident, being struck on his head while conducting a test on an experimental wing mounted on a rolling test stand. With loss of feeling in his limbs, he would have a long recovery. We grieved for this special servant of God who developed tools and technology appropriate for indigenous God followers to reach their own people with the Gospel. We were thankful that Steve's son Jaime came in his place to speak at a Saturday session and was our excellent Fair Emcee. He also introduced the Friday night film, "The Grandfathers" about Steve Saint's family going to live with the Waoranis who had killed his father, Nate. Jaime's brother Jesse also came to the Fair and flew the I-Tec airplane that was made in Ecuador. The Saint heritage continued!

The Saturday morning pancake breakfast served 500, again handled so well by our ABF class, and growing more popular each year. The Children's Program reported that a number of children accepted the Lord as Savior at one of their activity stations. On Sunday afternoon around 4:30 we got word that a storm with high winds was headed in our direction. At that point one plane was in the air with passengers, including my great nephew, Caleb. The pilot made a low pass to land, but instead went around to avoid a wind gust. Next try, thankfully he landed. We quickly packed up blowable items and shut the Fair down early. There was no major damage—just a few broken tent poles (including our personal dining fly).

Our Advisory Board had set a deadline of August 31 for the following actions:

1. Identify one big-name major speaker for next February's conference. (Several had been contacted and we were waiting for word from them.)
2. Have at least 5 churches actively involved in planning and running the events. (We presently had 3 doing that.)
3. Increase the number of sponsoring churches to at least 18. (Currently 13 were involved.)
4. Add at least 4 more Patron Donors at $3,000 each. (Or an alternative number of smaller gifts providing the same amount.)

While most of our events seemed to just about pay for themselves, the month-to-month operating costs of about $3,000 were a problem. For Missions Fest Lancaster to continue, we needed to be able to pay our bills on time, which included the rental office space for World Mission Associates, salary for our event coordinator and the receptionist, plus supplies.

By the end of August, we were unable to meet the Board's goals. The consensus was that the Mission Aviation Fair had more appeal for attendees than the February Missions Conference. To put on a large event like that involved an incredible amount of effort and resources. So, the Advisory Board decided not to continue the conference. Since that was the heart of the Missions Fest International organization, we ended our franchise with them. We felt that our three-year run had provided good opportunities for people to learn, connect and participate in missions, and we trusted the results to the Lord.

But we would continue the other events. We just had to regroup.

Chapter 13
Mission Aviation Promotions
Highlighting Technical Service

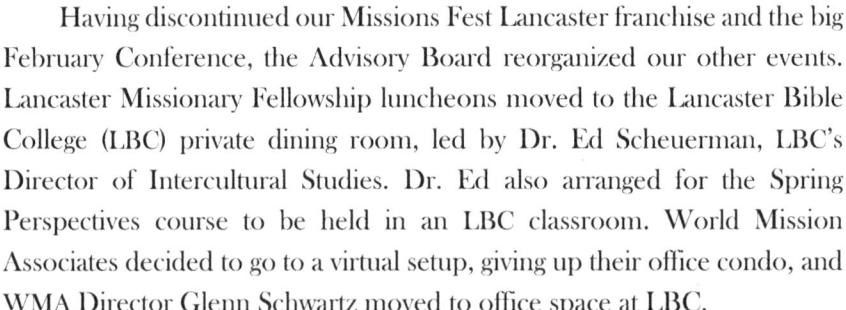

Having discontinued our Missions Fest Lancaster franchise and the big February Conference, the Advisory Board reorganized our other events. Lancaster Missionary Fellowship luncheons moved to the Lancaster Bible College (LBC) private dining room, led by Dr. Ed Scheuerman, LBC's Director of Intercultural Studies. Dr. Ed also arranged for the Spring Perspectives course to be held in an LBC classroom. World Mission Associates decided to go to a virtual setup, giving up their office condo, and WMA Director Glenn Schwartz moved to office space at LBC.

Our board set up a new non-profit 501(c)(3) called Mission Aviation Promotions (MAP) of which John was the director. Its goal was *"promoting the spread of the gospel through aviation and technology."* This permitted the Mission Aviation Fair to continue. The board members were actively involved. Marlin Horst, Smoketown Airport owner, offered John free space at the small terminal building near the airport's entrance. Charlie Kreider provided IT and technical help for our email and website setups as well as sound system, internet, and video setups for the Fair. Duane Tice handled finances, and Bill Snyder oversaw book sales. They all helped guide and promote the Fair—a talented and genial team!

John settled into cubicle space next to the office area of Mel Glick, the Airport Manager, and they became good buddies. John continued his various activities there under Wycliffe's Church Relations Department.

This also seemed like a good time for John to move to what we called "Reduced Assignment." In this status, basically everything remained the same, including our financial support, except that John would be responsible for only half-time involvement.

Without an Event Coordinator, I helped John as "Information Coordinator." That's when I learned how much was involved to hold the Mission Aviation Fair. As we prepared for the 2013 Fair, here's a behind-the-scenes look at the details:

The Missions Fest Lancaster website was discontinued and a new one set up as mission-aviation.org which I learned to maintain with occasional help from a free-lance computer specialist. I also set up a Facebook page for Mission Aviation Promotions. I designed a logo, based on an idea from one of the board members and set up a template for stationery and return address stickers. I prepared and sent out newsletters and kept the database file of our contacts up to date.

I needed to change 14 different Mission Fest Lancaster forms to Mission Aviation Promotions and update them, prepare signage for the Fair and the Program handout with advertisements. And I scheduled Welcome Tent volunteers.

Advertising could be expensive, so we endeavored to use the most effective means, with the least cost. There were posters to prepare, bulletins for churches, and radio ads for WDAC and WJTL. I sent event invitations by letter or email to the contact list, to former sponsoring churches and those listed in the Lancaster County Church Directory. I prepared an ad for the Dine & Clip Placemat and for Engel Publishing which went out to ten area weekly papers. In my retirement status, I was still very involved, working out of our home.

John and the board determined the event theme, budget, speakers, film to be shown, event schedule, and overall plans. He confirmed speakers and emcee, and reserved lodging space for outside participants. He contacted various businesses for donated or discounted food and drinks. He interacted with JAARS and MAF regarding aircraft they would bring. He led planning meetings with coordinators; developed the grounds layout; ordered tents, tables and chairs, porta potties, and dumpster.

John and Mel Glick were inspired to create our own barrel train ride for the children, making the barrel-cars look like little airplanes. They painted each one differently with logos of our main participating mission organizations. A friend, Don Stetter, made wooden propellers, and I designed a printed instrument panel. The Little Plane Train was to become a great hit!

John and Randy Pearson did a radio interview for a Saturday morning WDAC program. Two free aircraft rides rewarded WDAC call-in contestants. Charlie Kreider set up a newspaper interview with John, resulting in a nice article on the front of the Local/Business section in the Lancaster New Era Newspaper. John made plans with the Breakfast Committee, arranged pickups for the grill and serving supplies, worked with Mel Glick to have a refrigerated truck and the ice cream machine. He placed the big sign on the roadside. He kept us all going, and, as he said, "put out fires of any problems that came up."

Jean Hassel, our Volunteer Coordinator, took the big responsibility to find volunteers and schedule them for the various areas, like food service, children's tent, jump house, train rides, ticket sellers, audio visual help, on-site nurse, set up and close-down. She organized our new volunteer shirts and food vouchers. She also helped me put together Information packets for the exhibitors, speakers, and staff. She helped with exhibitor arrangements in the tents, posting signage, and whatever else was needed. Her experience working with Julie helped greatly.

Other coordinators were invaluable as well: Brian and Vicki Knisely headed up the food service. John M. Albright coordinated the parking—in the hot sun. Wilmer Smucker took responsibility for fairgrounds maintenance. Bonnie Leventry handled the silent auction. Julie Horst and Alicia Horst led the Children's Program. The month before the Fair was a crazy, busy time for us.

The 2013 Fair with the theme of "Aviation Maintenance" drew over 3,100 visitors, plus volunteers and staff. People attended from over 280 large and small churches, with many first timers. An exhibitor tent gave ample room for 21 mission displays and hundreds of visitors, with lots of significant conversations. The New Tribes Village-2-Go attracted many people, as well as the MMS Aviation riveting station, the MAF flight simulator, an airplane without its skin, and I-Tec's Maverick flying car.

Our Winsome Class again prepared and served a pancake breakfast for about 600 people, cooking 95 pounds of bacon and using 105 dozen eggs! JAARS gave 84 helicopter flights to 250 passengers and MAF gave many rides in the Cessna aircraft. Speaker sessions in Hangar F worked well. Our three neat speakers were: Dwight Jarboe, President of Missionary

Maintenance Service; Randy Pearson, pilot then serving with AuSIL (Australian Society for Indigenous Languages); and Gene Foltz with New Tribes Mission who described the development of the new Kodiak aircraft suited to demanding needs of mission and humanitarian aviation organizations.

Over 500 children participated in Kid-Zone activities, including passports to other countries; games, crafts, snacks from around the world, Don Billett from Creation Appreciation, world champion juggler Chris Ivey, face painting, balloons, story time, coloring corner, the debut of our "Little Airplane Train," and even a candy drop from an airplane!

Book sales brought in $1,500. Ice-cream was popular with 715 cones or bowls sold. With high attendance on Saturday, the food line backed up at noon. We had printed 1,000 programs on a printer in the rented Wycliffe office, but we ran out on Saturday. Thankfully, Wycliffe friend, Janet Morris, printed an additional amount on Saturday evening. We almost ran out of parking space. And we had a note to order more porta-potties next year. Good problems! The fun Silent Auction earned about $1,750.

We praised the Lord for a special Fair, as we sensed God working through the various aspects. We were thankful for safety in travel, the aircraft rides, and flight demonstrations. We prayed that all this effort would result in new missionaries serving globally, as well as prayer and financial partnering.

On Monday we cleared out equipment and supplies from the airport. John and I recorded our inventory as we stored it. Later I added new contacts to our database from the registration cards, then sent out a four-page email photo report to those on the contact list.

While our other events had required much preparation, none was as complex as the Fair. It took an immense amount of work (of which most people had no idea), but we felt the effort was worth it. It was a "vision-casting event." Hard to report immediate results, so we trusted those to the Lord. We occasionally heard that a new pilot serving on the field, was first motivated at our fair.

Since my retirement schedule was flexible, I joined a monthly Women's Missionary Coffee, an offshoot of a Philadelphia group. We shared and prayed with ladies from various missions, to encourage those in transition (heading to the field, on furlough, on health leave, or re-integrating into U.S. culture). It was a comfortable place to share candidly and encourage each other. Initially Lynn Henriksen graciously hosted us in her home until she had health issues. Then we began rotating to different homes. I was blessed to make new friends. *(In later years I became part of the leadership team.)*

We had become associate members of Calvary Church. For several years we were on the social committee for our large Winsome ABF (Adult Bible Fellowship). We had fun planning together for monthly class activities. John also served on the Cross Training Team, through which missionary candidates from the church were trained and mentored. Once when John interviewed a candidate to see how he was progressing, he learned that he had made a decision for missions at a recent Mission Aviation Fair.

We enjoyed getting away for camping trips, taking our dog, Frodo, with us. *(For Tolkien fans, our dog had big fluffy feet like a hobbit.)* He was lots of fun, and being with us was his greatest joy. I'm not sure if he enjoyed camping as much as we did, but it was a needed, inexpensive get-away. John enjoyed grilling and cooking breakfast, so meal preparation was easy.

Just before Christmas John's sister, Karen, suddenly passed away, after recuperating from back surgery. We missed her encouragement and prayers. She was a special sister and friend. To this day, we have reminders of her—the African violet she gave us which continues to bloom generously, the jacket, the leopard print shirt, the pink flamingo garden decoration, and books on writing which motivated me to start writing our story.

John and I were invited to be part of a Steering Committee to celebrate the 50th Anniversary of Calvary Fellowship Homes, with many events during 2013. John helped compile contact information for churches and mission agencies with connections to Calvary Homes to invite them to events. I served on the History sub-committee. We searched the Calvary archives for information and photos which I scanned to create a PowerPoint presentation for a banquet. I also prepared a timeline of Calvary history in a pamphlet and for a large wall hanging, which was placed in a building hallway.

John continued coordinating the annual Spring Perspectives Course. The 2013 course was held in a second level classroom of the Chapel building at Lancaster Bible College. Seven of the participants were LBC students. Someone kindly provided fees for a student's husband who wanted to join his wife in the study, making a total of 34 participants.

The 2014 class with 29 students, met in the tiered classroom of the Sebastian Academic Center at LBC. John scrambled to find a last-minute replacement for the Lesson Two presenter who had been urgently called to Chile. I helped by preparing the promotional folder and poster, and coordinated prayer for the class. Being the designated food runner, I picked up pizzas at Costco's or subs from S. Clyde Weaver, so that busy participants could come directly from work or school and have a light meal before class.

The 2015 Course had 44 students. In 2016, 30 inches of snow welcomed the 32 participants, with streets and sidewalks cleared in time for class on January 26. It seemed an oxymoron that the Spring course began in January.

For the 2014 Mission Aviation Fair, Mel Glick and John had fun adapting the tractor which pulled the Little Airplane Train. They added wings with twin propellers, covered the front to look like an airplane fuselage and added a big tail. The children enjoyed that, along with Chris Ivey's juggling, a candy drop and many other activities.

The Fair's theme, "Serving in a Changing World" was emphasized by the presenters. Ron Ensminger talked about Global Media Outreach's website, GodLife.com, to build personal relationships with their online missionaries.

I-TEC's unmanned aerial vehicle (UAV) demonstrated how emergency medications could be flown to remote areas. MAF displayed their beautiful new amphibious Kodiak aircraft, headed soon for Indonesia. Many of the 26 exhibitors reported hundreds who engaged in significant conversations. One exhibitor reported: *"I have much more detailed and focused conversations at Smoketown than any other venue that I participate in."*

Highlights of the 2015 Mission Aviation Fair included popular speaker, Nard Pugyao. A concert was presented by Melissa Hillard, Musical Ambassador for Mission Aviation Fellowship. Would-be pilots tested their skills at MAF's flight simulator. A new exhibitor joined us—the Ship Ministry of Operation Mobilization. Children enjoyed Jesse Rothacker's Reptile demonstration, caricature artists, etc. African jewelry was for sale—a project started by a teenager to benefit an orphanage in Kenya.

"It Takes a Team" was the 2016 Fair's theme. A record 622 people enjoyed the Pancake Breakfast. In the speaker's hangar we displayed a huge 477 square foot mural created by Lawrence Saint (a world-class stained-glass artist), father of the martyred missionary Nate Saint. It depicted men and women who walked with God. Starting In 1966 it had been displayed in the chapel of the Evangelical Seminary in Myerstown, PA. Later it was removed and stored during renovations. At the fair it was to be presented to Jaime Saint, on behalf of I-TEC mission where it would be housed. To our surprise, Steve Saint (Jaime's father and Nate's son) personally came to receive it, still learning to walk after his injury. In a touching talk, Steve remembered his grandfather, Lawrence.

A demonstration of 3-D printing attracted many. Ray Rising, radio technologist supporting Bible translation, shared how the Lord sustained him through a guerilla group's kidnapping for 810 days in Colombia's jungles. Significant rain and wind on Sunday afternoon lowered attendance, but activities and rides continued between the storms.

John and I were usually exhausted by the end of Sunday's activities, yet thankful for safety, for all who came out, and the many volunteers.

By this time, we were well past retirement age. I personally felt I couldn't continue to handle all I had been doing. I also needed to care for a friend with Alzheimer's. John had begun to have some memory issues, with short times of zoning out and confused speech. We looked for new leadership for the Fair, or maybe to cut back on some of the activities. Our volunteer friends were also getting older. Perhaps new approaches and ideas would be good for the Fair.

We also decided it was time for John to retire from Wycliffe at the end of 2016, after 46 years of service. We needed to slow down and enter a different phase of life. God had been faithful to us through past years, so we trusted Him for our future. We had been blessed with faithful financial partners, enabling us to serve. On retirement status with Wycliffe, we retained our membership and could continue to receive financial gifts as "pension income" with tax deductible receipts. John still planned to help with the local Perspectives Course, but he handed the leadership to Faith Flores, the Grader for the student's work and leader of the Fall Perspectives Course at Calvary Church. John continued to serve on committees at Calvary Fellowship Homes and helped on the Mission Aviation Fair Committee. As God enabled, we wanted to continue encouraging people towards mission service.

We decided to have a Retirement Celebration at Calvary Homes, and requested use of our Fellowship Hall. Friends from our Adult Bible Fellowship class volunteered to prepare a light lunch. I was embarrassed as

I called them several times adding to the number of those who responded with RSVPs.

On February 4, 2017, we were very blessed to celebrate with over 100 friends and family, maxing out the Fellowship Hall. What a treat to reconnect with some we hadn't seen for years.

The program included group singing of our favorite hymns ("Great is Thy Faithfulness" and "Day by Day"). John and I shared a PowerPoint presentation reviewing our work with Wycliffe. We had a time of open mike sharing of special memories. Wycliffe colleague, Don Toland, emceed and presented us with a retirement plaque. Our Wycliffe friends sang our Wycliffe theme song, "Faith, Mighty Faith." The lunch was generous, and folks enjoyed fellowship at tables in the back of the room.

We were privileged to have so many join us—a reminder that we had served alongside very special people, and been supported with prayer and finances from churches, family, and friends. We were surprised by many congratulation cards, some enclosing checks and gift cards.

Transitioning into retirement, we desired to simplify life, yet continue in meaningful pursuits. John thought he might need to work part time to help financially, but I didn't want work to tie him down and limit our opportunities. I had many home projects waiting for me. One was organizing our slides from the 60s and 70s, which our friend, Parks Squyres, then at Wycliffe's Tucson Center, offered to digitize.

(Parks has digitized over 100,000 slides for missionaries, using a special system he devised. After working in the aerospace industry, he volunteered to serve in Peru. Later he sold his newly built retirement home in Oregon to move to our Tucson Center to help our Mexico Branch people. In addition to his unique technical service, he came up with many ways to address unmet needs of Wycliffe staff. He said, "God gifted me with

inventive skills that my patents made lots of money for my employers. I now see how God used me for His purpose.")

Calvary Homes needed volunteers to set up and staff a Thrift Store. Proceeds from this benefited the Benevolent Care Fund, helping residents whose funds ran out. John helped paint and make shelving as we turned an unused apartment into a store. I signed up to help with advertising and ended up being the advertising person, with more work than anticipated. We both helped staff the store. It became very successful, giving us opportunity to interact with our community. John sometimes repaired donated furniture, and made some new items to sell.

Medical visits increased. We tried different medications for John's memory issues, but he had reactions to each of them. When John got lost a couple times, he began to realize that he had a problem. I researched natural supplements for memory loss and attended seminars, wanting to help in the best way.

On August 3, 2018, I was getting meat out of our garage freezer for supper. As I re-entered our house, I heard a terrible sound. John was slid down from his recliner breathing heavily with loud rasping sounds, and was unresponsive to me. I called 911 thinking it was a heart attack or stroke. An ambulance arrived shortly. In the ER they did tests after which John fell asleep. When he awoke, he seemed to be normal. They did more testing and determined that he'd had a seizure. Anti-seizure medicine was prescribed.

According to state law, he was not permitted to drive for six months following a seizure—not happy news for John. I was his new chauffeur. He kept pointing out where I needed to improve my driving. "Do you purposely drive over manhole covers?" he asked. We were both extremely happy when those six months passed.

Amazingly, John had no more zoning out issues. I concluded that they had been mini seizures. His memory was improving. Perhaps a sinus surgery helped also. In any case, the seizure seemed like an answer to prayer, a climax after which life was better. My good friend Jean Cooper affirmed there were reasons to "count it all joy." The seizure happened at home. John wasn't hurt falling. I was there to help. No one else was involved (like a car accident). Neighbors helped with our dog and in other ways. There were meds to help.

After taking a break in 2017, the 2018 Mission Aviation Fair was held in August under the leadership of IAMA (International Association of Missionary Aviation), directed by Glenn Ferguson (a JAARS pilot). IAMA is comprised of aviation-related individuals, schools, and ministry organizations encouraging collaboration and cooperation as they serve Christ globally. Our advisory committee stepped up to handle local logistics. They asked John and me to man the Information Tent during the event. It felt strange for us not to be in charge. It was a scaled down event, but good interaction took place. We enjoyed connecting with those who visited our tent. John also helped with other needs, as well as talking with a WJTL radio interviewer.

In the following years, John helped with the Spring and Fall Perspectives courses. He also continued on the committee for the Mission Aviation Fair.

In January of 2022, medical tests revealed that John had stage four prostate cancer, already spread to lymph nodes and bones. John took the news well. "I've had a full life," he said. "I'm ready for heaven whenever that happens." John responded well to hormone treatment, holding future spread of cancer under control. So, we trust that he will continue to tolerate the meds and that they remain effective. We carry on in our remaining time, thankful for God's many blessings.

Through our many adventures, we saw how our personalities and gifts meshed into a partnership, with challenges and blessings. As John and I say, "we help each other." We didn't feel too old, and we hoped to keep going as the Lord gave strength.

Epilogue

We had chosen to serve with Wycliffe Bible Translators because of their priority of Bible translation—for every people group to have the opportunity to understand God's Word in their own heart language. It was a mission where we could use the tools God had placed in our hands: John's aviation-technical skills and my teaching-secretarial experience. We never imagined the many ways we would serve.

We appreciated the opportunity Wycliffe offered to be involved in a team, each using our gifts and talents to help Bible translators be successful as they served in remote, challenging locations. We knew that some missionaries failed because they had been pulled in too many directions. We had seen how support personnel handling the nitty gritty of logistics enabled the higher-profile ministries to take place.

We felt God had led us even from our early years. During high-school days God tugged at John's heart as he read books about the five martyred missionaries on Ecuador's Curaray River while trying to contact the Auca Indians. John read Jim Elliot's quote: *"He is no fool who gives what he cannot keep to gain what he cannot lose."* He admired Nate Saint's ability to fly in a very remote area. John's life seemed to come full circle as the Saint family participated in our Aviation Fairs. When John had realized he could combine his love of aviation with missions, he set his heart in that direction. Years later, John's enthusiasm overcame my reluctance as I realized I could trust God to meet my desires as well as my needs. He certainly has done that.

Our mission journey took us from the JAARS Center in North Carolina to Bolivia, to Peru, to Kenya, and back to Pennsylvania. In each location we found God faithful. We were not perfect people, but were honored to be used of God as part of a team making God's translated Word available to people groups for the first time.

Technology made many advances during our time of service, and continues at an exponential rate, which can be used to accelerate Bible translation and ministry. That's good news for the 1,680 languages in the world that still need Bible translation to start. Could all language groups have God's Word in this generation?

Only God knows what ministry will look like in the future, but it will be exciting. John often told Perspectives students at the course conclusion, "Do something with your life that will outlast you." We end with this question from heaven: What's in *your* hand during this earthly pilgrimage?

To learn more about the ministry today of
Wycliffe Bible Translators and JAARS:
visit
www.wycliffe.org
www.jaars.org

List of Abbreviations Used in the Book

AIM-AIR	Africa Inland Mission Air Service
AMP	(First known as) Aircraft Marine Products
ATS	Africa Transportation Service
DRC	Democratic Republic of the Congo
ECG	Eastern Congo Group
EZG	Eastern Zaire Group
IAMA	International Association of Missionary Aviation
IT	Internet Technology
JAARS	Jungle Aviation and Radio Service (early meaning, later changed to "JAARS, Inc." when other technical services were added to the program)
LBC	Lancaster Bible College
LMF	Lancaster Missionary Fellowship
MAF	Mission Aviation Fellowship
MAP	Mission Aviation Promotions
MATA	Missions At The Airport
MFL	Missions Fest Lancaster
MK	Missionary Kid
NERO	Northeast Regional Office
SAMAIR	South America Mission Air Service
SIL	Summer Institute of Linguistics
SPEL	Strategic Planning on the Entity Level
STOL	Short Takeoff and Landing
TOTAL-It-Up	Taste of Translation and Literacy
WA	Wycliffe Associates
WBT	Wycliffe Bible Translators
WMA	World Mission Associates
WNE	Wycliffe Northeast
WOW	Window on Wycliffe

Biography for John and Elsie Bush

John is from Corning, NY. He trained at LeTourneau College in Aeronautical Technology and worked in the aviation industry in the U.S. before joining Wycliffe Bible Translators. Elsie is from Bellwood, PA, studied Elementary Education at Bob Jones University and taught in Christian schools.

John and Elsie began their service in **Bolivia**, South America in 1971, where John maintained a small airplane fleet, which enabled translator/linguists to travel quickly to *very* remote areas of the jungle.

Then in **Peru**, over a period of 14 years, John worked in aviation maintenance and management. It was exciting to see various groups receive God's Word during that time.

During 1992 to 1996 the Bushes served at the **JAARS Center** in Waxhaw, NC (Wycliffe's technical headquarters), where John directed the Africa Transportation Services. This program helped provide durable vehicles for land transportation of Wycliffe personnel serving in remote areas of Africa.

Then they served in Africa, first directing a Cessna refurbish project, then with our Eastern Congo Group to promote Bible translation programs in the Democratic Republic of Congo (formerly Zaire). Living in Nairobi, **Kenya** (because of war in Congo) John worked to coordinate Resource Development and Technical Services for the group.

In each of the locations, Elsie did desktop publishing, preparing items for publication—Scripture books and literacy materials in various languages. It has been her special joy to help prepare Scriptures for people for whom it was their first printed Scripture in their language.

Beginning in 2001 John served as the Director of Wycliffe's **Northeast Regional Office** located in the Lancaster, PA area. Then he was director of Missions Fest Lancaster, followed by Mission Aviation Promotions, which held events showing the value of technical workers and challenging people to be part of the Great Commission, becoming more actively involved as the Lord had gifted them. Elsie helped John as Information Coordinator.

John and Elsie currently reside at Calvary Fellowship Homes in Lancaster, PA.

Made in the USA
Las Vegas, NV
03 June 2023